Developing Writer

Developing Writers

Teaching and learning in the digital age

Richard Andrews and Anna Smith

 Open University Press

Open University Press
McGraw-Hill Education
McGraw-Hill House
Shoppenhangers Road
Maidenhead
Berkshire
England
SL6 2QL

email: enquiries@openup.co.uk
world wide web: www.openup.co.uk

and Two Penn Plaza, New York, NY 10121-2289, USA

First published 2011

A catalogue record of this book is available from the British Library

ISBN-13: 978-0-335-24179-8 (pb) 978-0-335-24178-1 (hb)
ISBN-10: 0-335-24179-4 (pb) 0-335-24178-6 (hb)
eISBN: 978-0-335-24180-4

Library of Congress Cataloging-in-Publication Data
CIP data applied for

Typeset by Aptara Inc., India
Printed in Great Britain by CPI Antony Rowe, Chippenham, Wiltshire

The *McGraw·Hill* Companies

Contents

Acknowledgements

Part of Chapter 1 first appeared in an earlier version as 'Shifting writing practice: focusing on the productive skills to improve quality and standards in *Getting Going: Generating, Shaping and Developing Ideas in Writing*, published by the UK government's Department of Children, Schools and Families in 2008. We are grateful to Sue Hackman and the Department for Education for permission to re-work and update this material. Thanks to Caroline Daly, Jon Davison and John Moss, editors of *Debates in English Teaching* and to Routledge for permission to include an updated and re-written version of 'A new theory and model of writing development' as Chapter 9 of the present book.

Richard Andrews would like to thank Roger Beard, Dodi Beardshaw, Frances Bodger, David Budge, Teresa Cremin, John Dixon, Myrrh Domingo, Gunther Kress, Peter Medway, Debra Myhill, Sue Rogers and Richard Sterling for support, critical engagement and new perspectives on writing development; David Scott and Mabel Encinas for permission to quote from draft material written for a national standards project; and Simon Wrigley and Jeni Smith for their work on the embryonic and successful Teachers as Writers project for Buckinghamshire County Council in the UK.

Anna Smith would like to thank LuAnne Forrest and Katie Oliver for their critical reads of early drafts; colleagues at New York University including Tim Fredrick for consistent support, and Richard Andrews, Glynda Hull, Niobe Way and Sarah Beck for their mentorship; and, finally, the young writers who inspired the questions addressed in this book, and those in New York City, particularly Sean, who helped her explore their writing development.

1 The Problem with Writing

Introduction

In a short paper, Dixon (2010) reminds us that tracing writing development was 'a new problematic for the 1960s' (p. 1) and that opportunities were taken to study the phenomenon in primary/elementary and secondary/high school classrooms. He describes the work of the London Writing Research group, set up by the Schools Council to map writing development in the years from 11–18:

> Their initial seminars in 1966–7 focussed on the problem and finally set about developing a model proposed by the linguist Roman Jakobson [and Halle, 1956/2002]. Three key components they came up with were: broad differences in function; in a writer's sense of 'audience'; and in the characteristic level of abstraction selected (from running commentary, through retrospective narrative, to various kinds of generalising).
>
> (Dixon 2010: 1)

These categories subsequently formed the basis for the work of the London Writing Research group, building as it did also on the work of Moffett ([1968] 1983), especially with regard to the question of abstraction. The work was seminal in many ways and has informed a generation or more of writing research on both sides of the Atlantic, as well as elsewhere in the world. It is a model based very much in classrooms and schools, and one that tried to align writing development with curriculum design in English.

Dixon goes on to trace some of the attempts to take the debate and research further forward in the years since the 1960s. In particular he notes the creation of the National Writing Project in the USA in the 1970s; some mostly small-scale but significant developmental work in the 1980s; some larger-scale studies of writing competences at 11 and 15 in the work of the Assessment for Performance Unit in the UK, also in the 1980s; and the shut-down in thinking about writing development in the 1990s after the imposition of notions of staged 'progression' in high-stakes testing regimes: 'fatally, the teacher's goal of finding optimal conditions ... for developing writers was pushed aside, in the interests of setting national tests' (p. 4).

The twenty years or so of high-stakes testing has had some effect in raising standards in reading, but less so in writing; and, as Dixon suggests, the question of writing development has been sidelined. It is as if a testing edifice has been built on a non-existent foundation. There has been no theory of writing development underpinning the notion of progression in writing from year to school year.

On both sides of the Atlantic, and in Australia and New Zealand, there is still (perhaps because of the testing regime) a problem with writing performance. It has lagged an average of 20 percentage points behind reading performance for 11-year-olds in the UK for over ten years. Whereas more than 80 per cent achieve national standards in reading, only 67 per cent do so in writing; the figure is worse for boys than for girls. In the USA, the No Child Left Behind policy has recorded reading scores nationally, but not writing scores, resulting in a lack of attention and focus on writing skills. Practitioners, policy-makers and researchers have all asked for a new theory of writing development to underpin teaching, curricula and assessment. Their perception is that there is no consistently applicable theory of writing development, and that writing practices are getting out of touch with multimodality and practices in the digital age.

The aim of this book is to put writing back in the position it deserves: alongside reading. We also wish to bring an understanding of writing development up to date by locating it, and writing pedagogies, within digital and multimodal dimensions. To fulfil these main aims, we need to discuss existing theories and models of writing, generate new ones that are suitable for contemporary purposes, and put the accent again on writing *development*.

The problem

The standard of pupils' writing in the UK has been increasing in the last few years. In terms of conversions, for example, those moving from Key Stage 1 (ages 5–7) in 2001–2 to Key Stage 2 (ages 7–11) in 2005–6 improved across the transition. Furthermore, the trend has been consistently upward in writing performance at Key Stage 2 since 1997, from 53 per cent of pupils achieving level 4+ (the average required standard at aged 11) in 1997 to 67 per cent in 2006 (an advance of 4 per cent on 2005 results). Since 2003, writing performance at level 5 has improved significantly (those attaining a level 5 in writing between 2003 and 2006 rising from 65 per cent to 75 per cent) whereas reading scores remain between 65 per cent and 70 per cent, without significant improvement. Writing performance continues to improve from Key Stage 2 to Key Stage 3, and from Key Stage 3 to GCSE, with a significantly better conversion from Key Stage 2 to Key Stage 4 than for Key Stage 3 to Key Stage 4. The above advances mark a considerable achievement by pupils and teachers working within the framework of the National Literacy Strategy (DfEE 1998) and Key Stage 3 National Strategy, which operated in England from 1997 and throughout the first decade of the twenty-first century (see Andrews 2008b).

The *problem*, however, is that since the mid-1990s, with the exception of the recent improvement in writing at Key Stage 3, *writing performance has lagged an average 20 percentage points behind reading at all key stages*. At Key Stage 2, the gap was 14 points in 1997, reached its widest at 28 points in 2000, and narrowed to 16 points again in 2006. Only two-thirds of Key Stage 2 pupils attain level 4+ in writing in 2006, whereas since 2000 80 per cent or more pupils per annum have attained level 4+ in reading. Not enough pupils gain level 4+ in writing at Key Stage 2, or advance sufficiently at Key Stage 3 (despite considerable improvements at this stage), to improve beyond 60 per cent of pupils gaining a C or above at GCSE. As the Office for Standards in Education (Ofsted) put it (2006, p. 55), 'many schools are finding difficulty in raising standards in writing'.[1]

The *significance* of the problem is at least twofold: a) that pupils are not developing the productive skills of writing sufficiently well to aid their schooling in English and across the curriculum, and b) that if pupils can attain level 5+ at Key Stage 3,[2] they are likely to have a good chance of gaining a C+ in the General Certificate of Secondary Education (GCSE) in English – the generally accepted level of a good working competence in the use of English at the end of compulsory schooling.

Challenges

The problems noted above, along with the sticking points mentioned later in this chapter, provide the challenges for the English curriculum, for teachers, teacher trainers, assessment designers and pupils. The major challenge is to reinvigorate writing practice and theory to increase engagement and to improve standards. To do so requires an understanding of the writing paradigm in which we now operate as pupils, teachers, trainers and policy-makers.

The history of teaching-of-writing approaches since the 1950s can be characterized in four phases (the first two pre-computer, and the second two informed by reciprocal co-evolution with ICT),[3] some elements of which have been and continue to be concurrent in the best practice:

> **1950s–1960s**: an approach to writing which set high store by quality within a limited range of genres derived from nineteenth-century rhetorical categories. Little emphasis on the processes of writing;

more on the finished product and on a distanced, 'academic' command of language types. Exercises (cf. the Renaissance and Elizabethan grammar school practice of *progymnasmata* – rhetorical models and imitation) designed to build up competence. The high point in the teaching of formal grammar in the hope of improving writing quality and accuracy.

1960s–1970s to early 1980s: more emphasis on expressiveness and the emergence of a personal 'voice' in writing. The foregrounding of the imagination and creative (in this case, literary) writing. A move away from given forms towards experimentation. The rise of narrative as a 'primary act of mind' (Hardy 1977) or 'human paradigm' (Fisher 1989). Celebration of self within societal contexts, best characterized by *Growth through English* (Dixon 1967). A gradual move toward recognizing the complex interdependency of speech and writing, as evidenced in the writing of Britton (1967) and Ong (1982).

1980s to early 2000s: a greater understanding of writing processes in expert writers that can be modelled in novice writers, deriving from the work of psycholinguistic and discourse modelling by Graves (1983) and Scardamalia and Bereiter (1987). Reified into a formal system for teaching writing (Calkins 1994) but creating an abreaction among schoolteachers and principals in New York and the USA (Harwayne 2001) who believe it to be fossilized. Emphasis on drafting, editing, peer conferencing (aided by use of wordprocessing) but still aiming to capture 'voice' in writing (we pursue this question further in Chapter 4 on process-related models of writing). Sometimes linked to or running alongside a widening of the range of written (and spoken) forms – a movement that reacts against the perceived narrowness of the narrative/expressive mode and prepares writers for the world. Such range manifested in the National Curriculum (later versions) and in the Australian (specifically, the Sydney School, e.g. Christie 2002) celebration (and calibration) of a range of genres in writing; as well as in the US equivalents: 'Writing Next' and 'Writing – a Ticket to Work'.

mid-1990s to the present, and the model in need of development: a tension between the functions of writing in wider society and those in schooling and assessment. Writing seen within multimodal communication, especially in its relation with the visual (still and moving images) in popular and indeed all culture(s). Writing processes moving from drafting and editing to design (Kress 1995). A move away from the notion of a single personal 'voice' to a multiplicity of voices. The advent of the mobile learner, accessing written, visual and audio material anytime, anyplace – an extension of academic and social space, especially for 11–16-year-olds. Writing as text-box filling, but not always briefly; much scope for extended writing, both *in-depth* and *functional*. The need for keyboarding skills. Web 2.0 applications which enabled synchronous, collaborative, networked literacies.

A fifth phase, yet to arrive (but likely to be here by 2015 – the date set in England by *English 21* as one to work toward for a full-scale review of the English curriculum) will probably see advances in speech recognition technology that might or might not obviate the need for keyboards or writing implements. The emphasis on composing written text (expression, articulation, framing, shaping) will shift towards oral composition, while not abandoning writing. There will be a renewed dynamic relationship between speaking and writing, with each finding their roles in a new economy of communication; and also more use of images in compositions, so that verbal text and image will seem natural alongside each other in 'writing' as well as in reading.

The major challenge posed by the fourth phase, as characterized above, is shaping a writing curriculum for 5–16-year-olds between now and five or ten years hence that will:

- recognize fully the *place* of writing within multimodality;
- acknowledge and explore writing in the *digital age*;
- re-engage and *motivate* disaffected or unengaged young people by a) bringing the genres of schooling closer to the genres of the wider social world and b) giving writing a *range* of real purposes;
- at the same time, use the power of writing to explore *depth* in thought, reflection and feeling;
- recognize the place of *creativity and imagination in non-literary forms* of writing, as well as in literary forms;
- recognize and exploit the fact that writing and reading are *reciprocal*;
- investigate the similarities and differences, strengths and weaknesses of *speaking and writing* in different contexts and for different functions – and thus re-establish the generative link between speaking and writing;
- provide a theory and model of writing development that take into account all of the above points.

Productive skills are the key to overall improvement in English

Speaking and writing are primarily skills of language *production*, whereas listening and reading are skills of *reception*. The word 'primarily' is emphasized, as theories and practices of listening and reading do employ active meaning-making on the part of the audience or reader. Meaning, it could be said, is the result of a negotiation between the listener/reader and the text.

However, it cannot be denied that speaking and writing can be demanding in that they require expression, articulation, framing and shaping. To explicate these terms briefly: *expression* requires motivation to speak or write and the intellectual and motor facility to do so; *articulation* requires clarity of intention and thought, or at least a move towards such clarity; *framing* requires selections from the repertoire of socially embedded and generated speech genres and text types (sometimes these genres are hybrid or newly created); and *shaping* requires the manipulation of language within the chosen frames of reference, often at the point of utterance.[4]

One possible reason for the fact that writing performance lags behind reading for the most part is that when listening or reading, the material is *given*. The intellectual load on the audience or reader might be said to be lighter than when composing in speech or writing, though that load will vary with content and substance in each case. It is generally accepted that writing is the most difficult, if not the most complex, of the four language skills, requiring solitary, creative, thoughtful, accurate and focussed *compositional* energy;[5] plus a higher degree of reflective thinking and (usually) personal engagement. Even though collaborative writing has come more to the fore in the twenty-first century, the compositional energy required to finish a piece of writing or a multimodal piece is undiminished.

Much has been done, for example, to introduce pupils to non-fiction text-types, and to improve their control of stylistic features associated with them. Where practice is weaker is in generating the motivation and purpose to write; without such direction, pupils know how to write but not why they write, how to start or how to engage an audience and how to generate and marshall ideas. *Producing* such writing of quality, along with other text-types, is one of the keys to overall improvement in English.

The relationship between speaking and writing

The relationship between speaking and writing is complex, and must be seen within the broader picture of how the language skills relate to each other. Essentially, the relationship between speaking and writing is *generative* in that both are productive skills, and they can complement each other by directly giving rise to expression in the other. The means of communication in each case are, however, different.

The relationship between writing and reading (like that between speaking and listening), on the other hand, is *reciprocal*: in these relationships, the means of communication (e.g. print or speech) are the same, but the difference is between productive and receptive actions within the mode.

In England, The National Curriculum in English and teaching within the National Strategies (which ended in March 2011), where teacher-talk continued to dominate pupil-talk (despite efforts to the contrary),[6] have until fairly recently (see DfES 2007) given precedence to writing and reading over speaking and listening. The latter two skills have been seen as more reciprocal than the first two, resulting in more curriculum time being given to writing and reading separately (with not enough time devoted to their reciprocity) and proportionately less to speaking and listening (which are almost always seen as 'going together') (Ofsted 2005). Often, speaking has been seen as a means to support writing and reading, rather than as an object of instruction in its own right (Cameron 2002, Myhill and Fisher 2005).

How can speaking continue to support writing, while at the same time establishing its own stronger presence in English and across the curriculum? The key is in seeing the generative relationship between speaking and writing as two-way.

First, speaking can be an important *rehearsal* for writing. Ideas can be discussed in pairs, small groups, in whole-class discussion and in larger forums, then distilled, translated and developed in writing. Such writing can be dialogic as well as monologic. Dialogic writing includes planning for Socratic dialogue (question-and-answer format), colloquia, playscripts and other dual- and multi-voiced text-types. Monologic writing includes the more conventional forms such as essay, story, letter and report, where translation from the multiple voices of speech to the single authorial voice of the writer can be more difficult.

Second, writing can be a *rehearsal* for speech. Individual and/or joint composition in writing can prefigure delivery in speech, as in the making of a speech, the production of an oral narrative, the composition of a persuasive case, or the scripting of a (radio) play or advertisement. Speech as a product in these cases is more than mere performance: it is part of a dialogue that invites response in spoken, written and other formats. It is in such transformation between different means of communication and different genres within those means that the day-to-day practice of English in classrooms takes place.

Lesson planning and curriculum design, then, need to cater for speaking to come both before, during and after writing. Such bridging between speaking and writing will require imagination and consideration of the strengths of each skill in classroom, school and wider contexts.

The problem of insufficient *space* for sustained speaking and writing is compounded by assessment practices.

It is the case that speaking and writing are used to provide evidence of the quality of listening and reading, i.e. they are used to assess listening and reading as well as assessing themselves. The dearth of *extended* speaking and writing across the curriculum and in assessment across the curriculum may well have contributed to the relatively poor production skills of learners as they move through schooling.[7] Pupils are not being given enough opportunities and enough support or incentive to *discourse* at length. As Britton pointed out as long ago as the 1960s (Britton 1967, p. xiii–xiv) 'a rough measure of [the teacher's] success in promoting the right kind of talk might well be the length of the span that can go on without word from him [sic]'.

What is clear is that speaking and writing are central to learning in formal education because they afford the learner the ability to reflect, think, compose and rearrange as well as respond spontaneously (particularly in the case of speech). Furthermore, as Meek (1983) proves, such emphasis on the productive language skills can be the key to improvements and even breakthroughs for weaker learners not only in speaking and writing themselves, but also in reading and listening as a result of increased motivation, commitment and investment in making meaning in language; and increased awareness and exploitation of the reciprocity between writing/reading, speaking/listening, mentioned at the start of this section.

What we know about writing practice – what we have been doing well and where the sticking points are

Speaking and writing share the following characteristics as productive skills, as mentioned earlier in this chapter. Here, these elements are elaborated further:

Expression is important because it engages the self or personae and releases what may be felt and/or thought. It affords channels of communication and creates contact with others.

Articulation aims to make such communication clear. In speech terms, articulation is associated perhaps most readily with surface features like clear enunciation of utterances; more importantly, the notion of articulation ('joining') is about logical or a-logical connections between ideas, thoughts, feelings and language, in speech and/or writing. Andrews et al. (2006b), in a systematic review of research on the teaching of argumentative writing at Key Stages 2 and 3, draw attention to the need for cognitive as well as linguistic work in improving writing in this mode.[8]

With *framing* (see Andrews 2011) and *shaping* the emphasis needs to move from a focus on the end-products – the frames (pedagogic 'scaffolds', genres, text types, forms) and shapes that language uses and that need to be learnt – to the act of fram*ing* and shap*ing* that is at the heart of *composition* (literally, 'putting things together'). Such a move will entail thinking more deeply about the early stages of composition: how ideas are formed; how they are framed; how inspirational ideas are supported by a climate for learning and development; how choices are made, early on, about the medium or media in which it is best to convey the message; how drafting and editing can be improved by critical dialogue and reflection at the deeper levels of composition (structure, voice, position, tone); how momentum and interest can be sustained; how speaking, reading and listening can contribute to the composing process in writing; how issues of design, balance and elegance ('when is a piece finished?') can be taught and learnt; and how a community of learners (speakers/writers/makers) can support such committed and high quality composing.

One of the considerable achievements of the National Curriculum, especially in its version since 2000, is in the range and balance of spoken and written forms that pupils must engage in. There is now, for example, a much better balance between informative, argumentative and narrative texts than was the case in previous versions of the English curriculum in 1989 or 1995, as well as a wider range of speech genres. However, there are a number of sticking points that partly derive from such success:

- an undue emphasis on form (and pedagogic techniques like scaffolding that induct pupils into these school genres), which can lead to a somewhat static and formulaic conception of what language can do;[9]
- a reluctance on the part of teachers (and thus pupils) to experiment with hybrid forms;
- insufficient engagement by pupils in their writing;
- too limited a sense of audience and function, so that writing becomes an activity that serves assessment requirements in school ('school writing') and the educational system, rather than a form of communication that can make a difference in the world;
- insufficient pace and verve in exploiting the potential of multimodal communication (verbal plus visual literacies, moving image, the advent of high quality sound in combination with words) and of seeing writing's place and special function within these multimodalities, i.e. what writing can and cannot do.[10]

Many of these sticking points might be seen to come under the banner of the need for 'creativity'. As *All Our Futures* (DfEE/DCMS 1999) suggests, creativity should not confine itself to 'creative writing' but should be pervasive across English and the rest of the curriculum, if creativity means the ability and capacity to make, shape, invent and articulate new meaning. The current English curriculum may have swung too far towards a catalogue of required forms of writing since the 1980s; but it does not have to swing back to a stereotypical creative formlessness/expressiveness. Neither polarity represents (or ever represented) the best of English writing teaching, which marries expression with structure, articulation with feeling/thought, and a range of linguistic competence with depth in engagement and imagination.[11]

The generation and marshalling of ideas for writing, mentioned in an earlier section, need more attention. Ideas for writing come from speech (e.g. a story *told* can then be *written*); in response to other writing and other media; commissioned for particular purposes; and 'out of the air'. Indeed, if – as we believe – writing is an act of communication between people, expressing a human need. In terms of writing development – and its converse but related notion of developing writers of all ages and at all times – writing is a central human activity. Providing a rich supporting context where a range of writing can be inspired and nurtured will require an appreciation of the written word. To develop such a climate, teachers and pupils will want to read and generate writing that gives pleasure (e.g. because it is funny, moving, well-crafted) and that makes a difference to personal lives and in the world. The early stages of the writing process – mulling an idea, developing the seed of an idea trying various 'voices' or styles, gathering evidence via research, allowing a gestation period for the rhythm of a piece to identify itself – are important to share and discuss so that the writing process is made more evident (and thus open to discussion and development). Writing the first draft is usually a solitary act (though increasingly there are chances for collaborative composition, and even if solitary, the written act is usually in response to an existing communication), requiring a high degree of concentration; but it is helpful to make the process public at significant stages, so that pre-writing, editing and proof-reading can play their part.

Implications for the pedagogy and assessment of writing

From a pedagogical point of view, techniques for improving writing will include practice in writing by the very teachers who are teaching it. In other words, English teachers will need to be *accomplished writers* in themselves, not only of literary and fictional genres but in informational and argumentative genres too. They will not only be able to produce final products in this range of genres ('Here's one I made earlier...'), but also to reflect on and model the processes of writing in the classroom. English teachers will also need to increase their knowledge of theories of writing and classroom interaction, so that they can justify what they are doing pedagogically. It is probably true to say that most English teachers are already accomplished readers as degrees in English and related disciplines are principally an education in advanced *reading* skills in literature. Writing receives less attention.

Like all good teaching, *engagement* of the pupils at whatever age will be crucial. It is probably true to say that lesson planning has moved away from initial and sustained engagement (which is much more than stimulus) towards learning outcomes, compliance with the curriculum, and comprehensiveness. Some of the excitement may have been lost from routine teaching, so a new balance needs to be struck between meeting targets and outcomes on the one hand, and generating impetus and significant communication on the other. Too much emphasis on atomistic targets out of context tends to devalue the learning experience itself; we are more likely to attain targets if we concentrate on the substance and quality of what we need and want to do.

Following from engagement will be a much greater willingness to go into *depth* in whatever kinds of writing are being taught. This will require commitment, time and imaginative energy. It involves critical engagement on the part of the teacher with the emergent written texts of pupils *before* and *during* the compositional process as well as after it. It also requires the engagement of the pupils as thinkers, establishing in them a purpose and giving them a sense of their independent choices and voices as writers. Greater consideration to different types of planning and composition will be required, e.g. argumentative writing requires hierarchical and sequenced planning (Andrews et al. 2006b), as well as a sense of what mode(s) of communication (speaking, writing, reading, listening) is/are best for what purpose.

Dialogic teaching (Alexander 2006) will be an important element in improving the quality of interaction and thought on the part of pupils in the classroom. Dialogic approaches to teaching can support both speaking and writing, though it is not always the case that productive and purposeful talk translates directly into writing of such quality. As suggested earlier, we need to look not only at the transition from talk to writing (and vice-versa), but also at dialogic forms of writing in themselves, thus adding to the repertoire of largely monologic written forms that dominate the school curriculum and assessment regimes.

Finally, *audiences* and *purposes* need to be diversified so that communication has meaning (and is thus motivating) rather than a performance in empty or purely academic 'school genres' (Sheeran and Barnes 1991) served up for assessment. The writing across the curriculum of the mid-1970s understood this principle in its promotion of writing that made a difference in the world; such insight was continued in Technical and Vocational Education Initiative (TVEI) projects in the 1980s, getting English beyond the classroom.

In all the above aspects, provision will need to be tailored for the differing contexts of primary and secondary schooling; at the same time, progression, personalized learning and attainment will need to be seamless across the primary/secondary transition. There is a task for the Primary National Strategy, the Secondary National Strategy and in post-16 provision (as well as the 14–19 agenda) for reinvigorating the approach to the teaching and learning of productive skills of speaking and writing, partly by giving them more space.

In terms of assessment, the range of skills tested will need to keep up with the actual learning requirements for assessment that reflects engagement, depth, range of audience and communicative *impact*. Such assessment may need to look beyond conventional forms to reflect and log progress ('portfolio assessment'); and use digitization to reflect an enriched, wider and deeper range and quality of writing.

The current generic statement on the use of information and communication technologies (ICT) across the curriculum does not recognise the nature and functions of writing within multimodality.

The *strategies*, as set out in the National Literacy Strategy (DfEE 1998), the Primary National Strategy, the Key Stage 3 National Strategy, (DfES 2003a, DfEE 2001a), the Secondary National Strategy and the more recent Primary Framework (see www.standards.dfes.gov.uk/primaryframeworks/literacy/) have been successful in raising standards to an extent, but for further progress in breaking through to higher levels of performance, teaching needs to be more consistently good and more focussed on engagement with and on the quality of speaking and writing in the curriculum. The key is to enable teachers to help pupils to see that speech and writing are powerful forms of expression and vehicles for thinking; and to encourage experimentation and judgement in finding the right forms for the meanings that are to be conveyed.[12] Work needs to be done through the existing frameworks and channels to support teachers and to enhance the current provision for the teaching of speaking and writing.

The likely impact of a greater emphasis on productive skills

Being *productive* in modes of language like writing and speaking can prepare the ground for advances and breakthroughs in the receptive skills –

reading and listening. One of the best contemporary examples of the close reciprocity of reading and writing is blogging, where the reader is writer and vice-versa. If the biggest gap in attainment is still that between pupils on free school meals and the rest, then one way to close that gap is to give *all* pupils the motivation, access and tools by which to express themselves, to articulate better, and to frame and shape via language within their lives and in society. Such an emphasis on engagement, production and quality will benefit all students, and contribute to a general improvement of literacy skills in the school population at 16 and beyond.

It has been noted above that a focussed emphasis on improving writing can have direct effects on the generative relationship between speaking and writing. Recognition that we learn to develop the range and depth of our writing through its reciprocal relationship with reading, and *vice-versa*, will further strengthen the bond between the language skills. At the same time, understanding the strengths of the spoken and written verbal codes within a wider multimodal context is important in terms of contemporary communicative practices inside and outside school. There is a much wider variety of genres (in the broader sense of text types *and* social action) outside school. The genres that operate inside school have much more significance for pupils and students if they are related to genres from the outside world.

Such increased emphasis on sustained productive skills will not only benefit young people's communicative abilities; it will also make them more employable and better equipped to play their part as citizens in an inclusive society.

Conclusion

This introductory chapter has identified some problems with writing performance, and with standards in writing in both the UK and USA. It has also suggested some partial solutions. These have included the recommendation for more emphasis on expression, sustained writing, framing and shaping, in addition to more space for teachers and children to generate topics in which they are motivated to write. Furthermore, there are recommendations here to link writing more closely to the other productive art in language skills: speech. These recommendations, along with an exploration of writing's role in the digital and multimodal age, are seen as some of the positive ways in which the writing agenda can be revived in an effort to increase writing quality and standards. Essential in this next phase of writing pedagogy is to move beyond the discourse of targets, commodification and product-oriented approaches.

However, many of the recommendations discussed above have been tried before. This does not mean to say they are unsuccessful; merely that they operated without an overarching theory or model of writing and writing development. It is to setting the foundation for a new theory and model of writing development that the book now turns.

2 Thinking About a New Model for the Digital Age

Introduction

Current policies and practice – at least in the UK, Australia and New Zealand – derive from 1980s models that depend on genre theory. Inevitably, perhaps, the pedagogic models that have derived from text-based (Australian) genre theory have been over-simplified and have become stale and rigid. They were the staple of the National Literacy Strategy in the UK and of various states' education curricula in Australia. Their 'scaffolding' and structured approach has left little room for creativity, for framing and re-framing on the part of students, or for extended writing in subjects across the curriculum in primary and secondary schooling. A consequence is that, although they have helped improve writing standards since the mid-1990s, writing quality has reached a plateau and teachers do not know how to break through to higher standards for a greater number of pupils. In the USA, the writing process theory of Graves (also 1980s) and his followers has had a great impact on many aspects of elementary schooling, but middle and high school level practice has largely been influenced by writing standards and measures at state level rather than federal (national) level (apart from recent National Assessment of Educational Progress (NAEP) assessments, the work of the National Writing Project and statements like *Writing Next*). There is thus a need for a new model of writing development internationally: one that will show progression on an individual basis as well as provide benchmark data in a more general sense. That model must take the contemporary environment for writing into account: the dimensions of digitization and of multimodality. While a chapter is devoted to each of these dimensions later in the book, in the present chapter we include initial discussion of these dimensions as they bear upon the emerging survey of theories and models in the field.

Why genre theory had an impact

There is no doubt that Australian genre theory had an impact, not only within Australia (to different degrees, according to state practice and policy) but also within the UK and elsewhere. In terms of writing, the models that were evident up to the mid-1980s gave broad vectors and categories for a writing curriculum. Those models tended to emphasize expressive and narrative forms of writing, perhaps reflecting the *zeitgeist* of the 1960s and 1970s. By the mid-1980s, however, there had been a series of articles in the USA and Canada, as well as work commissioned by examining boards in the UK, to suggest that argumentative forms of writing (e.g. the essay, persuasive pieces) were being neglected and not taught well (if at all). These suggestions were reinforced in larger-scale studies (e.g. by the Assessment of Performance Unit in the UK) which demonstrated that 11- and 15-year-old students were not good at writing argument. Interestingly, there continue to be studies (e.g. Ogreid 2010) that suggest that exposition and other forms of documentary, informational writing are still under-developed.

Against a background of expressiveness and a celebration of narrative, it was inevitable that a broader emphasis on a range of written genres would emerge. In retrospect, it is interesting to observe that Australian genre theory, which foregrounded written text-types under broader categories like narrative and argument, held sway in the UK and elsewhere; whereas the Canadian school of genre theory, based on a seminal piece by Miller (1984) entitled 'Genre as social action', and characterized, for example by the work of Bazerman (1988) and Freedman and Medway (1994), had less curricular effect. The principal reason might be that the mid-1980s neo-conservative political climate required tangible product-like categories via which to restructure the curriculum. The National Curriculum, launched in England and Wales by the Education Reform Act of 1988, provided a cocktail of expressive literariness combined with the beginnings of a move toward genres-as-text-types – a move that was reinforced in successive versions of the National Curriculum in 1995 and 2000. The genre-as-social-action movement was of a deeper nature, locating writing within a sociological framework; its impact has been at a more subliminal level, and is an important perspective we need to take into account as a new theory and model of writing development are built.

Australian genre theory had the greatest ostensible impact on curricular design in English teaching in the late 1980s and 1990s. However, the political dimensions of such theory, essential to its formation (and championing the cause of a wider range of written genres for all children so as to enfranchise them into the discourses of the adult world) were lost in a reduction to curricular *fiat* by the UK government. It was not so much the fact that a wider range of written genres was required, but the methods used to teach such a range. These included 'scaffolding', which again was reduced from a Vygotskian/Brunerian account expressed most clearly in the work of Cazden (Cazden 1983, Clay and Cazden 1990) to a worksheet mentality in which 'writing scaffolds' were presented to children to help them compose in the different genres. Such worksheets provided formulae for writing in different ways without much attention devoted to the functions of such writing. Thus the complexities of genre theory were distilled and reified into simplistic scaffolds for writing in a range of text-types, with little rationale for why these text-types had formed and what their function was – and certainly no sense that such text-types could be combined with others into hybrid forms, or indeed *transformed*.

Circumstances that suggest a new approach is needed

There are a number of circumstances that suggest a new approach is needed; part of that approach is the need for a new theory and model of writing development. These circumstances include: the tiredness of the text-based genre approach; exhaustion with targets and product-oriented assessment systems; a dis-connect between writing in the classroom and writing in the world at large, leading to a lack of motivation on the part of teachers and students; lack of professional development in writing for teachers; digitization of text; multimodality and its challenges to the pedagogy of writing; the notion and practice of digital writing (see Chapters 7 and 8); and a dearth of creativity across the range of written genres.

Tiredness of the text-based genre approach

The approach that builds on text-based genre theory has led to simplified worksheets which characterize genres by formulae. For example, an essay is seen to have an introduction, followed by points for the argument, points against, followed by a summing up or conclusion, stating the point of view of the writer. And yet we know from classical rhetoric that Aristotle, Cicero and Quintilian suggested at least seven variations on structural form between them, with Quintilian concluding that the number of parts must be determined by the function of the piece. Another version of such a formula is the American 'five-paragraph essay' consisting of introduction, three supporting paragraphs and a conclusion. This happens to be one of the many variations of form suggested by classical rhetoricians, reduced to a packaged formula for pedagogic use. An over-emphasis on form and structure tends to drain energy from the writing process which involves motivation to write, engagement with the audience, the formation of ideas or elements to be included and *then* a concentration on form.

Exhaustion with targets and product-oriented assessment systems

Targets are part of a business culture approach to education, and can divert attention from the process of writing. They are associated with product-oriented assessment systems which have contributed to the situation of high-stakes testing regimes. In such a culture, attention strays from the task in hand to the criteria by which the task is assessed; writing, in the case of our current focus, becomes a means to the end of attaining higher grades. While we wish to develop a theory and model of writing development that sees the act of writing as part of interaction in society, we feel that the over-emphasis on grading and examination success – itself a product of a meritocracy in which league tables and measurable performance are key elements – has provided the wrong sort of climate for students. Aspiration to be an excellent writer requires concentration on the task in hand.

Dis-connect between writing in the classroom and writing outside it

When written genres in classrooms – so called 'school writing' – become disconnected from the genres (we are thinking here of genres as social action) in the wider world, disaffection enters the writing classroom. It is a justifiable question for a writing student to ask 'What is the point of my undertaking five-paragraph essay training, or writing to this particular formula, when such kinds of writing do not exist outside the classroom?' The question is more likely in a secondary school or high school classroom, when students are more aware of genres outside the classroom; but even in primary and elementary schools, writing that is connected to real world experience is going to enthuse and engage students more than sterile writing exercises. There are a number of reasons for such inside/outside connection: real engagement with life outside the classroom gives young people an audience for their work; having an audience increases motivation, dialogism (writing becomes more like speech) and the desire to make writing accurate; engagement with the real world means that writing itself often takes on a transparent role, its function being to convey something clearly about the world. An example that could come from either primary or secondary education is that of a trip outside the classroom to observe, in writing, drawing, recording and photographs, an encounter with an old people's home, or with a nature site. The immediacy of the sensory experience makes the writing experience very different from that with the simulated world of the classroom (unless people and objects from the outside world are brought into the classroom). Writing is seen as a means to an end – but an end that is worth engaging with.

Lack of professional development in writing for teachers

The National Writing Project in the USA, which has been running since 1974, is a model of continuing professional development. Its function has been to develop teachers as writers so that they feel more confident and more skilled in teaching writing to their students. The setting up of writing communities, joint exploration of writing processes, publication of teachers' writing (some going on to become published writers themselves) and a more recent focus on digital writing have all contributed to an inspirational engagement for teachers. Elsewhere in the world, attempts are being made to set up similar networks in the belief that writing projects for teachers are beneficial in a number of ways. Since the early 2000s, the National Writing Project in the USA has been required to prove that not only is it beneficial to teachers and their self-confidence as teachers of writing, but that the impact is also evident on their students.

Multimodality and its challenges to writing pedagogies

Learning to write involves more than gaining command of an alphabetically-based system, or, by implication, any other system of graphic representation of meaning in handwriting or print. For a start, what is often acknowledged but rarely drawn on in practice is the relationship between speech and writing. These 'productive' verbal skills are interconnected. In the grapho-phonemic tradition, in the scripts of most European languages for example, the written system reflects the sound system to different degrees, depending on when the written system was 'fixed'. Spelling was normalized in the eighteenth century in England, for example, much to do with Johnson's *Dictionary* (see http://drjohnsonsdictionary.wordpress.com/) but the sounds of the spoken language have continued to change. Thus the spelling system in English has moved further away from the phonetics of the language as spoken English has diversified and developed.

But writing is indubitably visual too. Even when there are no images accompanying writing, written scripts have a strong visual identity. Some scripts move from left to right; others from right to left or from the top of the page to the bottom. The layout of script on the page, in handwritten or printed form, has a visual dimension. At a more localized level, the Chinese ideogram embodies within it visual and conceptual history: the elements that make up meaning are themselves derived from graphic representations of objects and ideas. The layout of the script has *meaning*: we know that paragraphing or the breaking of a text into other sections (bullet points, stanzas, clauses in a legal document) is significant. It is designed not only to help the reader manage the flow of information, but also to structure the composed text. Such visual arrangement is an essential part of composing in writing. For example, look at the current page you are reading: there are no ostensibly visual elements, but the page contains a certain number of words that are considered 'readable'; the line length is also designed with reading in mind; the subheadings of this section of the chapter are indicated in a particular size and type of font; there are paragraphs; and the white space is important to enable the reading process (black marks are made on white paper to distinguish significance from non-significance).

There is more to multimodality than speech-writing connections and the visual identity of handwriting and print. One of the contentions in this book, building on the work of Kress and colleagues (e.g. Kress 1997, 2010; Kress and Bezemer 2009) is that not only is it now impossible to conceive of writing without a more fully multimodal awareness; it is actually beneficial to take a multimodal perspective and to deploy other modes in the actual business of writing and writing development. Briefly for now, these others modes include still and moving images; spatial considerations (the immediate environments for writing); the relationship of writing development to physical being and development; and the relationship of writing to sounds other than those of the language being used. We explore the multimodal dimensions of writing development more fully in Chapter 7.

Digitization of text

This book was composed digitally, by one of us working in the UK and the other in the USA. We met initially on a number of occasions to plan the book, but most of the writing was done separately, on laptops and desktop computers in wordprocessing packages. Composing was done on planes, trains and portions were even composed on a cell phone in the subway system. From an early stage, we used Google Docs to compose the bibliography; at later stages in the process we shared the drafts of chapters on another file-sharing platform – Dropbox – in order to improve drafts and to check the overall structure, balance and quality of the writing. From the publisher we received digital mock-ups of the cover for which we discussed the messages implicit in the images, layout and fonts used in the design. After the manuscript (a vestigial term) was delivered to the publisher electronically as well as in printed form, the book was edited, designed and produced digitally. At any stage in the process from conception through to the actual production of the printed book, hard copy printouts of the emerging text could be made. But increasingly, not only the process of writing and book production are handled digitally, but e-books are replacing printed books.

Digitization of text is therefore now commonplace. Writers move from handwritten notes, back and forth to the computer. Some – those in the vanguard of digital use – never commit pen to paper at all, but make their notes in audio and written form through software packages like Evernote on handheld media devices. Digitization has transformed not only the writing process and the forms which writing takes in the world, it has also transformed the place of writing in relation to other modes; the length of writing (in that many forms of written communication approximate speech in their brevity and interactional nature); the design of writing (i.e. where writing comes in the process of designing communication); and the re-purposing of writing by other people.

A fuller account and exploration of writing in the digital age takes place in Chapter 8.

Dearth of creativity across the range of written genres

One of our motivations for writing this book is that we wish to see creativity in action across a range of written genres, and not just in 'creative writing'. There is a widespread assumption that creative writing inheres solely in the composition of stories, poems and plays – the so-called fictional genres – and perhaps in personal, autobiographical work, rather than in exposition, information writing, argumentation or other 'non-fictional' genres. To characterize a wide range of written genres via a negative definition – *non*-fiction – seems to us bizarre. It reveals the hegemony of the fictional in the imagination of readers, curriculum designers, booksellers and publishers. While we celebrate the fictional in all its forms, we also wish to give status to the so-called non-fictional forms, preferring to gather them under the heading 'documentary' texts. There is no doubt in our mind that such documentary texts (for example, essays, manuals, reports, letters, notes, annotations, speeches) have a creative dimension. That is to say, in the composition of such texts there are processes of imagination, arrangement, voice(s), position/stance, expression and metaphor at work. We wish to claim that the infusion of a creative spirit into such writing will not only motivate those developing writers who do not incline to the fictional forms; it will also improve writing in the documentary forms.

Conditions of a new theory and model

We now turn to the positive conditions that have to be taken into account in the design of a new theory and model of writing development. Above, we have set out why there is a need for such a theory and model. Here, we begin to lay the foundations for the theory and model themselves.

There are six headings which we think need to be taken into account: the nature of development, including progression on an individual basis (see Chapter 6); multimodality (discussed briefly above, and see Chapter 7); the digitization of text (see Chapter 8); biliteracy, by which we mean the ability to compose in more than one language; recognition that writing goes on outside as well as inside school; and pedagogic implications of the above (see Chapter 11). As four of these areas will be given full attention in the rest of the book, either side of the presentation of the new theory and model in Chapters 9 and 10, we focus principally here on biliteracy and on the in-school/out-of school issues.

The world is primarily bilingual or multilingual. Those who speak and write only one language are in a minority in the twenty-first century. To take English as an example: it is used as a first language in about twenty countries worldwide, and by about 400 million speakers. It is spoken by a further 1.4 billion people worldwide as a second or foreign language. Not all these people write as well as speak English, but 75% of the world's mail was in English in the 1990s. Despite the diversity and agency of spoken English around the world, the written form (broadly, written standard English) is a common currency. There are two other world languages: Mandarin and Spanish. There are an estimated 836 million to 1.4 billion speakers of Mandarin, with a lower proportion than for English of those being able to write Mandarin or Modern Standard Written Chinese. Spanish speakers number about 400 million.

It is our contention that, where feasible, it is beneficial to learn to write in more than one language. Increasingly, countries worldwide are encouraging the learning of a second language at aged 7 rather than at the beginning of secondary or high school. It is not necessarily the case that learning a second or additional language is primarily an oral/aural activity. Some learners prefer, and learn more quickly, in the writing/reading modes. Whether the second or additional language uses the same alphabetic system as the learner's first language, or whether the system is completely different, as in the case of Arabic or Mandarin for first-language English speakers, there is still the advantage of comparing the written system in one language to that in another. To take an example from two alphabetic languages, a large proportion of words in Spanish and English have a common, Latinate or ancient Greek, root: 'centro/centre', 'importante/important' and 'página/page'. Of course, many words do not share the same root, but have more tangential, sometimes metaphorical connection: 'corriente' as an adjective means 'running', 'instant', 'present' – rather like the English adjective 'current' with which there is a common root, and which is also present in the English word 'curriculum' – the course to be run. The fact that Spanish does not have a single word for curriculum, but uses 'curso de estudios' or 'programa o plan de las asignaturas' is a matter of interest and comparison. Such comparisons can only enhance language awareness, and particularly the understanding, conceptual mapping, use and spelling of words in English or Spanish. As a large proportion of words in any language uses root terms, as well as prefixes and suffixes (or other morphemic grammatical elements) and diacritical marks/accents to determine meaning and spelling, such developing awareness and knowledge is helpful in becoming a writer.

Biliteracy and multilingualism are not, as suggested above, unusual. In Hong Kong, for example, it is official language policy at present that a 'trilingual-biliterate' approach is employed across the city's schools. Essentially, this means that English, Mandarin and Cantonese are the spoken languages, and English and Modern Standard Written Chinese are the written languages of the curriculum (see Lam 2005; Lee and Lok 2010). The broad policy is not necessarily implemented in the same way in every school (in fact the policy is contentious, and has involved parents and their children migrating to schools which they see as fitting their own requirements in language terms), but the general principle is important: the education system is trying to equip its students to be biliterate. Learning to write and read in more than one language not only gives the learner access to a wider population in the world, and to a wider range of meanings; it also can enhance learning to write in one's principal language.

Recognition that writing goes on outside as well as inside school has emerged from a number of studies in the ethnography of writing since the early 1990s. In non-digital settings, Andrews (1998, 2011) noted in a case study of a 4-year-old's written and graphic production that of 55 pieces of 'writing' produced over a six-month period, 84% of them were produced at home; and that of 120 drawings during the same period, 92.5% were produced at home. Whereas the conventional assumption is that writing starts at school, and children move from an oral pre-school culture to a written school culture, this single case study (though it cannot be generalized) suggests the opposite: that home was a place for the bulk of written and graphic production, and school was the more public space for oral as well as written/graphic exchanges. Many other studies have explored the home/school axis, especially for early years development (see, for example, Czerniewska 1992; Kress 1997; Hall and Robinson 2003; Hall, Larson and Marsh 2003). Fewer have looked at the relationship between out of school written production and in-school written work for adolescent young people. A notable exception is the work of Domingo (2011a, 2011b) whose study of teenage Filipino composers in Hounslow, west London, indicates a rich biliterate and bilingual written culture outside school.

Rowe (2009) traces a longer history of studies on children's emergent writing, going back to a seminal work by Hildreth (1936). She notes the shift over the intervening decades (particularly from the 1970s onwards) from an emphasis on convention to one on intention: the idea of bringing meaning to print. As far as the school/out-of-school relationship is concerned,[1] Rowe's excellent review points us towards the work of Heath (1983) and Dyson (1989) and their exploration of writing 'in relation to the cultural patterns of their homes and communities' (2009, p215). Interestingly, Rowe notices a decline is such perspectives from the 1990s (including a focus on the relationship of play and writing in that decade) to the period between 2000 and 2008, indicating a contrapuntal (though related) movement towards sociocultural and social interaction studies in classrooms, as well as a focus on identities. Indeed, the largest growth in the study of early writing is seen to be in the last two areas, perhaps subsuming or assuming an understanding of the out-of-school environments for writing and composition. Such a sociocultural focus sees classrooms and other spaces as framed communities in which children learn to manipulate the semiotic resources available to them in order to make meaning. If that attempt to communicate is reciprocated, especially in a real world sense of an audience responding to writing in kind rather than a teacher responding according to a set of pre-ordained curriculum targets, the likelihood for an increasing sense of development as a writer is nurtured. Rowe's review is recommended for a state of the art update on where early writing research has focused, and where it might travel in the future. Not least, she provides for us important evidence for one of the conditions for a new theory and model of writing development: that we must look beyond the classroom to take into account the social literacy practices of children and young people as they develop their command of communication tools.

What are the affordances of writing?

In Chapter 8, we discuss the *affordances* of digital written composition. Because we are postponing the detailed discussion of digitization and its effects until then, it is important at this stage in the book to consider the affordances of writing itself as a mode, in whichever medium it operates. First, we need to clarify some of the key terms we are using. Writing is a *mode* of communication that needs to be considered alongside other modes like speech, still images, moving images, gestures and icons. It can operate in various *media* like print on a page of paper or on a screen; or in handwriting. Its affordances are what it 'allows' to be expressed – both its strengths as a mode of communication, but also its weaknesses. So, for example, we can say of a printed poem on a page of a book that it is in written mode, using the medium of print on a page. Its particular affordances are that it allows reading and re-reading at the reader's own pace; and the white space surrounding it allows and even suggests that we treat the poem as 'sacrosanct' in some way. Because the text in question is a poem and shaped by rhythmic intention (and partly reinforced by the affordances of writing), we tend to read it more closely, and more slowly, that we would any other piece of writing. We expect correspondence between the words that make up the poem: we look for echoes, resonance and other features that are 'afforded' by the structure, imagery, sound and rhythmic shape of the poem. Furthermore, from the point of view of the writer, writing in this particular genre (whether the composition is originally pen on paper, or type on paper or screen) is distinctive in that it allows for revision, the playful interrelationship of words, a visual set of possibilities (both in a direct sense, as in concrete poems, but also more typically via the form of the poem) and exploration of meaning ('shaping at the point of utterance'). There is also the expectation of permanence in the printing of a poem on paper: not just physical permanence in the expectation that the paper itself – especially if it is hand-made and cross-woven – will last a relatively long time; but also the idea or suggestion of permanence in the expression of feeling and/or ideas. It is as if the poem acts as a living monument to its subject.

Another example will indicate the different affordances of writing. A note to a post-man – or woman – will, by its very nature, be ephemeral. It is usually in handwriting on a note stuck to a door. It is brief and to the point: 'If there is no one here, please deliver the parcel to no 9 next door'. It is sometimes disguised so as not to suggest that the house is empty. But its presence *in writing* helps the cause of getting the post to the right place because leaving a spoken message would not be feasible; the post-man – or woman – can read, act upon it and then destroy it. There is no suggestion of permanence or any metaphorical significance beyond setting in motion the transaction in the world, at that time and place.

We have deliberately chosen two very different examples – a poem and a note to the post-man/woman for illustrative purposes, but our intention is not to suggest that the poetic and transactional functions of writing are to carry as much weight as categories as they did for Britton et al. (1976) where 'poetic' and 'transactional' writing accounted for the two main types, once the stream of expressive writing had divided into works to be spectated and contemplated for their internal resonances on the one hand, and works to 'get the world's work done' on the other. Rather, we would see a wider range of functions, all possible in any one text and certainly not polarized or exclusive of each other. In terms of our present argument about the affordances of writing, we would rather contrast writing to other modes of communication where the affordances are different. It would be possible to convey the message to the post-man in iconic and/or visual form, but perhaps not in moving image, gestures or any other mode of communication.

Writing systems

We are under no illusion that learning to write will be made easier by setting it alongside other modes, or bringing it into the twenty-first century by means of digitization. In whichever language writing manifests itself, there are well-honed and historically created *systems* to learn – and that may well take a lifetime to learn. A writing system has etymological history, particularly in the evolution of *words* over time. It also has system-wide rules, patterns and correspondences that need to be explored and learnt.

The notion of a self-enclosed semiotic system derives from the work of de Saussure (1916/1977) who suggested that signs operated on the basis of difference within a system. The emphasis in de Saussure's work was on the sign systems rather than on semantics or meanings generated. The fact that meanings in the world might be generated socially and might change did not divert him from a concentration of the internal system of language. De Saussure's focus was on the synchronic elements in language systems, rather than on the diachronic (historical) elements. Apart from his contribution to twentieth-century linguistics and semiotics, the legacy of de Saussure is to remind us that writing – in whichever language it presents itself – is a system to be learnt. Such learning does not imply, however, a systematic, logical series of steps towards competence in the chosen language. From a pedagogic point of view, and from the point of view of the developing writer, written language is closely associated with speech, reading and life experience, as well as with other modes of communication. It benefits from being integrated into these various systems, as its meaning is partly determined and circumscribed by them.

Writing development and developing writers

It will be clear by now that the focus of the present book is not just on writing development but on the activity of developing writers. In other words, the book has a two-fold purpose: to understand writing development better in order to help writers (of school age, but also of all ages) to develop their writing. We think that the development of writers-in-schools approaches to the teaching of writing has been only partially successful because writing development is only partially understood. There has been insufficient association and commerce between the study of cognitive development through writing, or the grammatical development of writing, or assessment regimes which attempt to capture stages in writing development, in order to fully integrate a model of writing development. So emergent writers of whatever age have been hampered by partial approaches to learning to write which emphasize one aspect of writing at the expense of others: a grammar-based approach, focussing primarily on the sentence as the unit of construction; or a genre-based approach, which focusses primarily on the whole text as typical of a kind or type of (verbal) text, and thus tends towards formulae for writing.

The model for writing development we wish to create in the present book, then, must address a range of factors at play as young people learn to write. These factors include the environment for writing; the resources available; the broad motivation and specific purposes for writing; the affordances of writing as opposed to other modes; the rhetorical context for writing, including consideration of the audience; the media in which writing operates; and the multimodal possibilities for composition.

It follows that a book entitled *Developing Writers* has at its heart the principle that all writers can be developed further, whatever their present state of competence in writing; and that to do so we need to diagnose fully what their present capacities and strengths/weaknesses are.

As we intend to show in the following three chapters, there are significant gaps in the understanding of writing development. We do not think we are yet in a position to propose a theory and model of writing development that is subtle and comprehensive enough to suit all purposes. What we will try to do is make clear where the gaps are, and then attempt to present a more comprehensive process- and product-based theory and model upon which practice, assessment, policy, curricula and further research can be built. Such an ambition can be too risky, in that it might result in our over-reaching ourselves in the pursuit of an ideal and all-emcompassing theory. But we feel that we have to make the attempt, and will do so by degrees so as not to stretch credibility and logic at too early a stage in the process.

Conclusion

To summarize the argument of the present chapter: writing and writing development can no longer be the preserve of a monomodal approach to communication, as if learning to write was merely (however difficult it is) the work of gaining command of a particular second-order symbolic system. The conditions for a new theory and model of writing development are so strong as to demand that some re-thinking has to take place. These conditions include the resurrection of multimodality as a central consideration in communication of all kinds; the tiredness of existing approaches which appear to be based on a watered-down version of genre theory; a need to move way from target-driven, assessment-driven models of writing; the ubiquity of digitization in contemporary communication; a desire for a more bi-literate world; an understanding and recognition that writing takes place out of school as much as, if not more than, it takes place within school; and the need for pedagogies that reflect the changing circumstances of writing and writing development. Furthermore, although we have implied as much in the book so far, writing development is not a phenomenon that is limited to young children; it is a serious matter for young people in their teens as they move from middle to high school, and then on to college, university and/or the workplace. But it is also a central concern for adult learners who need to learn to write in their native language and/or in a second language in order to play a full part in society.

The book now moves to a more in-depth consideration of theories (and lack of them) of writing and development; to process- and product-related models and their strengths and weaknesses; and to discussion of linguistic and/or social and/or psychological models of writing. We believe full consideration of the work that has been done to date, and practices and assumptions that have developed from them, are necessary before we move toward the proposal of our own theory and model of writing development. As ever, we will keep the multimodal and digital dimensions of writing and writing development in mind.

3 Theories of Writing and Development

Introduction

Before we address existing models of writing development – both process-related models and product-related models – we need to think about the relationship between learning and development; and also between writing and meaning-making. These are two large areas that need clarification, as well as a stating of our own position, so that subsequent chapters can be built on a relatively firm foundation. Part of the problem with writing development theory is that it has not addressed these two key issues. It has operated as though the development of writing can be studied in a vacuum.

Current theories of learning and development

Two books by Illeris (2007, 2009) provide a helpful guide to the current state of learning theory. What is interesting is that they have less to say about development. This is surprising, given that cognitive development has been a central preoccupation of learning theory for much of the twentieth century; and that other kinds of development (physical, emotional, 'maturational', experiential, social) must have a bearing on writing development. Indeed, if we look at the index of the first of these titles, *How We Learn: Learning and Non-learning in School and Beyond*, 'development' is given scant attention. Illeris notes in defining learning that: 'The term "development" is understood as an umbrella term for learning and maturation, and I thus regard the "classical" conflict in psychology concerning whether learning comes before development or vice versa (see Vygotsky 1986 [1934], pp260ff.) to be mistaken. Learning is part of development' (p. 3).

'Development', then, for Illeris is at such a general level of signification as to be hardly worth addressing in the book. This is an interesting position, as it assumes that learning and development are more or less synonymous; and/or that it is not worth considering development as a category that is useful in thinking about progress in learning. Later, however, he maps the position of various theorists in the learning field, and has as one of the axes of a learning triangle the work of *developmental psychologists* like Piaget (at the 'content' end of the spectrum) and Freud (at the 'incentive' end, though Freud is acknowledged as only addressing learning indirectly). So development does have a kind of significance: in mapping the field of learning, it provides one side of a (triangular) field, the other two of which are represented by activity theory and socialization theory.

In the later, edited book, *Contemporary Theories of Learning: Learning Theorists . . . in their Own Words*, there is no mention of development in the index, though the term occurs in many of the chapters. The assumption must be that development is of such pervasive significance in learning theory as to be of no significance.

Avoiding the polemical pitfalls of the classical conflict mentioned above – briefly, whether development precedes learning (Piaget) or learning precedes development (Vygotsky) – our own view is that it is worth distinguishing between learning and development. We attempt to define the terms of engagement here so that they can be clearly used in the rest of the book, informing our discussion of writing development models.

Learning we take to be a transformational process and *act* resulting from engagement with or within a community. It is an act that moves us forward in some way. Traditionally, that 'moving forward' has been conceived as a cognitive step or steps; and it is also seen as progression in knowledge, so that epistemological dimensions are taken into account. But the traditional cognitive/epistemological axis of learning does not seem to us to account fully for the act of learning. First, learning is *transformational* in that it marks a change from a previous state of being/knowledge/awareness. That is to say, the learner is different at the end of the learning process than he/she was at the beginning. He/she may have *acquired* a new (small) segment of knowledge – for example, he/she may have learnt that in some countries, you drive on the right-hand side of the road, and in others, on the left. At the other end of the spectrum, he/she may have undergone a major learning experience which will have changed the *paradigms* or *values* for learning completely – for example, learning that the world is a spherical orb in a galaxy of other planets rather than flat territory at the centre of one's personal 'universe' is a major transformational act.

Second, learning is an effect of community (Rogoff 1992). That is to say, the very fact of being part of a community leads to learning about the values, *mores*, knowledge and other aspects of that community, whether it is a family, school, special interest society, or a wider socio-political group. We can build on Rogoff's Vygotskian conception to say that learning is an effect of communi*ties*: we all belong to a number of communities, real-world and electronic, of varying degrees of networked intensity, which interact with each other through our own activities. Not only do we learn by being part of a community, then; we also learn by navigating between different communities and gaining from the tensions and complementarities at the interfaces of those communities.

We are not so interested in learning *outcomes*; to reduce learning to a set of identifiable targets and commodities seems to us to diminish its power. Rather, we see learning as a *process* that can transform us personally (emotionally, spiritually, intellectually, physically, and so on) but also help us to contribute to social and political dimensions of learning (adding to a socially agreed body of knowledge, using learning to change the world). Learning is thus seen as a verb in its original sense (the present participle of the verb 'to learn') but subsequently as a gerund (the noun 'learning'): remembering its origin as a verb reminds us that it is a process, an action. There is no doubt, then, that learning takes place both outside as well as inside school. Throughout the present book on writing development, we see the development of writers taking place in communities of practice: these can be formal schooling communities, or they can be out-of-school communities like writing groups, families, online communities or special interest societies.

Development need not be a transformational act nor result from engagement with a community or communities. So the first points to make about it stem from its differences from learning. Development can take place over a period of time. It is a result of a combination of any of the strands of separate development that we have characterized earlier: emotional, physical, spiritual, intellectual, cognitive, moral, experiential, social or 'maturational'. It results not so much from an act of learning, which could happen in an instant of time, as from a succession of acts of learning that add up to a stage in development. Furthermore, development need not be social or community based. It could be (and usually is conceived of as being) *individual*.

Later in this chapter, once we have also considered the relationship between writing and meaning-making and communicating in general, we will come back to the question of writing development (and of developing writers). For now, we need to explore in more depth the notion of development *per se*. In addition to the points that distinguish it from learning, we could also say that development usually has positive associations. That is true of learning too, though learning could be negative (we can imagine social situations in which learning about poverty through experiencing it could have negative consequences in later life). But *development* suggests positive individual maturation. Furthermore, to say that someone has developed suggests that they have integrated various aspects of learning along with normally occurring physical and social *growth*. Development assumes change in time. One of our key assumptions in the present book is that *writing development* is a complex, multi-dimensional (or, to change the metaphor, multi-stranded) phenomenon that has yet to be given full attention by the academic community, let alone by practitioners who teach writing. The temporal dimension is one that is important to any fuller account of how young and older people learn to write.

Writing and meaning-making

Writing is both a means of making sense – 'how can I tell what I think till I see what I say?' (Forster 1927/1976:99) – as well as a means of communicating with others. As we will explore later in the chapter on writing and multimodality, writing has particular affordances as a means of representation and as a 'language' or mode of communication. We will leave the discussion of its affordances in systemic terms until later. Here we look particularly at writing as meaning-making.

Writing has often been seen (for example, by Vygotsky) as a secondary symbolic system, based on speech. It is understandable how such a conception could form: speech comes first in the child; writing comes second, and seems in many ways to be used to represent speech; writing has dialogic properties that seem to be borrowed from speech; writing systems, at least in the alphabetic written languages, seem to be based on a broad (though often inexact) correspondence with speech-sounds. And yet it could not be said that the writing system in Modern Standard Written Chinese or its larger set of classic Chinese characters could be based on speech, as that system is ideographic rather than grapho-phonemic. Furthermore, it is the case that written systems have operated alongside spoken systems of communication – as far as we know – throughout time. It is more accurate to say that writing systems operate alongside spoken systems, often with close correspondence but sometimes not.

Learning to write in English, then, is a different matter from learning to write in Chinese. Not only do the two languages (English/English and Mandarin, or any other Chinese dialect/Modern Standard Written Chinese) have different written systems; the underpinning logic of those systems is different. The English alphabet, shared with other European languages, is predicated on a linear logic which suggests that strings of letters in particular sequences made into words, and then strings of words in particular sequences, constitute meaning. In Chinese and other ideographic written systems, the relationship between elements of the 'character' or concept are spatial rather than sequential. Within a square space, the elements are put together to compose a concept. Many of these abstract concepts carry the residual visual identity of the originally drawn characters; as spatial written systems, they are inevitably more visual than aural. And yet the changing of meanings in time results in the fact that the Chinese characters carry metaphorical nuances of their concrete origins.

If written systems operate *alongside* spoken systems, the implications is that they develop their own ways of making and representing meaning. These ways of meaning-making can be termed *affordances*. The affordances of writing in English is that they stand at an abstracted level away from felt or perceived experience: one can stand in an uninscribed landscape and speak to another person – perhaps a fellow walker or climber – and the voice leaves no trace on the landscape. But to write something in that landscape, whether it is inscribed on the ground with a stick in the dust, or carved into a tree; or whether it is less connected to the landscape, like a note left for future passers-by in a prominent place, or a recorded reflection or observation of particular features of the landscape or experience in a notebook – a notebook that will probably be carried out of the immediate landscape as the walker continues his/her journey – means that writing is to some degree or another *abstracted from* experience. Such abstraction ('pulled away from') is powerful because it allows non-figurative communication. New ideas can be imported; combinations of thought and experience can be made; new configurations explored; and all this can be preserved for future reference. (The same could be said for speech, especially now that it can be easily recorded and preserved. But speech is less considered, more narrow in its verbal range, more part of its immediate environment on the whole.)

Thus writing makes a particular kind of meaning: one that is, in general, transportable; readable; drawing on a wider vocabulary than speech; and preservable. In terms of meaning, it creates – again, on the whole – more orderly, managed, univocal messages than are usual in speech.

Why writing?

But the deliberations above do not fully answer the question of why we write at all. They address questions of the relationship of writing as a semiotic system. They do not answer a more fundamental question: why do we write? Why it is seen to be important? And why does education prize it so highly?

To start to answer the fundamental question – why write? – and its attendant questions, we need to go back to the bedrock of writing: verbal language. Verbal languages, which we define as languages that are made up of words, characters or other signs that can be represented in speech or writing, have as their driving force the need for social interaction between people. By 'verbal' we mean ' to do with words', not merely 'oral' languages; we distinguish verbal language, therefore, from visual, physical, musical, mathematical and other 'languages'. But we include the variety of world languages (English, Spanish, Mandarin, Swahili, etc.) under our generic term 'verbal language'.

Verbal languages have at least five characteristics that distinguish them from other languages. They are inherently symbolic; they are or can be relatively inexpensive in terms of production; they are relatively free in terms of copyright; they are flexible and develop; and they are carriers (and indeed creators) of a wide range of meaning, from the particular to the abstract, from the concrete to the conceptual. Let us explore each of these characteristics in turn.

The symbolic nature of language is evident in speech as well as in writing. Unlike most forms of visual, physical or musical representation (but like mathematical equations), verbal language is already one step removed from the sensory world of experience. Because words are either seen visually or heard aurally, there is a sensory dimension. But what we are reading or hearing is a symbolic representation of experience and/or abstraction, *not the thing itself*. Indeed, words operate in a realm of experience that is not primarily sensory. They map experience, in the way that an actual map charts a terrain rather than walks you through it. Each word (or element in other languages, like characters) is a small abstraction from the world of everyday felt experience. The way they are joined to each other – in utterances, sentences – makes for links between these abstractions that can be narrative and/or hierarchical and/or argumentational and/or classificatory in nature. But the words themselves do not all constitute 'concepts' as was proposed by Vygotsky; they constitute, instead, the raw material of concepts in the form of abstractions. Concepts are more like fully-fledged amalgams of abstraction, perhaps based on a series or collection of particularities, that have coherence and generalizibility. Abstractions come in all shapes and sizes, and their borders are less defined.

We need to qualify one statement in the previous paragraph: that verbal languages are a representation of experience, not the thing itself. There are many exceptions to this rule, for example in literature where the actual verbal construction *is* the experience (as in a poem); or in speech act theory where some utterances enact and stand in for experience (as in a declaration at a wedding – 'I do' – or a signature to an agreement, which have locutionary, perlocutionary and illocutionary force and import). But even in these examples of language-as-action, the verbal construct only appears to be standing freely from its context. In the case of a poem or experience, other modes of communication and significance are implied or suggested; in the case of a wedding or other legal ceremony, the words signify actions of agreement. So words rarely stand on their own, even in ritualistic and highly formal situations where they appear to do so.

The second characteristic of verbal languages is that they are economi-cal. Speech, at least, is relatively free. It takes air, vocal chords, intention; but these resources are available for other purposes too and seem not to draw heavily on human resources. Writing is different in that it requires mediation other than air: it is inscribed in the sand, on paper, via elec-tronic means. It is much more a part of the physical world than speech in the sense that it is tangible, visual and needs to be transported. When Yeats said of his poetry that 'he made it out of a mouthful of air' he was talking about the oral rather than the written version. Writing requires resources, even if these are a simple as a paper and pencil. When we com-pare written language to the other modes – the visual, physical, aural, etc. – we can see that each draws on a different set of resources. What is flexible about written language is that it can operate with scant resources as well as more expensive, high production resources such as computers, mobile phones and printing presses. What needs to be stressed is the flexibility of written language in terms of its representation and re-representation in various media. Because the individual units – words, characters and their constituent elements – are small and weightless, they are eminently transportable.

The issue of copyright is an unlikely feature to discuss in a book on the nature and development of writing. Nevertheless, the movement that has brought about a commodification and valuation of *intellectual* property finds itself in a relatively freer zone in the written world than it does in worlds of music and the visual. To suggest that words are more generally free of copyright than other modes is not to ignore the issue of copyright in the verbal domain; it is simply to say that combinations of words are less easily bound, less marketable and thus less subject to copyright law than other modes. It is hard, for instance, to patent an *idea* without it being framed in a particular sequence of words in the language. But an image or a musical work is more readily identifiable, and thus more of a commodity that can be protected. It is also the case that the music and visual industries fight harder to retain copyright than what we would loosely called the 'verbal industries' – except in the case of books, works, particularly achieved sequences of words and other verbal documents.

The flexibility and evolution of human verbal languages is another di-mension that requires consideration. Because words, even though they are abstractions, are sometimes close to everyday experience in that they not only describe the world but operate as an invisible fabric of connection in the social world, they reflect changes in the physical world and in the so-cial world. These changes are more readily and immediately observable in oral versions of languages, but they soon become reflected in written ver-sions too. The interesting phenomenon here is that if written languages are more *fixed* in their spelling systems (in alphabetic languages) or in characters and scripts, they are likely not to be able to keep up with shifts in pronunciation and dialect in spoken languages. The advantage of standard written versions of a language – standard written English, modern standard written Chinese, classical Arabic, for example – is that they are relatively stable as systems of communication and can this be interpreted by a wide range of people. But they need to be *learnt* because the spoken dialects, accents and languages change more quickly and the gap between the spoken and written version of the language can widen. The flexibility of written language is connected to its evolution. English, for example, has throughout its history absorbed and incorporated words from other languages, creating a colourful, hybrid, extensive range of meanings, allowing nuance between shades of meaning.

Lastly, in terms of characteristics of verbal languages, they 'are carriers (and indeed creators) of a wide range of meaning, from the particular to the abstract, from the concrete to the conceptual'. The axes suggested here denote something special about verbal languages: they can operate, indeed define and create, across a wide spectrum of possibility. An example is the way in which we use words as search terms in an electronic search engine: it would be hard to conceive of visual or aural or physical coding that could perform the same function. Words can be combined vertically and hierarchically, in terms of categories and concepts; and/or they can be strung in (horizontal) sequences to create logical, descriptive and narrative sets of meaning. It is also possible to *create* a field of enquiry and its terms of references in verbal languages: a new book on multimodality or on chaos theory will most likely be represented in words, even though part of its conceptions may have been in the visual mode or its initiating impulse may have been rhythmical. Because words can operate in multilayered, logical and quasi-logical sequences, they are particularly suited to describing complexity and making it explicit.

How does or could the teaching of writing reflect the above?

We could expect issues like those discussed above to be part of study in an advanced level language course in a high school, college or in the early years of university study; but how do such characteristics manifest themselves in the curriculum and pedagogies for writing that take place earlier in schooling, when most of the development in writing is most apparent? These characteristics may, at first sight, seem to be highly abstracted from actual written experience; but our aim in this section is to show that they are, in fact, highly practical and full of possibilities in the writing curriculum and in its pedagogies.

The answer to the question 'how does the teaching of writing reflect the above?' is short. In most cases, it does not. There is little awareness in writing curricula about why we write and what its affordances are. For example, questions of the symbolic nature of the written word; of its economy; of intellectual property issues; of its evolution; and of its range, complexity and nuance are rarely addressed. And yet there are practical ways in which such issues can be incorporated into teaching, thus infusing it with more meaning and contributing to greater motivational possibilities for students.

Exploration of the metaphorical power of verbal language could be incorporated much more integrally into lessons. This is not so much a matter of identifying metaphors and similes in poems, as recognizing that metaphor pervades verbal language. Studies such as Lakoff and Johnson (1980) indicate that metaphor works structurally through ideologies and assumptions that are represented in the language, as well as at the more micro-level of one thing standing for another. Media coverage, for example, will often be couched in terms of conflict and battle, winning and losing, because these dualities sell newspapers and make for engaging television and radio. But the conventions of seeing arguments solely in terms of battle can be countered by different metaphors that see it in terms of building or dance, or of a journey. To discuss such underpinning metaphors in the course of classroom interaction, as and when they emerge, can be highly illuminating. Simple phrases like 'I can *see* your point' or 'How *far have we come* in this discussion?' reveal underlying metaphors of landscape and journeying, in these cases, that are worthy of further exploration. Even in the business of writing itself, metaphors of, say, building and cooking can be brought in to enlighten understanding of the way in writing works. For example, we can say of an emerging argument that it needs to establish its *foundations* and then *build on that stage by stage*. Or, of a piece that needs further revision, that the *ingredients* of the piece need further *cooking* with the addition of some critical *spice* to enliven the work.

To pursue the practical implications further: issues of economy can be brought in by first considering with a class, at whatever age or stage in their development as writers, what the available resources are to communicate something to someone. Are we writing to someone close to whom we can pass a handwritten note; or is the piece longer that we wish to create, and does it need transportation across the world via electronic means? What are the means of reception? What is it going to cost us to make this kind of communication, and are there better ways of effecting such communication? Are we operating with our own material or with others' material that needs some acknowledgement, if not copyright clearance? Do we want to copyright our own productions so that others cannot appropriate them unfairly? How has verbal language changed, even with our own experienced generations, so that we need to think about our audience and whether they will understand what we are 'saying'?

These matters are not purely contextual or abstracted from the actual business of writing: they are intimately connected to the act of writing and can add meaning and import, thus increasing motivation. Writing is thus seen as a means to an end (communication with others) rather than a rather sterile, school-based exercise for its own sake.

Why do education systems prize writing so highly?

Although one of our arguments throughout the book is that school writing needs to connect with out-of-school writing in order to embrace 'the universe of discourse' (Moffett 1968/1983), we need in the current chapter to consider school writing (Sheeran and Barnes 1991) again, and in particular the place and function that writing has in schooling. Sheeran and Barnes suggested that schools fostered specific genres of writing that were not present in the world outside school, and therefore were of limited relevance in becoming a writer. An example of such a 'school genre' would be the *descriptive* piece, deriving from a nineteenth-century rhetorical category, in which the powers of describing with 'powerful' verbs and plenty of adjectives or adverbs would be the norm. Such cameo pieces, almost like writing exercises or the Greek *progymnasmata*, are arbitrary. As schooling has begin to reconnect itself to the outside world (we hesitate to call the spaces outside schools and the school day the 'real world', as schools themselves are part of that reality) attempts are being made to make writing more real, for real audiences, and in preparation for the 'real world'.

And yet, despite a movement to reconnect with the wider world, schools remain places with their own cultures. Institutionally, they have their parameters and their discourses. Writing plays a central role in schooling, and we need to know why as the status and development of writing has much to do with the nature of schooling itself. First, as in any institution, writing is used within school to regulate activity. Rules, conventions, instructions, statements of mission and aim and teacher directions are often couched in writing. They appear in notices, in handbooks and in letters to parents and students. Inevitably, these written missives carry the weight of authority and control; their attempt is to create a community, but it is a community that is run by adults for the benefit of young people. Part of the intent is to control and manage these young people so that they can learn. It is no coincidence that academic disciplines are connected to self-discipline and the maintenance of order in schools.

Second, writing is important in schools because it marks the kind of discourse that is highly valued. The transition from home to school (at increasingly early ages across the world in pre-school and kindergarten, but formally somewhere between the ages of 4 and 6) marks a transition from a primarily oral world of discourse to one in which writing takes pre-eminence. Writing is consciously taught in the early years of schooling – that is partly what elementary and primary schools see as their function – but writing also provides the medium and mode through which much of education takes place. Classrooms are places for writing, and for reading it. They move children from a 'natural' context in which communication is a means to an end as well as a pleasurable end in itself, to an environment in which communication has purpose, is boxed and packaged, and is systematized. We do not want to take a romantic position in which we see the period before school as Eden-like, and schooling itself as equivalent to the Fall, but something of that detachment of the purposes of writing from the systems of writing takes place as soon as the child enters the school on his or her first day. This is an institution that values writing highly, but which separates it from its contexts in the wider world in order to help children learn it as a system.

Third, writing is used by schools to assess progress. It is the principal mode and medium used in the examination system. Because of that, it carries with it associations of diagnosis, appraisal, control and grading – the concomitants of assessment. Much writing undertaken by children in schools is written for the teacher to assess – it is handed in as homework or as classwork/homework. Whether it is in draft form or is a finished piece, it receives a response from the teacher. That response can range from anything from a simple tick to show that the piece has been read and is generally approved (a sort of nod of acknowledgement), to a fully-fledged critical commentary, usually in the form of annotations. These signs of response and comments are sometimes accompanied by a grade. It is one thing to recognize the importance of writing to assessment, and the way the two are implicated with each other in schooling (we return to the issue more practically in Chapter 11); but it is also the case that assessment itself is interested in the kinds of knowledge that writing can represent. That is to say, writing makes possible and subsequently handles *abstractions* and *concepts*, as has been discussed earlier in this chapter. These form the basis of much assessment of understanding in the education system. Although that understanding can be expressed also in mathematical symbols (even more abstractly than in words) and in maps and diagrams, the expression of *understanding* or *explanation* and *exposition* is often in words.

For these and other reasons, then, writing is highly prized within schooling. It seems, in many ways, to be the *sine qua non* of schooling: school is where you go to write. The same is true of higher education. In a two year seminar series on the changing nature of the dissertation/thesis in the digital and multimodal age (see Andrews et al. 2011) in the arts, humanities and social sciences, the conclusion was that despite the turn to the visual – not only in arts-based theses but in the humanities and social sciences too – universities and colleges seem reluctant to abandon a dependence on words for the final assessment of a contribution to knowledge. Even where the regulations permitted the submitting of artworks, exhibitions, made objects or 'portfolios' of such non-verbal productions, most of them still required a 'commentary' – often of 40,000 words or so for a doctoral dissertation – in *writing*.

Writing development

What are the implications of the discussions above for the notion of writing development? And before we move into the chapters that review existing process- and product-related writing models, what other considerations need to take place?

Let us start with the point implied at the end of the previous section: that writing development continues beyond schooling into the college and university years. We can extrapolate from that and suggest that writing development continues (or could continue) throughout life. It is as much a concern for adult learners of whatever stage in writing development – from someone struggling to learn to write in an adult education class, or learning to write in a new language if they have immigrated from a part of the world and/or from a culture in which writing in the new language (or writing at all) was not addressed at one end of the spectrum; to an advanced writer in specific fields (like the writer of medical journal articles, or a human resources specialist designing job descriptions) at the other end of the spectrum. Writing development continues, and what is more, writing itself continues to develop and become more a part of everyday activities in the workplace, requiring the need for people to upskill themselves.

At the other end of the age continuum, writing starts before schooling. A number of studies have looked at pre-school writing (e.g. Kress 1997, Andrews 1988) and concluded that the writing/drawing/play nexus is a rich one in which writing is first seen as a means of communication, and then is gradually separated out as a system in its own right (a process that is accelerated at school). So writing development is a phenomenon that starts as soon as a child makes a mark with a crayon or any tool on a surface.

An implication of the lifelong process of learning to write is that tightly staged assessment/progress systems in the limited years of school-ing – although they are the principal focus of this book and the stages at which writing development is likely to accelerate most quickly – do not fully account for writing development over the lifecourse. It is important to for us, as writers of this book and for teachers, to look outside schooling to the wider contexts and environments for writing.

Conclusion: developing writers

Finally, in this chapter devoted to theories of learning and the place of writing, we switch the term 'writing development' to 'developing writers' – the title of the book. As well as to the business of helping to develop writers – the job of teachers of writing, addressed again more practically in Chapter 11 – we wish to draw attention to the human di-mension of learning to write: the fact that writers are people who develop their skills and capabilities in writing over the lifecourse.

It is interesting that writing development foregrounds the product, writing, rather than the act of writing or the person who is writing. As with many of the product-oriented models we will discuss in Chap-ter 5, such an approach is predicated on the development of written products, or the assumed changes that take place between one writ-ten product and another. But writers who develop are *people* who de-velop: they develop not only maturationally and cognitively, but also socially, experientially and globally by being exposed to different worlds, different people, different communities. Their range of discourses thus develops.

This somewhat different approach to the development of writing, by focusing on the writers, moves the ground of our common practice and interest to the role writing plays in people's lives. We think that no longer it is adequate to concentrate only on writing systems, and particularly on sub-sections of those systems that have been prioritized as central to the business of learning to write, like sentence grammar (see Locke 2010 for a move beyond conventional approaches to and debates about 'grammar'). Entire teaching approaches have been predicated on the teaching of a system; or on the systematization of the practice of writing that is already emergent. Our own approach is more integrated with other aspects of experience, in that it sees writing as one means of expression, one mode that is related to other modes; and furthermore, as a means of expression that is powerful in the contemporary world. This approach also wishes to lower the barriers between the school world and the world outside school. Such a widening of the aperture sees writing as a transparent window to experience and knowledge, rather than a self-referential system. At the same time, we do not underestimate that learning to write in one or more languages is a challenge that requires gaining the command of a symbolic system. We set high store by accuracy and elegance in the use of those systems; but we recognize that developing as a writer means being open to influences that may change one as a person – and therefore as a writer.

4 Product-Related Models

Introduction

Chapters 4 and 5 are based on a systematic review of writing development theories and models dating from 1968 to the present (Smith and Andrews 2009). Our approach to this search owes much to systematic literature review methodology (Torgerson 2003) in that we have undertaken a systematic search for books and articles about writing and its development. We searched libraries in New York and London, and used online databases (PsychInfo, ERIC, BEI, Dissertation Abstracts International, the Australian Education Index) as well as searched portals such as the Teacher Training Resource Bank (TTRB), the Evidence for Education portal, the Institute for Effective Education's Best Evidence Encyclopedia (BEE) and the Evidence for Policy and Practice Information and Coordinating Centre (all UK). In the USA, we also used the Campbell Collaboration's Social, Psychological, Educational Criminological Trials Register (C2SPECTR), the What Works Clearinghouse and the Promising Practices Network.

Our results exclude seminal studies such as Dyson (1997), which, we fully acknowledge, have influenced research and practice regarding writing, and even have important developmental implications. However, we have only included studies and series of studies that have posited theoretical models or generalized trends of writing development. We simultaneously conducted a review of writing development studies since the early 1990s to illuminate which theoretical models are currently being employed to see how the concept is actively being theorized (Smith 2009). From this review, we could determine which models have remained relevant and salient in the field. As such, findings and influence from several more studies than are discussed in this text remain critical, but outside the scope of this review.

Our search resulted in several theories of writing development popular in education, beginning in the 1960s. We created a comparative matrix to analyze how these theories are related and distinguished from one another. We included the following categories for each theoretical approach: definition of writing; definition of development; focus (linguistic, process/product, multimodal); contextual frames; methods of researching; and population (on which the model is based and to which the model applies). We found that most writing theories and models are based on an analysis of written products – examples of children's writing. Certainly those theories and models created in the 1960s, 1970s and 1990s (there have been none that we can identify in the 2000s) were product related. For this reason, we dedicate this chapter to studies that locate development in students' written products.

In the next chapter we will consider the theories that approached writing development by questioning the processes people go through to create written products. These two approaches to understanding writing development, product-related and process-related, capture the two most prominent historical approaches to writing in education. They inform the current teaching, assessment and curricular practices in education across continents and the personal theories of many as to how writing develops and should develop in schools. By reviewing these existing theories, we build the foundation for a renewed theoretical approach for the twenty-first century.

Product-related models of writing development

Written products permeate education. Students not only learn to write, but they write to learn and write to demonstrate understanding, as well as discover and express their opinions. A well-written response can mask misunderstanding and poorly worded writing can be mistaken for the same. The written product, then, is an obvious place to look for evidence of writing development. Not only is it the clearest and most tangible remnant of the act of composing, but the effectiveness of a written product to communicate an intended message to a particular audience is of interest to both the reader and the writer. With improving communicative effectiveness as an educational goal, it makes sense that some of the first attempts to measure development in writing focused in on the written product.

In this chapter, we will review three product-related approaches to theorizing writing development that have shaped writing instruction, assessment and policy. First, we look at studies from both Hunt (1970) and Loban (1976) who analyzed the syntactic strategies employed by writers in written products. Their studies did not result in a 'model' of development *per se*, but the findings of these studies suggested trends of change in syntax of students' written products through the school years. Next, we take a look at Britton et al.'s (1976) study of written products in the upper grades, which has had major impact on curricular planning worldwide. Finally, we'll take a look at Wilkinson et al.'s (1980) and Arnold's (1980) proposed models of development beyond the printed text of the written product. Like analytical rubrics for correctness or effectiveness, which are used as common assessment tools in large-scale assessments, rubrics were employed in these final two approaches; however, their studies extend the notion of what is possible to learn about the writer behind the written products. These five theories of writing development have implications for understanding the types of changes to written products we can expect to see over time and the types of written products students are able to practise in schools. And although written products in the twenty-first century have changed through the inclusion of multiple modes, interactive features, and also in terms of the physicality of the written product itself, they will remain an integral measure and source of evidence for a model of writing development in the digital age.

Developmental trends in syntax

Before the studies of Hunt (1965) and Loban (1976), several linguistic, semantic and syntactic studies existed. However, the results of studies in this field were not comparable, because each counted the sentence, the fragment, the clause and the run-on differently. Thus the general consensus of educators and researchers was limited to the idea that with age people wrote longer sentences. Unsatisfied with such a crude understanding of linguistic development, Loban, whose longitudinal study began in 1953 and was published in 1976, argued that word counts, even comparable word counts, could not capture syntactic development. He called for an accounting of the ability of writers to use clauses to 'coil thought more tightly' (p. 17). Answering this call, Hunt's 1965 report reframed linguistic analysis for studies of writing development in schools through the creation of the *T-unit*. Defined as 'one clause plus any subordinate clause or non-clausal structure that is attached to or embedded in it' (p. 4), the T-unit satisfied the need for a comparable, distinct unit of measure of syntactic changes across writers and time (see Figure 4.1). Loban used an equivalent syntactic unit in his study, which he termed a 'communication unit'. Hunt's term – the 'T-unit' – however, has been more widely used, showing up in studies of varied foci from tracking revision, to measuring motivation, to assessing product quality.

Hunt (1970) based his developmental findings on a series of studies utilizing free-writing, speech, and sentence-combining exercises from students in different schools in a cross-sectional design to compare grade-level subgroups. Hunt found that at 2-year intervals, older students write longer clauses and T-units, but not longer sentences. He reasoned that people learn methods of combining concepts in ways other than using 'and' between separate sentences. Hunt found that in the sentence-combining exercises, older students retained a fewer number of the

One T-Unit

The teachers cheered.

The teachers cheered on the last day of school.

The teachers, not the students, cheered on the last day of school.

It was the teachers who cheered on the last day of school not the students.

Two T-Units

The teachers cheered on the last day of school while the students were sad to leave.

Three T-Units

As the last day of school came to a close, the teachers cheered and the students began to cry.

Figure 4.1 Examples of T-units

original sentences and main clauses, reducing them to subordinate clauses or to units less than that. The number of subordinate clauses per T-unit increased up until the middle grades and then decreased. Older students embed more elements into a single clause, and can do so with fewer words; so, the clauses get longer, but in more succinct and varied ways.

In a longitudinal study, Loban (1976) analyzed the language behaviour (reading, writing and listening) of 211 students in each of their school years from kindergarten to twelfth grades. For the writing portion of the study, at least one sample of student writing was collected and analyzed each year from grades three to twelve. In terms of trends over the thirteen years, the number of the words per communication unit increased and decreased with higher performing students consistently using more words per unit. Increases of words per unit in one year were consistently followed by drops, 'pauses, or consolidations' in the next year (p. 41). Along with frequent recursions, the transformation strategies (the ways in which units were elaborated or consolidated) employed by the students were evidenced in speech one to two years prior to their use in writing. Loban reasoned that with the increase of complexity in desired expression, fluency of expression faltered. More recent studies using T-unit measures have provided additional possibilities for the erratic growth in syntactic structure found in student writing. In a study of the relationship between motivation and writing, Potter et al. (2001) reported that students in their case studies found themselves with a 'current inability to write with [their] earlier fluency' (p. 49) when their present philosophical status was in conflict with schooling.

Both researchers also analyzed students' syntactic strategies in relation to their general academic ability, which they designated based on standardized test performance and teacher recommendation. With this analysis two additional features related to development were brought into focus: quality and experience. In Loban's (1976) study, around grade nine, the lower-achieving group made gains on the higher-achieving group in terms of words per unit; however, these sentences remained less coherent or organized. Hunt (1970) reported that writers of all ages created sub-ordinated nominal clauses; however, the less experienced writers wrote clauses that were repetitive and awkward. Within grades, higher-ability students in Hunt's studies wrote longer sentence parts; however, higher-level ability students did not typically write longer sentence parts than the lower-level ability students at the subsequent grade. These findings suggest that both ability and experience influence the increase in words per unit, not merely age.

Though Hunt's (1965) and Loban's (1976) studies differed in research design, their use of similar units of measure resulted in findings that support one another. Like researchers before them, Hunt and Loban counted words per sentence, but with their new precise and comparable measures, they were able to document the ways or strategies writers employed to embed concepts within the sentence. The trend that T-unit, or communication unit, analysis showed was that with experience, writers not only write longer sentence parts, but they also transform and subjugate information within sentences in effective, varied ways. The length of a sentence was no longer the single determiner of mature writing. Rather, elaboration within sentence parts, and succinct embedded concepts resulting in syntactic complexity were defined as signs of mature writing. A developed writer, then, was one who could 'compress ideas into more mature, meaningful forms' (Loban 1976, p. 13). The growth within this trend was identified as erratic – increasing and decreasing in intervals at each age and ability level – and based on the individual's writing experiences. Additionally, the quality or effectiveness of the resulting sentences did not relate to the syntactic strategies that were employed or the final word count.

Trends: descriptive to prescriptive

Hunt (1965) and Loban's (1976) studies were born out of an era of focus on syntactic structures. Sentence-combining exercises existed long before the 1960s and 1970s, but their use in teaching reached its fever pitch after the determination was made in these studies that mature writing is defined by highly-embedded, concise sentences (cf. Connors 2000). Textbooks still have students learn the difference between compound, complex and the epitome of the developed sentence, the compound-complex sentence. Champions of sentence-combining instruction and practice show that students can learn how to not only edit sentences for correct punctuation, but revise sentences for tighter construction by practising different ways to combine two 'complete thoughts' into one. Not only is sentence-combining teachable, it is, more importantly, measureable change. Proponents can show that teachers are able to speed up students' development. Dissenters of this practice argue that though students can demonstrate multiple ways of combining thoughts in more concise ways through these exercises, students are not practising the core ability at which this measure is targeted: 'coiling thought more tightly'. Though students can complete exercises, the results are often awkward prose. Mellon (1968) had established sentence-combining as more effective scholastic practice than the traditional grammar exercise for the understanding of grammar. But sentence-combining in isolation has been criticized as fiercely as detached, formal grammar lessons. Sentence quality and variation are lacking in writing by students who merely practise with sentence writing exercises without attention to the written product as a whole. Many argue that writing products as a whole provide the environment in which students increase their sentence-combining skills. This is sometimes called 'natural' growth and some suggest that quality sentence-combining cannot be directly taught, but only grown in experiences with writing.

On either count – whether we aim to speed up development by practising the component parts of sentences or we foster development by creating an environment rich with writing experiences – we must remember that studies such as Hunt (1965) and Loban (1976) were descriptive accounts not prescriptive statements. They were fashioned in reference to a particular population in particular conditions. So though it informs us of patterns that were seen and may be representative or generalizable, it is certainly not an account of how syntax *should* be. Quite simply, a compound-complex sentence with several subordinated clauses and embedded concepts is not the goal of every type of writing. One of the tenets of the disciplinary literacy movement is that expectations of the syntactic structure of sentences vary by field, discourse community and academic discipline. Moje et al. (2008) argues for a focus on teaching metadiscursivity, which would mean that rather than learning to write one type of highly-embedded sentence, students need to be prepared to match the style of their sentences to the purpose and audience of each product. Finally, the developmental nature of growth – erratic and regressive – is cited in both studies, but it is often disregarded. Whether syntactic maturity is considered as either taught or experienced 'naturally', we must account for an understanding of development that is dynamic.

Hierarchies of abstraction: audience and function

The research team of Britton et al. (1976) found strict linguistic approaches to measure writing insufficient to render the development of written products in their entirety. Turning to a form of rhetoric as an alternative orientation inclusive of the communicative aspect of writing, the researchers sought to map the development of written products through secondary school. Previous rhetorical categorizations of written products, the researchers critiqued, were based on how writers *should* write rather than how they actually *did* write. The researchers set out, instead, to theorize writing development in such a way that took into consideration the actual 'series of interlocking choices that arise from the context within which [a student] writes and the resources of experience, linguistic and non-linguistic, that he [sic] brings to the occasion' (p. 9). In order to map multidimensional development inclusive of writers' engagement, teachers' expectations, language resources outside school and pragmatic use of the product, Britton et al. proposed a four-part deductive inquiry project in which they analyzed over 2000 school-based written products from students aged 11–18 from 65 different secondary schools in the UK. However, the researchers quickly found that they did not have the means to identify and account for several aspects of a written product. For instance, though a writer's engagement and intentions for a piece of writing are reasonably influential on the resulting written product, access to these aspects is limited when all that is before you is the end product. The researchers noted this limitation: 'A writer's intention, we saw, may be highly personal, unique and sometimes hidden: he may, moreover fail in his intention so that "effect" and "intention" are out of joint, and there will be cases wherein all traces of intention has been lost' (Britton et al. 1976: 75). The research plan was thus reduced to a two-part plan in which only the rhetorical aspects of a written product – sense of audience and function of text – were assessed. In essence, then, the theory is two-dimensional rather than multidimensional. Where the researchers could not – because of the lack of developed methods, technology or access to data – systematically address the complexities they wished, they acknowledged the limitation and called for future inquiry.

Britton et al. (1976) drew from existing psychological and linguistic developmental schemes, namely from Moffett ([1968] 1983) to explain the developmental scale of the actual audiences and functions they had identified in student pieces. Moffett's ([1968] 1983) work was informed by psychological theories of Piaget that centred on the prevailing idea that growing in maturity (or learning) is an act of de-centering from egocentricity – that cognition develops as learners become further removed from the subject of their thinking. At the basic level of abstraction, this means that to express to your friend your excitement of being on a rollercoaster right before it begins its descent requires a simple cognitive and linguistic capability. Explaining to someone who wasn't there about your excitement when you rode the rollercoaster last week requires a more mature set of skills. One even more mature or abstracted step would be to explain why an activity, such as riding a rollercoaster, is exciting. Moffett reasoned that it is through time, space and the distance between the speaker and listener that concepts become abstracted, and thus require more mature cognition. Britton et al. set out to order the 2000 writing samples according to just such a cognitive-distance scale, from the most mature – deemed adult cognitive capacity – to the least, or childlike cognition. As opposed to typical scales of writing – equating immature writing status with less stylistically effective products or those written by younger individuals – immature writing was thus labelled when it did not clearly fit within a category determined as mature in the rhetorical features of audience or function.

In part one, the team analyzed the students' written products in order to establish their categorical scheme based on the rhetorical components of audiences and functions. In this scheme, a writer's sense of the audience included not only who was reading the text, but why the audience was reading it and whether the text served a practical purpose or was just an exercise. Audiences for the written products included: self, teacher, known wider audience, and unknown public audience. Each of these categories included subcategories based on the purpose and use of the written products. Within the teacher category, for instance, the audience subcategories included younger person to trusted adult, student to teacher, student to a particular teacher and student to examiner. Following Moffett's (1968) logic, the developmental sequence for a written product extends from the self or intimate, personal relationship to the distant, abstracted sense of a general or unknown audience.

Analyzing the linguistic and structural patterns of the text as a whole, the researchers mapped the functions the written products of students in secondary schools were serving. The researchers were interested in the function of the text as a whole, rather than the many functions that exist within a text, even the many functions that single words or groups of words may serve. The researchers concluded that the written products' functions could be best described in a hierarchy with the base or least mature function serving expressive or emotive expression. At a more cognitively abstract level, the products ranged from the poetic – those where message and form were equally important – to the transactional, in which the linguistic resources were a *means* to the end message. The transactional category included several types of text functions including to persuade, to inform and to entertain.

Implications for practice

In the second part of the research project, the researchers assigned the categories to a subset of written products (n = 500) to analyze the inter-sections of audience, function, grade level, gender and effectiveness. The influence of audience is one of the most well-known findings from this section of the study. Fifty per cent of the written pieces deemed as imma-ture, i.e. with no distinguishable function or audience, were from work completed for English language arts courses. Many of these pieces were considered by the researchers to be 'dummy runs' or student products written merely to show a teacher capacity to complete a certain written task (p. 106). To this day, the importance of creating written assignments with 'real' audiences or audiences logically aligned with the purpose of the written task and beyond the teacher is looked upon as instrumental in ensuring student engagement in writing a product, as well as higher quality end products.

The researchers also reported that of the written products deemed transactional, those that functioned as informative (as opposed to persua-sive) were most often assigned. Of the subcategories of informative tasks, analogic tasks in which students classified 'particulars within a relatively highly wrought system of generalizations' (p. 163) were the written prod-uct most often assigned. Throughout the grade levels, teacher-specified demands for assignments with informative functions increased. Thus, not only were students afforded more practice writing informative tasks, particularly analogic tasks, they were receiving the most instructional di-rection with these types of tasks. Britton et al. (1976) noted that within the varying functions existed a range of quality among the end products and generally those students who had more experiences writing a partic-ular function wrote better quality products. Thus, Britton et al. suggested that within the functions of writing exists another developmental scale – a scale of quality or product effectiveness rather than a cognitive ab-straction scale. The research did not entail a full investigation of how or which products were better suited for the audience and function or those more eloquently written. The researchers just noted that there seemed a pattern that suggested that the students who had more opportunities to write for the function and audience in question wrote better prod-ucts. The researchers also proposed 'use of an increasing range of genres and structural devices' (p. 197) as a form of writing development. Thus, though this study was limited by the researchers' ability to account sys-tematically for multiple dimensions, they concluded that there existed parallel developmental scales for aspects of written products, particularly quality of end products and students' capacity writing a range of genres, which should be considered in order to understand writing development.

Both the quality and range scales, the researchers suggested, are related to experience, or number of times a writer has written a text for a particular audience and function, and determined the mastery or effective use of that function.[1] With this observation the researchers raised a pedagogical concern: within the informative hierarchy, the subcategories which were deemed the highest cognitive maturity such as speculative or tautologic writing were rarely assigned. Thus students have the least experience of writing at the highest level of cognitive abstraction, and would logically then write poorer texts of this type. Compounding such a concern was that as one function began to be assigned more often all other types of writing decreased, thus limiting the range of purposes in which students were gaining experiences in writing.

Implications for taking up this theory

As the audiences and functions of students' written products aligned closely with the writing tasks assigned to them in school, the researchers reasoned that the range of written products in schools was the result of teaching curriculum and methodology rather than students' independent writing development or skills:

> We are clear about one thing: the work we have classified cannot be taken as a sample of what young writers can do. It is a sample of what they have done under the constraints of a school situation, a curriculum, a teacher's expectations, and a system of public examinations which itself may constrain both teacher and writer.
>
> (Britton et al. 1976: 108)

Applebee (2000) argued that rather than a maturational or developmental sequence of cognitive and linguistic resources used to address audiences and functions, the researchers' findings about students' performance could be summarized as such: 'To a very large extent, they learned what they were taught in the order in which they were taught it' (p. 3). In essence, then, the developmental model offered by Britton et al. (1976) is a model of the development of school curriculum – how to characterize the sequence of tasks assigned to students in first, third, fifth and seventh years of secondary school in the UK. The order of assigned products aligned with and further reflected a pre-existing scale of cognitive abstraction. As with the studies that defined syntactic maturity, this descriptive study of school curriculum quickly became the recommended sequence of audiences and functions for schooling. The suggested sequence of increasing cognitive abstraction is pervasive in the field in both curricula (e.g. in the first version of the National Curriculum in England in English) and studies (e.g. McKeough and Genereux 2003).

The implication of this study to theory is that writing development is intricately tied to the writing experiences that have been afforded; and a common denominator to young persons' development is the experiences required in school. Britton et al.'s (1976) developmental scheme, however, is not an indication of students' cognitive or writing capacity, nor reflective of the entire range of audiences or functions of students' writing. For one, students are involved in institutions other than school, such as clubs and churches, as well as informal discourse communities, such as their families and friendship groups. The twenty-first century has also brought us communities that bridge formalized discourse with informality in correspondence, such as in gaming communities and fan fiction sites. Each of these communities has its own expectations for written products. Students participate in multiple discourse communities concurrently with school, and a theory of writing development is incomplete without an accounting of these experiences. Skilton-Sylvester's (2002) case study of one immigrant student's school and home literacy practices found that her practices involving genres, writing status, functions, volume and quality never converged in and out of school. The participant continued to be considered illiterate at school, while at the same time successfully conducting various and complicated literacy practices at home and in her community. To take up a theory of writing development centred on the written products students write, we need to account for each community within which the student writes, the expectations of writing and types of writing experiences afforded, as well as the logic of the order and types of written products required in that community. In schools, Britton et al. found a sequential logic of abstracted thought and distance between audience and writer. It is unlikely that every community has the same written product developmental sequence.

Beyond the written product: comprehensive models

The following two models of writing development differ from the previously discussed product-based models in that they attempt to provide systematic ways of measuring comprehensive or multidimensional writing development. Arnold (1980) argued that an individual's writing development was too complex, recursive and simply slow-moving to be captured by existing measures. She set out to devise a model inclusive of societal influences and representative of dynamic individual development. The research team of Wilkinson et al. (1980) of the Crediton Project in England similarly critiqued existing measures of writing as too narrowly focused on linguistics or cognition to be representative of individual human elements involved in composing a written product, such as emotion or belief systems. Each of these approaches to measuring written products utilized analytical rubrics to identify changes in or differences between written products. The rubric categories demonstrated the range of developmental aspects evidenced in written products – beyond changes in linguistics, syntax, content, or audience and function. Rather than assessing the products, as is the typical use of a rubric, these were used to inform models of development.

Modelling situated, dynamic growth

Published in 1980, Arnold's 'Spiral Model of Psychodynamic Discourse Development' was founded on several existing studies, including that of Britton et al. (1976), as well as a series of 35 experimental studies she conducted with the same student population over four years. Students at the intervention sites of these studies were asked to write self-expression and reflective tasks which the research team measured with a rubric of four categories: audience, creativity, thinking and language. From the results of both the control and experimental groups, Arnold designed a visual model of writing development that could be characterized as both socially situated and dynamic. The nature of writing in the model was inclusive of the social influences noted but not theorized in previous models. The model was also a rare attempt to model dynamic growth – the erratically progressive and regressive nature of growth cited in previous studies of written products, as well as her own. Rather than graphing her studies' data into trend reports or drawing a diagram of factors found in her studies, she modelled writing development metaphorically.

Arnold (1980) modelled writing development as extending from what she termed the 'core self', which was represented in the visual model as a small dot from which concentric circles (representing written products) spiralled upward and outward until bounded by three very thick and widening vectors (representing discourses) that angled out from the core self to the upper reaches of the visual model. The model is a visual metaphor of the ever distinct and dominant discourses the 'self' experiences over time. The discourses were an idealized sequential progression of the expressive, transactional and poetic discourses designated in the Britton et al. (1976) study. Development was represented as growing circles. As they became wider and closer to the three vectors, they represented both the widening range of a writers' repertoire, and closer approximations to the discourses represented in the vectors. Unlike many theorists and researchers of her time, Arnold (1980) theorized the reading audience as an integral part of writing development. She used the metaphor of mirrors to describe the way the audience, or the vectors in the visual model, reflect back to the writer the appropriate societal and discursive expectations for the writing discourse. She explained writing as an exchange, an attempt to 'match [a writer's] discourse intentions with society's expectations while still engaging an expressive experience' (p. 22). In this sense awareness of audience and sensitivity to a range of audiences is one way the writer develops up and outward in the spiral.

Arnold (1980) intentionally drew a few of the circles in the visual model as dashed or attenuated. She explained that they were drawn this way to account for the written products composed by a person that are – for one reason or another – not successful or not closer to the discourse expectations than previously written products. Arnold did not attempt to represent visually all the factors or how these factors influence the written products in the model. Rather these attenuated lines were one of the ways she drew attention to the students' seemingly erratic success rate in creating written products. The visual model, as a spiral, was intended to suggested dynamism or a springing energy between self and discourse as well as previous written products and current products. The least linear or hierarchal of existing product-based theories of writing development, the model accounted for both the sequential patterns of discourses afforded in school (cf. Britton et al. 1976) shown in the strong linear trajectories of the vectors along with the recursive nature of resulting products as people engage in an interplay between their social experiences, their thoughts and their patterns of expressive language. Arnold made an impassioned plea for dynamism and complexity in models of writing development:

> [S]tudents progress and regress in quite unexpected ways. Hence the need for a comprehensive theory of writing development and sensitivity, responsive monitoring of students' writing (and reading and related discourse experiences) over a long period of time. Writing development is slow to occur and difficult to detect by valid measures. To believe otherwise is to ignore the complexity of writing development processes and possibly to sell our students short.
>
> (Arnold 1980: 133)

Indeed, her focus on the student is demonstrated in the model itself. It is the 'core self' that changes or develops rather than the student's written products or the discourses in which they are writing. Arnold (1980) is one of the first to locate development in the person rather than the products.

How can you tell, when writing is what describes the "core self"?

Multifaceted development of the individual

As part of a teacher research project called the Crediton Project, Wilkinson et al. (1980) critiqued the often used, but ill-defined educational concepts 'development', 'maturity' and 'growth'. They attempted, by using students' written products with teachers' analyses of those texts to describe, in detail, what their team of researchers and teachers noticed was developing and what was seen as evidence of that development in the written products. Students aged 7, 10 and 13 completed the same four writing assignments in classes in two schools. These assignments differed in topic and function and included: 1) an autobiography about a happy or sad day; 2) a narrative based on one of three pictures; 3) an explanation; and 4) an argument. The researchers felt that differing the task and topic allowed the students to demonstrate different uses of written language to meet the topical and functional tasks.

The researchers argued that the locus of development resides in the individual, and that the written text that results on the page when a child writes is evidence of that development. Focused on development of the writer rather than the written product, the research team looked for growth in four areas: cognitive, affective, moral and stylistic. Based on existing theories of human development, and informed by the content and style of the student written products generated and analyzed in the course of the project, each of the four areas was described as a model of development, each having its own growth trajectory.[2] These trajectories, in sum, defined development as 'movement from a world of instances to a world organized by the mind; from dependence to autonomy; from convention to uniqueness, from unconsciousness to awareness; from subjectivity to objectivity; from ignorance to understanding; from self to neighbour as self' (Wilkinson et al. 1983: 45).

The Crediton Project's cognitive and stylistic models of development were similar to pre-existing models. Cognitive development was based in Piagetian notions of de-centering from the self in which products with descriptions limited to concrete details of the writer's personal experiences were indicators of the lowest level of cognitive development. The highest cognitive levels were evidenced by the inclusion of generalized and speculative ideas. The stylistic model of development included typical rubric categories: organization, cohesion, syntax, reader awareness and overall effectiveness. Not only was style modelled as developing, but characteristics of the writer's style were used as evidence of development for the cognitive, affective and moral models.

Growth in affect and morality are rarely operationalized in writing development studies. Typically, these areas of human expression are limited to prefaces of curriculum guides to act as guiding principles or overarching goals of the writing objectives which follow. As one of many examples, in Massachusetts the English Language Arts Curriculum Framework (Massachusetts Department of Education 2001) is prefaced by citing research that connects a person's resilience in times of personal trial to reading and writing skills. The model explains that English language arts courses are places to explore the wide variety of beliefs and values in the world, while simultaneously to develop a common ground with classmates that will facilitate their future functioning as citizens of the United States. In general, affect and morality are left out of official standards sections of such statements for many reasons, including issues of validity and reliability in assessing the achievement of such objectives. It is questionable that attributes such as emotional state and moral reasoning can be reliably accounted for in single written documents. The concepts of affect and morality themselves are hotly debated. Whose morality? What kind of emotional reaction is more mature than another? What would be satisfactory evidence of emotional content and moral reasoning?

As controversial as these questions may seem, these components of a written product have been central to teachers' interpretation and continue to be so. The prevalence of 'voice' in pedagogy and assessments is a current manifestation of this interest in expression of affect and morality. In Jeffery's (2010) three-part study of the ways voice is identified in the language of written texts across genres, employed in teachers' responses to writing, and used in evaluation criteria, she reported that voice accounts for a wide range of features in a written product that work together to express passion, reveal personal struggle, discuss values and opinions, and convince the reader of honesty or authenticity in the written composition. An amalgam representation of the writer behind the writing, *voice* appears as a criterion in half of the end-of-level high-stakes writing assessments across the United States (Jeffery 2009). Whether the concept is broadly conceived as 'voice' or directly as morality and emotion, when students are writing in school, these features will be present and integral to the end product, and will be assessed whether directly or indirectly. In the Crediton Project, the researchers decided to address the components directly, noting that their models of affective and moral growth were culturally defined, implying that the models themselves are in flux with the wider social and cultural environment in which students write products.

Like the cognitive model, the team's model of moral development was based on a pre-existing model of development in the field of psychology – Kohlberg's (1969) stage model of moral development. In the students' written products, judgements made of self and others were classified. Development was described to extend from immediate, concrete experiences that resulted in judgements, to judgements less directly tied to experiences. Specifically, the factors used in judgements were lined up in a scale starting, at the lowest level, with development judgements based on physical characteristics to judgements based on a personal value system. In between and in order from least to most developed were judgements based on punishments/rewards, status quo, norms and conventions, motives or status and abstract concepts such as respect. Affective development was modelled in terms of how emotion operates – in relationship with self, others (including the reader) and reality. Each of these instantiations of emotional possibility evidenced in the products was rated as to whether the emotion was implied, expressed, evaluated or discussed. Evidence of development, for both moral and affective models was looked for in the autobiography and narrative pieces through both content and style. When writing about a sad day, for instance, the student described the day and either the emotion was implied or it was explicitly stated. The researchers noted that often whether the explicitly stated emotions were then evaluated or discussed was determined by the stylistic prowess of the student in finessing both a full, explicit description of the emotive quality of the day they were writing about, including conjecture and further discussion. In other words, those most developed in style were able to demonstrate higher levels of affective development.

To this conception the researchers added that younger children may not have the same range of emotive register or the understanding of how to punctuate a more complicated sentence that could express emotive quality or abstracted thought. This lack of range did not mean, however, that the child actually used a lower form of abstracted thought, moral sensitivity or emotional complexity. Though the researchers add this as a short note of discussion, it highlights the limits of this theory of writing development. Such a disconnect could indicate several developmental issues. It could indicate that written products cannot provide conclusive evidence of human development – even when considering four products of differing topic and function. It could indicate that stylistic development runs parallel or slightly behind development in these other areas, or that certain facility with stylistic devices could indicate development in morality, emotion or cognition that is not actually present. Thus, our developmental claims are quite limited. However, this study does indicate that written products can be evidence of development beyond the text. Which features of the written products conclusively and directly are indicated by this development is not clear.

Conclusion: what we learn from the product approach

Consideration of written products is necessary to understand how writing develops. Three broad approaches to written products were reviewed in this chapter. From them we see several factors that must inform a theory for the twenty-first century. First, idealistic models are problematic in theory and in practice. Based on a sequence of examples of writing, often from different genres (e.g. narrative, argument, description) and derived from nineteenth-century rhetoric, these theories and models make assumptions about what characterizes written products among various ages and stages. Interpolated from the data actually gathered, these theories provide simplified linear trajectories of growth from one year to the next. When the data from Hunt (1965) and Loban's (1970) studies, for instance, are applied to a maturity scale with which students are expected to write various types of sentence based on their ages, secondary problems arise. Students can be labelled deficient if they do not exemplify a particular type of sentence on demand. They can also be misled that all forms of writing look alike. We learn from Arnold (1980) that it is possible to model development realistically. We can account for growth that is regressive as well as progressive, and therefore theorize writing development that is more reflective of actual experience. Arnold achieved this dynamic modelling through the use of metaphor and symbol, which can be taken up in our model.

We also learn that a theory of writing development will need to account for the full range of writing experiences afforded by various communities. Britton et al.'s (1976) study makes a foray into understanding the written genres of schooled literacy. While it is accepted that tangible evidence of writing progression is a good way to track writing, there has been little or no collection of such evidence in the 2000s as digital composition and multimodal composition (and sometimes both together) have established themselves outside and inside the classroom. We need a theory of development that is self informed, by which we mean that the expectations of a range of written products in multiple communities have shaping power on the actual developmental trajectory of the students' experiences. We also need to account for quality or effectiveness of these written products. Once the written product is situated – meaning expectations for its form, style and content are located by the community for which it is written – we must account for how closely that product approximates to the expectations.

Finally, electronic social networks have collapsed the time and space abstraction element of Piagetian thought that guided most of these studies. Electronic communication is at times even preferred over speaking. Students who have access to electronic communication have more experience of and contact to audience through writing than ever before. As a single example, at the time of writing this book all students in Smith's nephew Kaden's fourth grade class have received their own laptop computers, and Kaden was proud to report that they could now go 'paperless'. Kaden is most excited about the ease he believes laptops will make his work in school. 'I can get my ideas out so much quicker typing,' he reported. Kaden can experiment with and revise his syntactic patterns with much more ease than without this digital tool, which could allow for new kinds of linguistic development. Kaden also noted the ability they will now have as a class to research and manipulate text by cutting, copying and pasting, creating images, slide shows and videos simply with the click of a mouse. The compositions he creates are also immediately accessible to his chosen audiences, which extend both in and outside of school for projects he composes in both spaces. The digital media also make interaction between audience and creator possible. Kaden receives feedback through comments posted by classmates and strangers when posting to YouTube, by members of his extended family on his family blog, and on a small online cartoon community to which he sometimes posts. The accompanying software, programs and networks allow Kaden multimodal, multimedia designing options that would not have previously been available to a student composing a text with pen and paper.

5 Process-Related Models

Introduction: writing processes

The minority of existing theories and models of writing development are process related, meaning they describe and predict the processes writers go through as they compose. These processes can include: pre-writing activities like planning or brainstorming; the actual processes of committing words to the page or screen; and processes of revision, editing and proof-reading. Approaching writing as a process or as interrelated processes focusses attention on the act of composition in the present tense – as the person is compos*ing*, writ*ing*, design*ing*.

A process view of writing presumes that writing is made up of a series of actions or steps. Terms used to describe processes, such as *series*, often suggest an element of order – chronological or procedural – as in the steps taken to complete a task. The process of getting your car registered in the United States, for instance, is an ordered series of steps. This process varies from state to state. Finding out the steps to take in your state, as well as the order of those steps, is critical if you want to avoid delay, backtracking and a reprimand from the Division of Motor Vehicles. The processes of writing discussed in this chapter, however, are not necessarily systematic. Rather, the writing processes we will discuss have been theorized as *dynamic* according to the writer, the task, rhetorical goals and context. Instead of an ordered list of tasks to complete, the processes of writing are more akin to processes involved in a large social event. Imagine, from a bird's eye view, a large educational conference. Educators from around the world are milling about the vendors' tent. Some are returning to their hotel rooms to pick up forgotten items, and several more are moving chairs into the overcrowded conference room where a keynote speaker is just being introduced. Seemingly chaotic, there are still recognizable trends of movement, identifiable constraints on these movements, and decisions that typically follow other decisions. The processes of attending a conference are multiple and unpredictable, but can still be traced and understood; so are the processes of writing.

In this chapter, we will review two seminal approaches to researching and explaining the processes of writing; namely, the 'writing process', an approach popularized by practitioners such as Graves (1983), Murray (2003), and Elbow (1973), and a 'cognitive processes' approach most notably from the teams of Flower and Hayes (1981) and Bereiter and Scardamalia (1987). These two approaches differ from each other in important and distinct ways, but they contrast even more dramatically from the product approaches discussed in the previous chapter. Both of these approaches to the processes of writing focus our attention to the micro level of writing *en vivo*, that is, these theories of writing highlight the range of decisions made during the composing processes, as well as the range of approaches writers take to frame and solve compositional problems.

Another similarity between the writing process approach and the cognitive processes approach is that both of these schemes are primarily theories about the act of writing, not development. Rather than setting out to reshape the concept of writing *development*, the intention of the writing and cognitive processes work has been to reframe the conception of writing itself. Because of this, in the following sections we will outline the theoretical statements, research and work that reframed the general understanding of writing in education. We will then look at the developmental claims from research using theories of writing processes in their design. Though not developmental theories themselves, these two theories of writing processes have made a significant impact on educational practice, as well as the scope of what is considered 'developmental'.

The writing process movement

Rather than a theory derived from a series of research studies, the 'writing process' was more of a social movement in which practitioner-researchers such as Emig, Murray, Elbow and Graves acted as revolutionaries, dethroning the written product from its place of prestige in the composition classroom. The opening scene is situated in an era of weekly themes in which the student's role was to replicate the characteristics of a model text. The teacher's role was then to labour over the student's writing, marking errors. Enter the writing process movement actors. Emig (1971) published her dissertation in which she conducted case studies of 12th graders. She watched them write. She asked them to think aloud as they wrote. She analyzed the writing they produced. Her methods of observing writers in the act of writing were as revolutionary and influential as her findings that illuminated the complex series of writing activities high schools students employed to accomplish their writing assignments. Murray (2003: 3–4), a writer turned writing teacher, claimed, 'When we teach composition, we are not teaching a product, we are teaching process ... the process of discovery through language.' Meanwhile, Elbow (1973), from another angle, published *Writing Without Teachers*, in which he argued that current-traditional approaches which include outlining and an emphasis on correctness are fundamentally flawed. Rather, he suggested, writing is a learning transaction in which the writer discovers and learns as they write.

Though the emphasis of each of these practitioner-researchers' work varied, taken together their work resulted in a dramatic shift in the norms of writing instruction, particularly in the USA. Even though activities reminiscent of the traditional approach, such as model texts and the 'five-paragraph essay', still figure prominently in classrooms, their use is underpinned by a notion that these pieces are written through a process. Providing time, instruction and structures in the classroom to support the writing process has become commonplace. The fact that it makes so much sense to educators to think of writing as a process, characterized by thinking of an idea, writing down ideas and reviewing and making changes to what has been written, is evidence of this movement's success. Petraglia (1999: 53) humorously noted, 'We now have the theoretical and empirical sophistication to consider the mantra "writing as a process" as the right answer to a really boring question'. It is only boring because it is now so commonplace.

In the following two sections, we will outline the writing process approach that developed from this practice-based theoretical position, and the limited research that concurrently shaped the movement. Then we will take a look at the place of 'development' in this model of writing.

The writing process in research and practice

Process theory

Rohman (1965) is often cited as one of the first researchers to conduct an empirical study designed to understand what the writer is doing while composing school-based tasks. Based on his research findings, he suggested a simple linear, stage model of writing: pre-writing, writing and rewriting. The order and isolation of the stages in Rohman's (1965) model were questioned by researchers who conducted their own observation and case studies. Emig (1971), Sommers (1980) and Perl (1979), for example, documented the processes of various populations of writers. Perl (1979) documented five cases of writers who were deemed 'unskilled' due to the poor quality of their written products. In four 90-minute sessions that varied in audience and topic, she asked the participants to compose aloud. Though she witnessed a shift in the dominance of one phase of writing to another – a phase before the text was written on the page, then a phase in which text was produced, and finally a time when the text was reviewed – she described a very different picture than Rohman's three-stage linear model. She explained that within each phase was a series of varied activities in which the writers 'shuttled' back and forth between activities associated with other phases: generating, then editing by discarding text, followed by planning, then rereading, then generating again. She brought the concept of 'recursive' to the writing process movement.

Further descriptions of the writing process from both anecdotal and empirical inquiry supported this idea and further described ways in which each of the activities of pre-writing, writing and re-writing are embedded in the other (Sommers 1980). For instance, when writing a letter of complaint to a business, a writer may draft in order to pre-write. Rather than starting at the beginning, the writer may start with composing the paragraph that gets to the heart of the complaint in order to figure out how he or she wants the tone of the letter to be. Later, when the writer gets stuck, he or she may start either revising that paragraph or composing the beginning of the letter until he or she figures out what should be written in the next section of the letter. Murray (1984) also explained that while three overarching phases of writing – pre-writing, writing, and re-writing – is descriptive of this writing experience, the shifting and shuttling within the process are a singular series of activities, distinctive to each and every writing situation and varying according to the purpose of writing, the author's familiarity and comfort writing about the topic, and even the personality of the writer. In other words, there is not one process that should be replicated in learning to write.

In addition to the overarching stages of writing and revising, Murray (1984) proposed three distinct pre-writing phases – collecting, focusing and ordering – highlighting the range of activities with which the author is engaged before the moment print is formed into recognizable sentences on the page. Graves (1983) similarly proposed five stages in the writing process, teasing out some of the activities within pre-writing and re-writing: topic choice, rehearsal, composing, reading and revision. The work of Murray, Graves and other researchers during the writing process movement broadened the definition of writing to include activity surrounding the moment when pen meets paper or fingers tap on the keyboard. From this perspective, writing is highly complex, encompassing a range of mental, social and emotional activity. Even during the stroke of the pen, a writer is reconsidering the word they just typed, laughing at a joke a friend just posted on Facebook, deciding if their paragraph looks too long, and a myriad of other types of activities that are all a part of composing.

Simply put, the writing process is a recursive, idiosyncratic, situation-dependent set of activities we engage in to produce a piece of writing. These activities are embedded within broader categories or phases, the hallmark of the writing process: pre-writing, writing and re-writing.

Process pedagogy

Writing process theory is sensitive to the social situation for which the approach was posited – the classroom. Since the earliest work in the writing process movement, the work of teachers has been intertwined in the theory of students' writing processes (Pritchard and Honeycutt 2006; Boscolo 2008). For instance, Murray (1984) argued that teacher and student interaction should incorporate both the activity of writing and instruction for writing as the student is writing. He suggested that teachers meet this goal by employing writing activities and social structures that reflected the kinds of practices successful adult authors use to compose text:

- pre-writing – brainstorming, collecting realia in a journal, researching, listing;
- writing – 'brain dump', or brainstorming, writing without looking, dictating;
- re-writing – peer response groups, teacher conferencing, revising and editing.

Activities such as journalling, freewriting and conferencing epitomize the writing/instructing interaction Murray suggested. These types of activities are often suggested within descriptions of the writing process theory. In fact, the activities and structures suggested for classroom practices are often mistaken for theory itself. They are, rather, types of activities that may or may not be engaged in while in the phases of one's writing process. They are not components of the process. For instance, a writer may brainstorm as a form of pre-writing, but they may also collect realia or talk to peers or engage in a number of other pre-writing activities.

In addition to activities that are similar to the ones adult writers utilize, Murray (1968) also recommended that teachers should adopt a laboratory classroom structure with work areas and conferencing tables to replace the traditional lectern and rows of student desks. This physical rearrangement, Murray reasoned, would facilitate a shift in the classroom activities, relational roles of teachers and students and dispositions towards writing. Graves (1983) and his student Calkins are best known for the promotion of just such a classroom environment and structure commonly referred to as 'Writing Workshop', a laboratory of guided self-exploration through writing. Although there are variations in the way the Writing Workshop is implemented in different classrooms and programmes, the typical structures of a Writing Workshop, such as a class meeting, independent writing time, response groupings and one-on-one conferences with the teacher, avail the time necessary for the types of activities that support the writing process.

Whereas previously a teacher presented a task, described the necessary components required for an adequate response and students then wrote independently in order to be assessed (Applebee 1984), in the new arrangement students became engaged in writing in the classroom and the teacher acted in response to the students' writing. As the teacher moved from assigner and assessor (Durkin 1978) to guide and audience, the student moved into the central position of activity. Instead of an empty vessel to be filled with knowledge by the teacher, the student was actively writing to learn. The 'expressionists' such as Macrorie and Elbow argued that by writing through the experiences of self to understand the wider world, the student is engaged in motivated learning – the goal of many teachers.

In the classroom: from processes to orthodoxies and protocols

For educational purposes, implementation of the theory of the writing process, and its closely aligned pedagogy, was problematic. Early on in the process movement Graves (1983: 185) spoke out regarding unintentional orthodoxies about writing process pedagogy that he saw in teaching practices, such as: students should revise and have multiple drafts of every piece; the writing process is used only when writing personal narrative pieces; and teachers should limit their direction to students. Couture (1999: 30) questioned: 'How did the emphasis upon process, like so many ideas about writing that were derived from scholarship and research, lose so much when applied *en masse* in our classrooms?' As is typical in education, something as complex as a writing process and its pedagogy gets simplified in order to be mass produced. Its simplified version ends up being passed on. The fidelity of the process is compromised. Like the flat, lifeless characters in a sorry sequel, the nuances of practice that aligned with the writing process theory were distorted.

The pedagogical activities that were suggested for pre-writing, such as brainstorming, webbing and outlining, led to increased emphasis on pre-writing in classrooms. However, in the classroom, these activities became assignments. We hear of teachers assigning 'process papers' in which students are required to complete a series of these activities teachers have created as a lockstep protocol intended to prod the students to 'go through' a process. Step one may consist of filling out a brainstorming web in which students receive credit based on the number of ideas and sub-ideas generated. Step two may be a freewrite about the topic, and filling a page with text as a measure of success. In this type of 'process paper' the end product may or may not be graded. Rather, students often receive points for completion of each step's specific teacher-created activity.

Applebee (1984) concluded from his research of writing instruction across the curriculum that when teachers were using 'process writing' there was no connection between the rhetorical problem, the task posed, and the teacher-prepared writing activities students were required to complete. Post-process theorists argue just this point, that in implementation, teachers teach the process as content in and of itself rather than a description of how to write (Breuch 2003). Not only is the recursive and idiosyncratic nature of the process lost in class-wide, lock-step protocols, but so is the flexible nature of the writing activities as dependent on the writing situation. Students complete teachers' planned activities rather than practise responding to the writing situations before them, which would result in learning a conditional type of knowledge about when and under which circumstances different activities are well suited to meet compositional problems.

Institutionalized: mandated curriculum and commoditization

The limited impact of theoretical statements and results of research studies on classroom practice is widely known. As a practice-based theory with clear pedagogical instructions, the writing process theory has had more impact than most academic educational advances. Now that it has reached near common acceptance, the writing process is appearing in curricular directives and policy statements (Patthey-Chavez et al. 2004). If school systems and teachers missed or rejected the process in the first go around, they may now be mandated to address it in the classroom. The 2010 US Common Core State Standard Initiative is one such directive. Rather than a national curriculum, within the United States educational curricula are designed and administered at the state level. In a radical move made by a collaborative of several state agencies and organizations, the Common Core State Standard Initiative (2010) has set out to align existing curricula across states 'to provide a clear and consistent framework to prepare our children for college and the workforce' (http://www.corestandards.org/). It claims to promote only those standards shared across the curriculum-adopting states. It is significant then that the writing process phases or stages have a prominent place in the standard that addresses writing: 'Develop and strengthen writing as needed by planning, revising, editing, rewriting, or trying a new approach'.

In order to be mandated at such an official level, standards must be limited to teaching practices that can be implemented broadly and use similar measureable outcomes across the entire school system. Aspects of writing process theory and pedagogy, such as developing positive dispositions toward writing, student choice and discovery through writing, for instance, cannot be reliably assessed across varying classrooms, schools, states, etc. Thus, these components of writing process theory and pedagogy have not been incorporated into standards. Many of the suggested activities and learning targets listed in these standard sets are streamlined as to be mere shells of the theory and pedagogy.

Publishing houses would be foolish to ignore the marketing possibilities that come from such mandated curriculum, classroom activities and structures. The commoditization of the writing process movement has further removed writing activities from the writing process as it was originally described – recursive, idiosyncratic and situation dependent (Ede 1994). Though teaching aides such as brainstorming worksheets, classroom sets of Writing Workshop 'first draft', 'second draft' folders and rubrics for grading the various assignments may be quite handy for the classroom teacher, the process becomes ever further reduced to series of worksheets and predetermined activities.

Development and the writing process

Studies regarding development within the writing process are nearly nonexistent in educational literature. In fact, developmental implications for the writing process have been quite limited. A dearth in attention to development is understandable when remembering that the writing process movement was much more interested in a person's individual, idiosyncratic experiences with a particular piece of writing rather than trends or scales across writers or long-term mapping of one's writing processes across several written pieces. Murray (1968) went so far as to claim that it is a myth that a student's grade level in school matters. He explained this as a 'fallacy that there is a group of writing problems peculiar to the tenth grade, the seventh grade or the twelfth grade' (p. 107). Instead, Murray recommended that teachers teach in response to what they see happening in their students' writing, rather than according to what has been predicted that they might have learned. Also, the writing process movement is not concerned with the phenomenon of writing development outside the context of teaching. The movement's parallel focus on describing the writing process and changing teaching practices convolute possible generalizations about writing development. Researchers (e.g. Perl 1979) have demonstrated that composing – across ages and settings and abilities – is a 'naturally' occurring recursive process of pre-writing, writing, re-writing or process that stems from the writing situation itself rather than something to teach or that develops. Perhaps skills or activities used within the phases could be improved, but the process itself is part of the contextual learning landscape.

That said, development within the writing process has been addressed in three general ways:

1. improvement of product characteristics, i.e. spelling and the amount/kind of changes between drafts, while a student is engaged in the context of some variant of writing process pedagogy, as an evaluation of the effectiveness of writing process pedagogy;
2. development of the use of activities within certain stages of the process, again, during writing process pedagogy;
3. inferred implications from the variance of standards and directives for different grade levels.

Development of products as a test of effectiveness

The effectiveness of the writing process pedagogy such as freewriting, Writing Workshop and emphasis on revision to improve a student's written products is of interest and debate. Graves (1983) conducted his most systematic and extensive study of the effectiveness of the writing process pedagogy for the National Institute of Education. For this study, his team of researchers followed 16 students over two years of schooling. Graves's report claimed general improvement of certain product characteristics such as spelling, handwriting, grammatical construction and correct punctuation. He also described a general trend in which young children's concerns shifted from spelling to handwriting to conventions to topic and finally to revision. Graves was careful to point out that each concern observed by his researchers was mentioned by every study participant at every age and at all points during composition, meaning there was not a writing situation in which each of these concerns was not being juggled or an age when each of these was not a concern to the writer. Rather, what shifted was which concern was most dominant across the ages. The research team found no other similarities in the progression from one concern to another either by age, or genre, or teaching structure or strategy.

As the implementation of Writing Workshop or other writing process pedagogy varies widely, the body of comparable research on the effectiveness of writing process pedagogy is quite limited (Pritchard and Honeycutt 2006). Hillocks (1986) concluded from cross-analysis of several studies that pedagogy that involved pre-writing (what he more broadly conceived as inquiry) was more effective than having students study model texts and focus on revision. Conflated in such reports, however, are the writing process and classroom activities that offer time, space, resources and instruction on the process itself. Additionally, across such studies, the ultimate test of the pedagogy is the improvement in students' products.

An underlying assumption of the theory is that with similar processes come similar products. Like the theories presented in the previous chapter, *development* is again located in the characteristics of end-products.

Development of process(es)

Calkins (1983), a researcher involved in the NIE study as a student of Graves, focussed on one particular child in her study, mapping the child's experiences in a Writing Workshop environment. Calkins described a gradual internalization process for the various activities the teacher assigned during each stage of the process. In a later study, Honeycutt and Pritchard (2005) described the improvement of written products over 16 weeks of writing instruction using a process approach. During the weeks of the study, students practised the activities of the various processes and increased in automaticity in using these activities independently. The concepts of gradual internalization and increasing automaticity of activities have developmental implications, but the import of these studies' developmental findings is limited by parallel studies that showed that no matter what the classroom writing activities were, students gradually internalized and increased in their automaticity of those activities (e.g. Mahar 2001).

Developmental implications are also found in practitioner literature written to promote the writing process. Recent literature emphasizes students' consciousness of their personal processes (e.g. Dornan et al. 2003), and the controlled use of a growing repertoire of activities within the phases of the writing process (e.g. Dean 2006). Consciousness of one's personal writing process is often described as a mechanism for growth; whereas the idea that students build a repertoire of activities or ways to deal with writing situations within each writing phase is considered to be a way to measure change over time. A student's repertoire – the quantity and variety of writing tools or activities – is referred to as a set of skills or writing knowledge they can use across a range of situations. Instead of vertical development through higher and higher grade levels, which is a common way to understand development in education, a writing repertoire represents horizontal development that a child takes with them to the next grade.

In a practitioner-friendly book *Strategic Writing*, Dean (2006) offered teachers a new view on what it means to teach the writing process. First, she provided an expanded range of activities (such as researching and inquiry as possible pre-writing activities) for students to try and eventually add to their repertoire of writing activities. Second, and more importantly, she reframed the teaching and learning goals for writing process instruction. Instead of providing activities aimed at teaching the stages of writing and instructions on how to complete those activities, she recommends that teachers ask students to reflect on each writing experience to understand when and under what conditions various process activities were effective in meeting their goals. They are asked to consider what components of writing are active in a situation – rhetorical, technological, contextual – and then which writing activities work well with those contextual constraints. The teacher's role is to facilitate students' understanding of writing as an ever-changing experience, and help them gain control and become strategic about the activities they use to compose.

Developmental implications from curricula

Let us look a little closer at the classroom implications regarding development found in the grade-level specific objectives of the US Common Core State Standards Initiative (2010), which promotes writing in the classroom as a process in Writing Standard 5: 'Develop and strengthen writing as needed by planning, revising, editing, rewriting, or trying a new approach'. Across a range of grades K-12, differences in the standards for each grade level have developmental implications for understanding characteristics of writing, written products and the youth who are doing the writing. These differences involve:

1. a degree of guidance and support;
2. phases within the process;
3. US conventions of written English;
4. attuning students to rhetorical problems; and
5. the specificity of grade-level descriptors.

In kindergarten, the writing process objective is prefaced by the phrase 'with guidance and support from adults', and by second grade, 'and peers' is added. This guidance and support from adults and peers holds steady until the sixth grade at which time students are expected to accomplish writing process objectives with only 'some' guidance and support. By ninth grade the phrase drops completely from the standard. Developmentally, this trajectory of guidance seems to follow and promote the US ideal of creating an independent learner, rather than other approaches to teaching and learning such as a Vygotskian approach to an ever shifting zone of proximal development and a more collective spirit in composition (as discussed elsewhere in the book in relation to digital composing).

Within the phases of the writing process, specific skills and activities, such as responding to feedback, revising by adding details, and focussing the topic are targeted in K-2 grades. By third grade, these specific activities are dropped from the wording of the standard and in its place are the general process stages of planning, revising and editing. The developmental implication here may be that for students in K-2 grades, the activities of planning, revising and editing should be limited to the particular listed skills. Whether these activities are based on a presumed ability for these grade levels or an attempt to limit the scope of planning, revising and editing activities to ensure adequate time and attention to particular skills, is unclear.

For the third to twelfth grades, a new element, editing, is added to the Standard's objectives. Editing should result in the students' demonstration of 'language command of the English language up to and including the grade of the student'. Language development, in terms of US written conventions, is the only changing descriptor of writing process across third to fifth grades. Writing development is then implied to be the mastery of particular writing conventions. Seventh and eighth grades are the same as third to sixth grade, except now the rhetorical problems of purpose and audience are targeted with the expectation that during revision students should 'focus on how well purpose and audience have been addressed'. For grades nine to twelve, students will be 'focusing on addressing what is most significant for a specific purpose and audience'. Interestingly, the practice of rhetorical problems moves from general to specific, whereas the skills of process progressed from specific activities to general phases of writing in K-2 grades.

As noted, the Standard's objectives for grades three to five are the same and grades nine to twelve are the same. This implies that changes to students' writing processes occur from grade to grade in K-2 and then in larger and larger swathes of grades. As with several developmental theories, development is a process for the young. The younger a person, the clearer are their delineators of growth or development, but once a young person reaches adolescence, they are in a nondescript stage of undetermined growth in their writing. With clear delineators of development, dramatic shifts in growth become evident. Take for example physical changes in height or weight. We often miss the subtle changes in the people we see every day. Without markers or scales, the gradual changes go unnoticed, and it is not until a friend, child or colleague has been away for an extended period of time that we notice weight or height changes. Adolescent writing development is particularly problematic – consistently low levels of improvement in products through the teen years – but is it because they are not developing or that we do not have markers that can identify subtle changes?

Also particular to this developmental implication, it is not the young person who is developing but the products that are improving in quality. By the third grade only the correctness of written conventions of standard US English and the rhetorical concerns of purpose and audience are developing – and both of these are evidenced by the quality of a written product. In fact, in Standard 5 regarding writing processes, the phase of drafting or generating the actual text is not mentioned. With no growth indicators for the moment of composition – be it with support or without, with general or specific tools – the question can be raised as to the teacher's responsibility for teaching a child to compose text. In terms of a theory of development, do the processes of putting words on the page then not evolve?

While all curricular documents come with developmental implications, they rarely, if ever, include the theoretical explanations for the minute changes between grades despite their huge consequences – not just for that particular standard, but for how youth in that grade level are positioned. We interpret the statement with our pre-existing tacit theories of ability, expectations and dispositions toward youth. Although the implementation of standards varies, assumptions about the importance of particular skills and abilities in writing, as well as the nature of the youth that are inherent in such curricular directives, extend beyond standard-based lessons and are infused in educational orientations toward youth and writing.

Cognitive approaches to the processes of writing

While players in the writing process movement shifted their focus from written products to the multiple tasks and activities involved in writing a product, the researchers taking a cognitive psychology approach narrowed this lens even further to the act of actually composing text. Out of view is the classroom context and activity before and after a piece is composed, and brought into focus are the complexities of how people make compositional decisions. With heightened focus on immediate thought processes of composing, the recursivity of pre-writing, writing and re-writing, as well as the embedded nature of the activities within those phases were substantiated through a series of empirical studies.

Stemming from a psychological research orientation that values controlled experimental studies and requires several replicated studies before theoretical claims are made, the methods employed and the conclusions reached in the series of studies conducted by both Flower and Hayes, and by Bereiter and Scardamalia, were innovative and continue to draw criticism from the psychological field, though they are generally accepted in the applied field of education. In the two models of writing we review here, neither of the research teams considered its theories of writing processes development as finalized. Flower and Hayes, in particular, explained that theirs was a 'theory and distillation of data' which guided 'the kinds of developmental questions they addressed' (Flower et al. 1986: 20). Likewise, even though part of the design of Bereiter and Scardamalia's studies and their models of writing processes are focussed on developmental aspects of writing, they stated that they do not have definitive conclusions for the development of the cognitive processes occurring while writing.

The studies conducted by the research teams of Flower and Hayes and by Bereiter and Scardamalia are seminal works in the cognitive approach to writing, referred to in the design and findings of several current studies and approaches (e.g. Smith and Andrews 2009). Their models provide two fundamentally different ways to understand the processes and development of those processes. As such, we will review their models of writing processes separately. First, we will take a look at how the Flower and Hayes model of writing processes informs our understanding of the nature of composition as a goal-driven and highly embedded, yet distinct series of processes. Second, we will outline Bereiter and Scardamalia's two models of writing, highlighting their developmental components. Finally, we will consider both teams' models and research designs together to understand the developmental implications of cognitive processes in writing.

Flower and Hayes: orchestrating cognitive processes

Flower and Hayes (1981) constructed a model of the cognitive processes of writing based on several studies they conducted over at least five years of research. These studies employed protocol analysis, a research technique in which participants – usually adults or young children – received a writing task and were asked to think aloud while producing the written text. In these studies, Flower and Hayes identified a set of embedded yet still distinctive thinking processes. Their studies suggested that certain cognitive activities, such as generating text, typically instigated other particular cognitive activities, such as translating ideas into words on the page. Flower and Hayes also found that a writer's compositional goals were the guiding force behind the writer's type of cognitive activities. They argued that writing could be characterized as a problem-solving process. They found that as a writer produces a piece of text, the complexity of problems and solution-finding increases. In terms of development, Flower and Hayes (1981: 373) argued, 'The act of defining one's own rhetorical problem and setting goals is an important part of "being creative" and can account for some important differences between good and poor writers.'

In the design of several of Flower and Hayes's studies, participants were selected that they considered good and poor writers. Important to the purposes of this book, developmental differences between 'good and poor' (the distinction they used the most) is comparative only. This means that the designations of good and poor were pre-determined and based on past performance on writing tasks. At times, the studies were designed so that the age of the participant (designated as 'older or younger' or 'more experienced and less experienced') determined the comparative dyad. In this sense, the *process* of development was not the focus of these studies. Rather, the developmental findings are implied in the comparison, but how or why a better writer wrote differently than a poorer writer was not researched. For instance, in terms of goal setting, Flower and Hayes (1981: 379) found that poor writers depend on very abstract, undeveloped general goals, such as to write a page, or get 'locked in by the myopia' of procedural low-level goals, such as spelling a word correctly; whereas the better or more experienced writers created goals to direct their writing that were not overly focussed on either local or global concerns, but which met a criteria that could be called a middle range. Thus, the difference between good and poor writers is in 'both the quantity and quality of the middle range of goals they create' (p. 379). *When, how* or *where* this developmental shift is made for a writer was not researched or theorized, nor should these aspects of development be inferred. Bereiter and Scardamalia similarly used this type of novice/expert design choice. We will return to this design choice and its implications and limitations for understanding development of cognitive processes after considering both Flower and Hayes's and Bereiter and Scardamalia's models.

Processes of good and poor writers

In addition to goal setting, Flower and Hayes found processing differences between good and poor writers. As we describe their model of the cognitive processes of writing, we will point out these identified differences.

Flower and Hayes' model of writing processes is multilayered. In graphic form, the model includes multiple flow charts filled with double-ended arrows pointing to boxes that indicate additional flow charts of sub-processes. The broadest of Flower and Hayes's processes are Task Environment, Writing Processes and Long-term Memory. Within these processes are multiple sub-processes. The Rhetorical Problem (the process of problem-solving to address the needs of the audience and task at hand) and Text Produced So Far (the process of reading and connecting the produced text to the previously identified goals and problem-solving from that point on), for instance, are a sub-process of the Task Environment. The Rhetorical Problem has distinct influence on all other sub-processes, as Flower and Hayes discovered. More mature writers juggled the demands of writing tasks efficiently; whereas poor writers reduced 'large set of constraints to a radically simplified problem' (1981: 369).

Within Writing Processes, Flower and Hayes identified three sub-processes – Planning, Translating and Reviewing – that sound akin to the pre-writing, writing and re-writing of the writing process movement. Like Graves and Murray, Flower and Hayes documented a second level of sub-processes within Planning; namely, Generating, Organizing and Goal Setting. And within Reviewing, Flower and Hayes described the distinct sub-processes of Evaluating and Revising. They found that better writers have more conscious control of their writing process activity and give themselves several instructions to reach their organizing, drafting and revising goals. Interestingly, whereas awareness of goals and problems was found to be a sign of mature or better processes, automaticity is the feature of more mature or better writing in the Translating component.

Flower and Hayes also documented an overarching process, Monitoring, that acts as the rudder that guides writers' shifts between the other processes. The significant difference between younger and older participants' process of Monitoring was the ease or automaticity with which the older participants shifted between processes. Likewise, in addition to goal-setting, the other major developmental implication found in this model of writing processes is that older and better writers more effortlessly orchestrated the several competing and embedded cognitive processes during the act of composing.

To review, Flower and Hayes (1981) considered their model with all its layers and dynamics as a model of competent writers' processes. Flower and Hayes have been able to identify a few critical differences in the processes of younger and less competent writers from those of older and more experienced ones. For one, somewhere along the way from childhood to adulthood, we start to see writing tasks as more rhetorically and situationally nuanced. We also switch, with greater ease, between the cognitive processes that will help us reach our more nuanced rhetorical goals. We can consider the task, then edit, then generate text with much less consciousness than our younger counterparts. Flower and Hayes also tell us that the better writers among us set small sub-goals within each of these processes and tell ourselves many instructions to accomplish these goals successfully.

Bereiter and Scardamalia: telling and transforming

Bereiter and Scardamalia had dual research goals. Similar to Flower and Hayes, they set out to understand the nature of the cognitive processes involved in writing. Additionally, they hoped their research activities would *advance* young writers' composing strategies' (1987: 245, italics added). As such, they designed a series of quasi-experimental educational intervention studies, which resulted in a model of cognitive writing processes that differed from Flower and Hayes's model in visual shape, conceptual scope and developmental implications. Like Flower and Hayes, the findings of these studies primarily contrasted processes of elementary school-aged children with adult writers within various topics such as memory-load, planning and comprehension. Children who produced poor quality writing and those who produced high quality written pieces were also compared, and participants were often paired in these poorer and better dyads, or were paired with a researcher who employed instructional guidance during writing. Though intentionally instructional, these observed interactions did not result in developmental implications that extended much beyond an individual's internal thinking processes.

One of the major sticking points for children who participated in Bereiter and Scardamalia's studies was handling the cognitive load of writing. Bereiter (1980: 78) explained that at its most basic form, writing entailed several activities, including:

1. creating a personal intention for the piece that aligns to the writer's understanding of the task;
2. coming up with a game plan to accomplish the task and personal goals;
3. accessing topical content from memory;
4. looking for additional information that is not readily available from memory; and
5. tuning the written output to the writer's intention and understanding of the discourse for which it is being written.

Accomplishing these tasks requires constant comparison between the mental representation of what will be written and the actual output forming on the page. Many cognitive psychologists believe that children also have less basic memory capacity than adults. Described in this way, it is no wonder that the cognitive load of writing is difficult for young children.

Bereiter and Scardamalia modelled this complex cognitive activity after the first of two processes they witnessed participants engaging in while writing. Called the knowledge-telling model, this process is described as the simpler of two models, which Bereiter and Scardamalia claimed was required for simplistic regurgitation of knowledge. They found that children used this model much more often than adults, though adults were found to use the model to accomplish some writing tasks as well. As such, several of Bereiter and Scardamalia's quasi-experimental studies using educational interventions with children involved cueing cards or other memory trigger devices that the researcher would invite the child to use while writing. Bereiter and Scardamalia (1987: 213) found that the older the child the less they exhibited 'dependency on external conditions and events to organize and stimulate ... thought'. In addition to this independence in generation, Bereiter and Scardamalia (1987) found three additional abilities that could be placed on a developmental continuum:

1. learning active search for content;
2. shifting from local to whole-text planning;
3. learning to go beyond the text as written, i.e. revision.

These three developmental aspects are captured in the differences between the knowledge-telling process and Bereiter and Scardamalia's second model of writing processes, the knowledge-transforming model.

The knowledge-transforming model is a far more complex model that subsumes the knowledge-telling processes. The cognitive activities in this model are directed by problem-analysis and goal setting in relation to the understanding of the writing task. Whereas Flower and Hayes described this difference in goal-influenced writing as characteristic of poor and good writers, Bereiter and Scardamalia considered the knowledge-telling and knowledge-transforming to be completely different processes. Additionally, Bereiter and Scardamalia suggested that writers using the knowledge-transforming model not only drew on existing memories of content to write about, and the discourse within which it was to be written to fit, but that their understanding of that content and the discourse was informed by the written text as it was produced. Dually influenced by the discourse within which they were writing and the content that they had written, the pre-existing knowledge was shaped and reshaped – or 'transformed' – as the piece was written rather than just regurgitated as in the first model.

Bereiter and Scardamalia discussed a range of approaches to the knowledge-transforming process. They found several novices – writers who were new to the task's content or discourse – who 'side-stepped' the problem-solving aspects of the knowledge-transforming model, and in essence just enacted a knowledge-telling process. They also found several children and adults who made unsuccessful attempts at the knowledge-transforming process, explaining, 'The novice possesses productions for transferring information from the content space to the rhetorical space, but lacks productions for the return trip' (1987: 303). In other words, they would access existing content or discursive knowledge, but then did not know how to adapt what they were writing to fit the parameters of the content or discourse. Finally, the more mature writers often used the knowledge-telling process, but in reference to the problems and goals understood from the task, content and discourse knowledge and the written work as it was being produced. In other words, they were successful at gauging when to take up the more complicated production of text and when to produce text in a less conscious and simple way. Bereiter and Scardamalia explained one possible mechanism for this last difference, namely that as the capacity of memory and knowledge-telling processes became automatic, i.e. the writer was older, attention could be employed on increasingly difficult process problems.

Bereiter and Scardamalia (1987: 356) argued that development does not cease once the writer is working within a knowledge-transforming process:

> Mature writers ... [are] people who can carry out purposeful, strategically guided operations on a variety of kinds of mental representations of the text or of the writing task. It is easy to see how, starting with that kind of competence, writers who keep at it can acquire extremely high levels of expertise. Through repeated experience trying to achieve similar goals and wrestling with similar problems, they evolve increasingly refined representations of goal types and problem types.

Like Flower and Hayes, the quality of goals and understanding of problems gets more sophisticated with more experience and with practice in writing toward similar goals and similar problems.

The authors posited that one difference between novice and expert writers is in the process employed, but also highlighted that any writer at any age and skill level may engage in either process at any time. They noted children who engaged in very astute knowledge-transforming actions, such as writing dialogue and attuning that dialogue to the discourse of story. They also witnessed the use of knowledge-telling in highly functional adult writers resulting in successful pieces of writing. In other words, moving from one model to another is not the developmental endgame, nor is always writing in a knowledge-transforming way the sign of a highly developed writer.

To review, older writers and writers more experienced in a particular content or discourse utilized the knowledge-transforming process more often and with more ease. The more often this process was used with a particular type of writing task, the more refined the goals and problems were analyzed for the specific task and the better the results met the demands of the task. Finally, maturation – and thus building memory capacity – was deemed critical to managing the cognitive load of either writing process model.

Developmental implications of cognitive writing process models

Upon close examination of the cognition involved in writing, the research teams of Flower and Hayes and Bereiter and Scardamalia raise awareness of the multiple developmental systems involved when writing. The biological development of memory capacity is central to both research teams. Additionally, the development of a child's linguistic capacities including register and linguistic complexity affect the ease of translating ideas into words and tuning writing to an internal intention. Bereiter (1980) also claimed that both moral and social development impact on the development of writing. Considering the rhetorical, content and discursive problem-solving highlighted in both approaches to cognitive processes of writing, it only makes sense that a highly refined understanding of social relationships, roles and interactions of discourse communities and rhetorical situations would play into the ability to understand writing tasks, address rhetorical problems and reach the writer's goals.

As previously noted, Flower and Hayes's and Bereiter and Scardamalia's comparisons of poor and good writers are problematic when considering the question of development. Based in a novice/expert research tradition, poor and better writers are discussed interchangeably with similar dyads: less experienced and more experienced writers, and younger and older writers. Basically, any person can, at any time, be both a novice and an expert, depending on the research frame. For development, this construct is particularly problematic as the scale – novice to expert – is predetermined by means outside the phenomenon studied. Developmental claims are then limited to identifying where development might be located, i.e. socially, morally, cognitively, rather than increasing our understanding of what the developmental evolution of writing is like.

Most often the predetermination of 'developed writer' was in regard to the quality of previously written pieces or the participant's age in comparison to another's age. Although both research teams documented the use of all processes – even effectively used by all participants in all comparative categories – the findings were still explained using these predetermined categories. Designs such as these that predetermine physical age as the evidentiary site of transformation characterize development as 'naturally' occurring as one gets older. The role of instruction is often lost in such models. For instance, it could be inferred from Bereiter and Scardamalia's studies that younger children use the knowledge-telling process more often solely because of their lack of cognitive capacity to handle the problems of rhetorical situation and discursive goals. Studies such as Applebee's (1984) study of writing instruction, however, raise the question as to whether these children are employing a knowledge-telling process because of capacity or because of their understanding of the instructional context in which they are writing. Applebee and his team found that only 3 per cent of the time in classrooms was used in writing a paragraph or longer. Each and every writing episode was a test of the students' retention of the subject knowledge previously studied, that is, a regurgitation task. In such instructional contexts, are we, in fact, inadvertently teaching children that writing means fulfilling a knowledge-telling task? If consistently faced with such tasks in the school setting, it is reasonable that students would put their efforts into accessing the content memory and restating this knowledge as directly as possible. Do we, then, see the knowledge-telling process used more often by our younger students because they are unable to do more in their writing or because we have necessitated that response? Learning contexts – in and out of schools – are critical to understanding the actions we see students take while writing. Writing processes, as with products, are a function of the scholastic environment, opportunities and experiences involved in certain types of writing practices. Further, often measuring instruction and learning is reduced to measurements of *amount* of time, i.e. a year in school or the age of a participant, as opposed to directly accounting for, mapping and taking into consideration what has been learned and experienced over time.

Conclusion

The advantage of process-based theories is that they come close to writing development in one sense, *viz.* they track the immediate processes involved in composition. But the disadvantage is that they do not consider writing development in the medium and long term. Focussed on the processes involved in composing a single product, process-based theories contribute to thinking about writing pedagogy; however, they are not suitable for curriculum or assessment design. In research regarding the processes involved in writing a single piece, neither the changes in processes over time nor the mechanisms or catalysts of those changes have been researched or theorized. These process-based theories, instead, have drawn attention to areas of development outside a piece of writing. Such interacting systems or areas of learning include:

1. the experiences provided through particular pedagogies and learning environments;
2. biological, social and moral development;
3. the individual's repertoire of writing activities, and the effectiveness of their reflection and control of the use of those activities; and
4. the dispositions toward writing, plus situated and transcontextual motivation for writing.

We do not yet have a model or research data to map reliably trends in these areas across time that could inform the broad educational goals of curriculum design and assessment design. However, from what we learn from these researchers – that writing processes are always shifting rhetorically, situationally and from person to person – trends of changes over time may be a misguided goal. Not only have we learned the places to look for growth in a person's writing processes, we have learned that we should not expect to find similar changes and trajectories across people. Rather than trends – which we have seen repeatedly being reverted to deficit models, as was the result of many of the product-approach models – we should instead build on the components identified as growing in a person's writing processes and find new ways to both map and understand what these changes over time mean for the individual writer.

6 The Question of Writing Development

Introduction

Findings from the seminal studies we have reviewed shed light on the nature of writing. Although they have developmental implications for education, it is a theory and model of writing *development* that is needed, according to teachers, researchers and policy-makers. The changes we witness in a person's products or processes are often mistaken for development; they are but signs of the development of a person in society. We will now approach a theory of writing development that positions the writer – as opposed to their written products or writing processes – at the centre.

With the individual as the developing subject, we will examine just *what* is considered to be developing, and *how* that development can be re-imagined to better align with what we have learned about writing development from previous theories. First, what is developing? Learning does not occur in a vacuum. We need to broaden our notions of what we accept as evidence of development and include social, cultural, technological and pedagogical influences. But, how will we account for these multiple, interacting social contexts in an individual's development? In this chapter, we propose what this might entail.

As discussed in Chapter 3, learning is a transformational process and an *act* resulting from engagement with or within a community. In each of the seminal studies we have reviewed, the researchers presented case after case in which transformations were paired with moments of suspended or recursive growth. A student's sentence length increased until a certain age or grade and then became stagnant for a year or two before suddenly increasing again. Another student started writing more complicated story-lines and then inexplicably seemed to regress in their focus while writing. Changes such as these in a student's writing are currently considered an interruption to growth; negative consequences that should be overcome if development is to continue. If we look at development as encompassing an individual's learning within the sociocultural contexts in which writing occurs, we need a broadened definition of *growth* in writing that reframes these moments of stalled or regressive changes.

In the following sections we introduce Sean, a 17-year-old writer who lives in a large metropolitan area in the USA. With samples of Sean's writing and reflections on his writing, we will use the established means discussed in the previous chapters to map the development of his products and processes. We will broaden what we accept as signs of writing development, noting the educational benefits of widening the scope of evidence. We will then pause to consider development as an educational concept – one that is notoriously linear and deficit-based. We offer three metaphors of nonlinear development borrowed from other fields – development of a photograph, development of a piece of music, and development within the complexity sciences – to discuss what we can learn about Sean's development which includes suspension and regression, and is informed by the multiple communities with whom and for whom Sean writes.

Taking a case: Sean

Meet Sean. At the time we were writing this book, Sean was a high school senior who dropped out of his regular high school at the age of 16. After a year, he decided to re-enroll and is attending an alternative high school. He is anxious to graduate as quickly as possible. Sean is taking extra courses after school hours and feels like he is just 'toughing it out' in this final year. He does not feel challenged by the work he is asked to do in his classes, and thinks he is wasting time on the kinds of writing tasks that will neither make a difference in his life nor impact the world for good. Sean is African-American, has been in and out of foster care for most of his life, and is currently living in low-income project housing.

This profile of a low-performing, low-income, urban ethnic minority student is not uncommon in the USA. Teenage males in the USA persistently underperform on assessments of writing. On the National Assessment of Educational Progress (2007) this gap is approximately 20 points on a 300-point scale. The gap in academic performance data is even wider for males disaggregated by race and socioeconomic status. Various theories of male literacy underachievement have been offered as males' underachievement has been a quandary for educators and researchers alike. The limited biological linguistic capacity of males is one theory (i.e. Maynard 2002). Attributing feminine – or passive and anti-masculine – qualities to literacy practices and schooling in general is another (i.e. Walkerdine 1990; Martino 1998). However, what have yet to be questioned are the very scales upon which we are measuring these deficits.

We got to know Sean over a three year period of time as part of a wider study of urban adolescent writing development both in and out of school

(Smith 2011). Coming to know Sean outside school was critical: if we had just looked at his scholastic profile, we would have missed the majority of his writerly life. Sean is an accomplished spoken word artist, recently taking first place in the USA in a highly competitive national spoken word festival. He travels to all corners of his city to compose, promote and perform spoken word poetry. Sean has also written and put on repeat performances of a one-act one-man play. He composes and produces hip hop tracks and he is a social activist for race and gender equality.

In writing development, *what* is developing?

We begin our discussion of development by focusing on Sean's *written products*. By examining the texts he has produced over the previous three years we can learn much from Sean's use of the conventions of standard American written English, the complexity of his sentences, and the adherence of his written texts to expectations of the genre in which he has written. We can see that Sean has a wide range of genres in his repertoire, favouring academic writing, page poetry, spoken word and hip hop. In Table 6.1, we have provided a continuum outlining how closely these genres relate to each other and how these genres are distinguished in terms of register (tone and vocabulary), structure (internal organizational patterns), modes (communication channels) and discourse communities (communities in which the genre is used).

The genres Sean uses when in school – academic writing and page poetry – have remained static, meaning that neither the genre characteristics nor the quality of his pieces have changed. In fact, comparing one essay from his tenth grade year to another in his final year of public education differed little in established measures of products, like sentence complexity and topic. This is consistent with the findings from several studies that have reported very little change in characteristics of written products from early to late adolescence (e.g. Loban 1976; Fitzgerald and Shanahan 2000). It also reflects the trend of expectations in state standards for English language arts which have similar, if not the same, writing standards for grades 6–12 (e.g. Common Core Standards Initiative 2010). Reflecting on any of the established approaches for measuring development in products that we have discussed in previous chapters, it seems as if Sean has not been developing in school. However, there is more to consider.

Over three years, Sean's page poetry and spoken word genres have changed by growing in similarity. Over time, spoken word has come to resemble page poetry with less word play, more layered meaning, and increased use of literary devices. Sean is currently mining spoken word

Table 6.1 Continuum of similarity in observed genres

	Academic writing	Page poetry	Spoken word [Spittin']	Hip hop
Register (tone and vocabulary)	Ceremonial quality, limited content-specific terms.	Carefully crafted and affected tone – often serious. Metaphor and symbolism for wit and layered meaning.	Often serious. Word-play, allusions to popular culture and political climate.	Original word-play integrated with rhythmic beat. Hyperbole and allusions to popular culture.
Structure (internal organizational patterns)	Prose, often three paragraphs with at least introduction, body (discussion of issues from introduction) and conclusion.	Line-breaks and stanzas to emphasize intended meaning. Repetition of both words and phrasing.	Often narrative elements such as plot or characters. Line-breaks and stanzas to emphasize intended meaning. Repetition of both words and phrasing.	Line-breaks and stanzas in verse. Repetition of phrasing. Several call and answer sections with collaborator.

Mode and medium (communication channel)	Composed on a computer with wordprocessing software. Printed on paper and distributed.	Composed on cell phone and in a small notebook. Typed on a computer on a social networking webpage or with wordprocessing software. Distributed electronically on social networking site or rare oral readings to small audiences mostly at workshops from the phone or notebook.	Notes are written on cell phone and saved via email. Oral delivery most often for a large group. Nonverbal cues such as bodily movements and breath particularly important. Occasionally posted to social networking site.	Lyrics written on cell phone and texted between collaborators. Music tracks are created with software that provides beat and mixing capability. Several tracks are recorded as read off cell phone.
Discourse community	Officials at schools and colleges as gatekeepers, and students as novices or applicants (in college application essays).	Sean does not have a separate discourse community within which he writes page-poetry. Rather, page-poems are written in workshops as a bridge to spoken word.	Out-of-school organization members, interacting participants at readings and competitions. Large online following through YouTube and MySpace.	A limited number of out-of-school males create hip hop tracks, but the out-of-school organization members, participants at readings and online following are the same as for spoken word.

pieces he wrote a few years ago to this end. In Figure 6.1 we see the first stanza of a poem Sean composed to discuss the lack of universal health care in the USA. In his first version, originally composed and performed over a year before, he uses two similes and a strong explicative in what he calls 'hot lines.' He explained that his old goal was to affect a strong response from his audiences, and such lines were just the ticket. He says that he is less concerned with hot lines now that he has a new goal of effectively communicating about the social issue itself, and does not want to distract from the message. To this end, he has used the same comparisons, but with more nuanced figurative language, more complex syntactic structure, and has removed provocative language.

Original first stanza

There's a girl
laying close to her death
like a flag wrapped on a soldier's coffin.
She has a cough
like a fourth of July
f***ing in a barrel of gun powder.

Revised first stanza

Laying closer to her death
than a flag wrapped around a soldier's coffin,
there's a girl
who has a cough
like a firecracker crying cancer.

Figure 6.1 Two versions of Sean B's composition

The development of Sean's writing produced in school differs considerably from that produced out of school. Had we considered only Sean's in-school written products we might have concluded he is not developing as a writer at all. As most existing theories are based on evidence collected in classrooms or in experimental situations, there is little recognition of composition and its development in contexts outside school. Yet Sean is a prime example of how learning and development take place, potentially, in a number of communities: school, home, clubs, in public life, in friendship groups, and so on. The first step to an inclusive theory of writing development is to account for the multiple contexts writers participate in and across.

In addition to written products, the changes to Sean's *writing processes* across contexts both in and out of school also reveal writing development.

Sean was asked to record writers' memos – reflective accounts of the processes of writing several pieces at differing points of completion. From these we have determined that Sean has two main processes for writing. Sean will only compose spoken word and page poetry in an emotionally-charged state, and so he often waits for a dramatic experience to happen before he will compose. He composes by stating lines aloud and repeating them, then jotting notes in his cell/mobile phone to trigger the memory of each line. If Sean only writes a few lines during a particular emotive time he will wait for a new state of strong emotion during which he will 'play' with the old lines, but for the purpose of writing about the current emotional experience: 'I take that line, put it in that [new poem], and just completely cancelled out the [original] poem.' In essence then, when we met Sean, he did not pre-write, revise or edit his poetry. The pieces either 'flowed' or they did not. He did re-imagine particular lines or phrases, but for new products. Now, three years later, Sean's processes have shifted. He often uses a technique learned in an out-of-school workshop to write a free-association list when composing a piece with a new topic. As shown in Figure 6.1, he is also now revising, returning to products written previously to clarify the message and maintain the emotion of the pieces, not to re-imagine them for a new emotion.

When writing hip hop or writing in school, Sean explained that he is 'comfortable writing,' 'accustomed,' and 'great with words just right there on the spot.' When he experiences writer's block with hip hop and school-based writing, he does not wait for new emotion. Instead, with academic work, he just waits until it is convenient to write and then completes the piece in the second sitting, composing and revising simultaneously. With hip hop, he continues to generate a different section of the piece and simultaneously repeats the phrase that he was stuck on until he has figured out the exact wording he wants. One could say he fixates on the wording and word play.

Independently, any of the aspects of writing products and processes paints a picture of change and stasis over time. Together, not only do we have a broader view of Sean's growth, but the details of when, how and for what reasons change occurs are brought into focus. In each of the genres listed above, Sean's approaches to composing (e.g. brainstorming a list before writing; composing aloud then writing) were used both in and out of school, but only with the most similar genres. From observations in and out of school, we noted that Sean used the approaches to composing presented in school only in class with specific assignments that required academic writing or page poetry; whereas the approaches that were practised in workshops were transferred between page poetry, spoken word and hip hop across contexts. Such findings complicate studies of out-of-school activities in which it is reasoned that improvement in writing abilities similar to those listed in academic curricular standards mean students have these same skills and knowledge available for use in other settings (e.g. Mahiri and Sablo 1996; Jocson 2006).

The developing *writer*

With the focus on trends in the changes to Sean's genres and written products, his sustained and changing processes, and their intersections with instruction, one important detail slips out of focus – the individual. Sean's waxing and waning motivations for school work, Sean's social prowess, Sean's awareness of social responsibility and fascination with word play are not just interesting items to note; they are intricately interwoven throughout every aspect of his life. David Kirkland (2009, personal communication) posed the insightful question: 'Where is the power located? Are we talking about the development of the written work, a person's writing or the writer himself or herself?' While Sean, himself, is not a factor in existing theories and measures of writing growth, value is given to the evidence Sean has left on the page. This evidence may be a fine example of Sean's abilities and skills or a far cry from his potential. Though distinctions between orienting our focus on written products, processes or persons may seem insignificant, that is hardly the case. Like the pivot on a large wrecking ball, entire assessment systems, curricular and instructional approaches and theories themselves turn upon the orientation to what is considered to be developing. The orientation we take toward that which we see as developing has very real consequences for our students' learning. How writers are positioned in the question of development affects what we imagine is possible for students, and what opportunities we provide.

Thus, our understanding of a young writer's development should be informed by our understanding of youth, motivation and identity. The concepts of identity and motivation are intricately linked to each other, and to writing, through young people's preferences and practices. In a review of research on motivation, adolescents and literacy, Reed et al. (2004) argued that *affiliation* was found to be especially influential in the adolescent years. As a social group, teenagers are positioned with heightened attention to the social roles they want to play; in this context, adolescents identify and 'disidentify' with literacy – affecting the cognitive attention youth give to writing. Reed et al. (2004) argued that adolescents similarly need *self-regulation* strategies to remain engaged in literacy tasks.

Though individual intentional acts, such as identifying or self-regulating, are evident in Sean's writing history, they are not salient in Sean's experiences, performances and composing processes. He rarely, if ever, 'motivates' himself to compose outside of school. Either he is in the mood or he is not. In school, he writes or he does not. Instead of individual-based reasons, contextual-based factors – such as having a validating mentor, organized events to attend, and a place to live in proximity to an active community – are the factors that sustain Sean's motivated state. McCaslin (1990: 36) explained, '[Motivation] involve[s] both incidental and intentional processes within the learner and within the social instructional setting, hence to understand the dynamics of an individual learner, one must attend to the changing social contexts within which the developing learner emerges.' We often focus on the intentional actions of an individual, locating motivation solely in the individual, but as Geoffery Cohen (personal communication, 12 November, 2008) explained: 'the effect of motivation on achievement is best explained as a story of identity and situation.' In research with first grade students, Turner and Paris (1995) similarly found seven attributes of lesson design that contributed to motivated learning: choice, challenge, control, collaboration, meaning construction and consequences. Motivation and a person's sense of self are both drawn from individual as well as social context.

So, what about context?

By centering a theory of writing development on the writer, it may seem that the surrounding factors of context, culture and situation will be considered secondary in development. The opposite, however, is true. Scribner and Cole (1981) were one of the first to call writing a *social practice*, which means that when we write – be it in school, work or home – we are acting within certain social systems. What is considered writing in one community may not be in another. Scribner and Cole (1981), for instance, found three distinct written scripts and communities in the same geographic area, leading them to reason that: 'Literacy is not simply knowing how to read and write a particular script, but applying this knowledge for specific purposes in specific contexts of use' (p. 236). Not only do we need to keep in mind that most existing theories of writing and writing development have been defined by school literacy, there are aspects within the school context that have not been considered in a substantive way in existing theories. Dixon (2010) has recently called for attention to be drawn to the 'individual differences in developmental routes' arguing that this entails understanding how the teacher-student interaction in the classroom can be optimized. Langer and Applebee (1986: 171) made a similar plea: 'We will argue here that [individual development and instruction] should be integrated through a more general theory that systematically relates individual development to the social processes that surround it.'

Giving us a start on how to systematically account for social processes, Schultz and Fecho (2000) posited six sociocultural dimensions to consider when addressing writing development, viz that writing:

1. reflects social historical contexts;
2. varies across local contexts;
3. reflects classroom curriculum and pedagogy;
4. is shaped by social interaction;
5. is tied to social identities; and
6. is a nonlinear process.

We add a seventh dimension to this list:

7. the affordances and constraints of the technologies, broadly conceived (i.e. pen, memory devices, word processing, social media) and modes with and within which writing is composed, represented and disseminated (Kress 2003).

Kell (2009), in work studying how writing evolves across time and space, argued that technologies, settings, relationships and even events without text deserve more attention when studying how writing practices develop with a community and across communities with individuals.

What does theorizing the sociocultural landscape mean for understanding Sean's development as a writer? Violence, aggression and battle are prevalent themes in Sean's work from love poems filled with war imagery to the way he describes his writing processes to the performance of his poetry. Sean describes the purpose of being a poet this way: 'It's our responsibility as poets to speak for those who can't speak... That's what we do. We wage war with words... If you are a good poet you have an arsenal of poems.' We could easily attribute this to a performance of masculinity. Maynard's (2002) findings typify research regarding topic choice of boys: males have been found to 'write aggressive, blood-thirsty stories, often about authority and control and containing superheroes and bad guys' (p. 39).[1] Once sociocultural dimensions have been taken into consideration, however, we can see that Sean had been encompassed with hypermasculine structures and practices in his out-of-school poetry workshop, which had become over time more like a sports team than a writing group in its training for and focus on competitive slams (Lesko 2000). In this context Sean received support via being 'pushed' to go harder, be competitive and to 'prove' himself. In turn, he compares his poetry performances to the performances of other poets: '[Mentors] let you know that other poets gonna be there, that there's gonna be tough poets. So you gotta go hard. You gotta step it up. You gotta go harder than them, twice as hard, three times, know what I'm saying?'

The genre of spittin', which has a long history in adult spoken word communities, increased in popularity among these youth as a hybrid genre. Sharing characteristics with both spoken word and hip hop, its distinguishing characteristics are spontaneous composition with simultaneous performance, negative tone and use of derogatory terms. Though participants did not associate spittin' with competition, its rise coincided with several newly initiated competitive poetry slams with increased competitive language and metaphors across levels of the discourse in workshops, writers' memos and interviews.

In six months' time, just as quickly as hypermasculine practices had entered the poetry workshop, spittin' dropped from the discourse. This occurred when youth, including Sean, initiated efforts to de-emphasize competition throughout the organization by organizing non-competitive poetry readings and establishing forums in order to provide input to the planning of the organization. It is at this time that Sean's purpose for writing shifted from affecting a strong response with hot lines to communicating a clear message regarding social injustices, evidenced in minute changes to his poetry as detailed in Figure 6.1, but also by an entirely different approach to his participation in workshops. Instead of competition, he often wrote with the intent of encouraging the other writers. He often gathered teens around in a huddle for pep talks after workshops, encouraging them to stay true to their voice.

The poetry organization's mission, which had always been to provide a free, safe space to nurture youth to find their own voices, might also be considered as developing hypermasculine modes of instruction and structures – albeit unintentionally. From years of research focused on the emergent literacy development of young children, Dyson (1995, 2007) concluded that 'over time... not only may individual children develop as skillful participants in literacy practices, but cultures – configurations of shared practices – themselves develop' (2007: 116). Shifts in schools, curricula and assessments need to be reflected in the measurement of the individual's development. It is too simplistic to conclude that Sean is a young man therefore he writes aggressively. Developmental inquiry must not only attend to the participants' development, but also acknowledge the ways contexts of practice are developing concurrently.

In writing development, *how* is the writer developing?

We have argued that reframing writing development to centre on the developing writer necessitates a broader scope in what is currently accepted as evidence of development. This suggestion follows the most current trend of existing theories of writing development, which are more and more explicitly inclusive of the social, cultural, pedagogical, technological and modal impact on a writer writing. What we have yet to do in this chapter is address what effect a change in scope has on how we conceive of development itself. Even as the nature of writing has been redefined by theorists of writing development, the nature of *development* has remained static in definition and application. Consistently, writing development has been used to refer to discrete changes in one aspect of writing along a linear trajectory. For researchers like Hunt (1970) this linear trajectory meant longer and more complicated linguistic units. For Bereiter and Scardamalia (1987) this linear trajectory was steadily more complicated cognitive processes handled with greater ease. Across all the varied approaches we reviewed, 'development' is reduced to one aspect of writing and idealized as a linear trajectory on a scale indexed by age or grade level (Illeris 2007). Even recent studies designed from a sociocultural perspective conceptualize writing development as closer approximations or increased participation in a discourse community's genres (e.g. Schultz 2002; Guzzetti and Gamboa 2004; Jacobs 2008), reducing the concept of development to mean a trajectory of literate acts toward one particular type of participation.

This reduction and linear projection has positive and negative educational consequences. For teachers, it can provide clear goals and direction for planning instruction. Something inherently complicated to teach, such as the effective use of sentences, can be simplified. If writing development to us means that sentences increase in complexity, we start with mastering simple sentences, then compound sentences, and only then, complex sentences. However, we posit that this common conception of development in education – that youth learns content and skills in a linear, chronological fashion – actually contributes to the deficit model of education (Stevens 2008). Any youth whose writing is not similar – in terms of linguistic complexity or alignment to genre expectations – to his or her age-based peers' writing is seen to be at a deficit and the youth is considered to be in need of remediation or intervention. The conception of writing development as a function of a sliding linear scale, no matter how it is packaged in assessments or instruction, results in similar solutions: a game of catch-up. Recent political measures in the USA actually discipline school systems that cannot demonstrate change in student practices that adhere to an idealistic, linear scale; in England, the prevalence of league tables of schools' performance since the late 1990s, with scores partly based on performance in English at 11 and 16, has a similar intention.

Beyond these practical problems, a linear idealization of writing development does not align with what we have learned from research from varied perspectives. If trends and trajectories are not sufficient to capture the nature of students' linguistic ability within the mode of writing or to describe the genres employed, it is clearly insufficient to capture multiple components of writing (i.e. practices, processes, design) and interrelationships among them. It does not account for moments of erratic and suspended growth, regression in a skill or the variance of writing situation. We have seen the integral nature of context, the situation, genre, topic, technology and community in our observations of Sean. An acontextual prediction of what another student with a different developmental route will produce at a specific year is not a meaningful standard.

The concept of development informs every aspect of our educational system from curriculum guides and standards to autonomous, in-the-moment decisions at the classroom level. But what do we mean when we say to each other that one student is developing and another is not? New notions of development are needed if changes over time in writing – as have been noted in the theories and foundational research studies – are indeed idiosyncratic, unpredictable and intricately tied to context. Dyson (1995, 2007) shows us that we need a theory sensitive to the interrelated nature of the co-developing contexts in which writing practices occur. Schultz and Fecho (2000: 59, emphasis added) suggest:

> A sense of writing development must entail a meta-awareness of how these dimensions are implicated in the composing process and an understanding of the impact they have at various times in the process... *learning how to consider and weigh these dimensions is crucial to research on writing development.*

Development re-imagined

In addition to calling for a broadened scope to help understand writing development, we are challenging assumptions of its linear progression supposedly inherent in educational development. What would an approach based on the concept of development that was not linear, not idealized and did not result in deficit thinking look like? To begin, increased age or grade level would not be assumed to be indicative of increased ability or experience. This approach to development is multidimensional and recursive rather than linear. By multidimensional we mean changes in development affect and are affected by several interactions and dimensions of a person's development. We are interested in the multiple interrelated dimensions of growth: emotional, physical, spiritual, intellectual, cognitive, moral, experiential, social and 'maturational.' By recursive, we mean that improvement in one aspect of writing may be paired with a regression in another aspect. Sean, for instance, has a strong voice, knowledge base and interest in social injustices. When Sean takes on a new genre, it is most likely he will return to writing in reference to issues of social injustices of race and class. One might interpret this return to the same topics as stalled growth. But we could also view this repeated revisiting of topics in new genres and within new communities and audiences as an occasion for deepening of understanding and discovery. Guastello (as cited by Willis 2007: 345) explains nonlinearity this way: 'A nonlinear relationship between two variables is one where an incremental change in one is not met with a proportional change in the other. Rather, a small change in one variable, at the right place and time, can produce a large effect elsewhere in the system.'

No model of writing development – as of yet – has depicted this process as idiosyncratic and branching out in several directions, where multiple dimensions of growth and recursion are an accepted part of development. Kuhn, a philosopher of science, is attributed to have said, 'You don't see something until you have the right metaphor to let you perceive it' (Gleick 1987: 262). The kind of developmental growth we are suggesting is far removed from the traditional approach. It is not immediately clear how to conceive of development that is multidimensional and recursive. In this section, we explore three alternative nonlinear metaphors of development from fields outside education – development of a photograph, development of a piece of music, and development in complexity science. Each of these metaphors has limitations in how representative it is of reality; however, each provides a fresh perspective on what it can mean to develop as a writer.

Development of a photograph

If you have ever spent time in a darkroom, other than the pungent smells of chemicals and bleach, you probably remember the seemingly magical transformation as a white piece of photographic paper is dipped into the treatment baths and colours begin to slowly emerge, seemingly rising to the surface of the page. First, just a hint of grey begins to take shape, and with each subsequent treatment, the definition of the image comes into focus. After washing the image and hanging it to dry, there is a sense of awe at how quickly the image begins to take shape.

First, we know it is not magic. Each chemical bath holds different carbocyanine dyes and each has spectral absorption characteristics. In fact, the intensity of the dyes introduced is directly proportional to the amount of exposure the layer received. However, even though this is not magic – something that human development often feels like – it still works in our metaphor.

In developing a photograph, photographic paper is treated by a series of chemical baths that instigate the formation of varying colours. This metaphor lends explanatory power to how contextual experiences are like treatments with particular effects. In Sean's case, the increasing and decreasing focus on the discourse of competition at his out-of-school spoken word organization is the contextual 'treatment' that instigated the development of a hybrid genre of spittin' and the subsequent competitive approach to spoken word. Limits of this metaphor include the false analogy of a series of contextual experiences as treatments with known results.

This metaphor also draws attention to the possibility of simultaneous development in several aspects of writing products and processes, as multiple colours appear in phases of photographic development. Colours on photographic paper do not regress; rather they may seem to fade as other colours become more dominant. What would it mean if rather than seeing students' ability erratically progressing and regressing, we consider differing aspects of a young writer's products or processes fading in comparison to other dominant interests, practices or genres?

Development in music

In music, development is the way an idea or theme is communicated through a musical score. The idea is developed through contrapuntal techniques such as inverting a line of the melody or augmenting the rhythmic patterns in the theme with embellishments in the melody. These techniques add interest and push the idea forward. In certain musical forms such as the sonata, the theme as originally presented in the beginning returns in the final portions of the song, reminding the audience of the journey of sound they just experienced, and creating a satisfying ending. Another way composers develop a piece of music is by using counterpoint. Counterpoints are additional lines of melody that retain their independent sound while being played against or in unison with the main melody creating intricate harmonies. The forward moving sound of a fugue is achieved through this type of technique.

Though this metaphor is quite limited in that a musical score is a composed, controlled and designed work of art rather than an organic, experienced phenomenon, the idea that development could be achieved by recursion to a previous theme or by juxtaposition to another melody is a powerful one. What has been perceived as instances of limited change, or suspended development in Sean's school-based genres and essays can be re-imagined as repeating themes. Like an eddy's effect in a riverbed, we are pulled to established practices and with each return, the practices deepen. Sean may be embellishing, augmenting or otherwise developing ideas – such as his focus on social activism for gender, social class and racial equality – or writing techniques – such as his fixation on word play in hip hop – as he returns to these practices. In fact, when we see any component of writing 'stalled out' – topics, processes, product characteristics, genres – we may be witnessing moments of deepening understanding.

Similarly, with the harmonizing effects of musical counterpoints in mind, we can reconsider how dissimilar genres or styles could be reimagined in the classroom. Often we hear teachers and parents bemoaning the latest techno-speech as being the downfall of writing capacity. Indeed, Britton et al. (1976) were particularly concerned that as one function or audience was emphasized in the classroom all other genres were dropped. A teacher viewing differing styles and genres as counterpoints which, when played against each other, clarify the distinctions of genre, style or tone, might welcome Sean's use of texting and emailing by cell/mobile phone, as it actually increases instructional possibilities.

Development in complexity science

This brings us to a final metaphor, one of organic growth: chaos and complexity science. Complexity science, the study of the dynamism of adaptive systems (Gleick 1987), suggests that organic, changing systems – e.g. teenagers' learning in and out of schools – while complicated, erratic and unpredictable, are also patterned and ordered. The ways in which complex systems are viewed and described is the simplifying factor. Patterns in chaos were first discovered when scientists moved from graphing phenomena on two-dimensional, linear graphs to using super-computers to chart phase space, which allowed the consideration of multiple dimensions of a system as well as the systems in which it is nested.

Once multiple dimensions were taken into consideration – as we are suggesting needs to occur in order to theorize writing development more accurately – researchers noticed patterns of growth, even in the most chaotic of systems. One such pattern is similarity across levels of a system or within nested systems. With the concept of system similarity in mind, we might have helped Sean move beyond his exclusive use of war and aggressive imagery by looking beyond the most obvious of issues, the hypermasculine features of his written products, processes and practices. Rather, we would have looked right away for similar conditions and structures in other levels of the discourse (Fairclough 2001) and in other social systems in which Sean writes.

Although complexity science is often applied to human social systems, most established approaches to the study of complexity involve observation and description of natural phenomena such as weather patterns, life cycles of animals, or pure mathematical inquiry. As such, complexity will be relegated as powerful metaphor in this instance. As a metaphor that is yet unfamiliar to most of us, its pragmatic value as illuminating is currently limited.

Conclusion

We have considered three alternative metaphors that each present *development* in a meaningful way. We see 'linear progression' as yet another metaphor for growth. Pictorially represented in graph form, linear progression seems to simplify a complicated and extensive amount of information into a manageable chunk. However, not only is the simplified version unrealistic, it has also informed a deficit orientation to education. The full theory of a writer's development presented in Chapter 9 will address a broadened sense of both the nature of writing and nonlinear development.

7   Writing within Multimodality

Introduction

Research and theoretical development in the field of multimodality suggests that it is no longer possible to conceive of 'English' and writing development in terms of teaching and learning a single, monomodal system: written script. Writing itself always has a visual dimension. Furthermore, even when writing appears by itself (e.g. in a handwritten letter, in a book, in a report) it is framed by space around it that helps the composer and reader shape their response to it. That space invites the reader or composer to bring other forms of imagination and conception to the business of writing (and reading). We could say, in this case, that writing *implies* the other modes. Furthermore, writing appears *alongside* other modes in newspapers, magazines, on television, in films, in children's books and in a host of other texts and contexts. Indeed, it is more common to see writing in a multimodal situation than in a monomodal one. As well as learning the internal dynamics of the written system, pupils and students need to take account of these multimodal dimensions as they compose (and read).

The visual dimension of writing

Look at this page from a distance. You may not be able to make out the individual words or discern any meaning as such, but you will be able to see the layout of words on the page, the title of the chapter and headings, the fact that the right-hand margin is justified, and the page number. You will also notice the white space around the text. Each feature of the page (and there are more, like the 'leading' or the degree of space between the lines, the nature and size of the type, and whether any of the headings are in bold) contributes to the act of communication. Because you are used to reading academic, research and/or professional books, you will recognize the layout as typical of such a book. Even without seeing any of the individual words, you could work out the nature of the book, and possibly its provenance, date and country of origin from these features.

Writing is inescapably visual, and always has been. From the first mark made on a wall or on the ground, to highly sophisticated typographical creations and computer generated verbal text, writing has visual identity. In the case of looking at the present page, the layout is conventional and has limited significance. It frames the text (see Andrews 2011) but does little more. It also helps to make the text readable (the length of each line, the type size and the leading all contribute to this effect). The right-hand justification is simply to make the column of text look well designed; it would not change the meaning if there was no right-hand justification. Justification is not strongly significant: it is simply there because books are of a certain size and there must be white space at each margin. But take a poem, for example. As once defined by an 11-year-old, it 'does not go up to the right-hand edge of the page' (Andrews 1992):

The view from Hadrian's Wall

Nine days out of ten
it's damp, miserable, dark;
you can't see beyond
the next field, the next milecastle.

One day out of ten
the sky clears itself out
into a Mediterranean blue
and Rome appears.

The first point to make about the setting of the poem in these pages is that we have indented it, so it already stands out, like a quotation, as something different from the main body of the text. But on whichever page this poem might appear, there is no right-hand justification (that would change the nature of the poem) and, more importantly, the individual character of each line would be affected if it was. It would become a prose poem (if we defined it as such) or merely a chunk of prose. We will set it as a quotation to make this clear:

> Nine days out of ten it's damp, miserable, dark; you can't see beyond the next field, the next milecastle. One day out of ten the sky clears itself out into a Mediterranean blue and Rome appears.

In this version, the line endings are not significant (though they could be read as such). There is no divisions of the lines into two four-line stanzas; the rhythmic shape of the lines, as indicated by the line endings and overall visual look of the poem in the first version, is lost; the pace of the reading changes because the longer lines require or invite faster, less attentive reading; and, associated with the last point, because we are reading it as a prose poem or as a prose quotation, we are not bringing to it the expectations that we would bring to the reading of a poem, *viz.* that the individual words will be resonant, that there will be correspondences to discover between the words; that there is an underlying metrical/rhythmical shape to the poem which itself carries meaning; that we might want to provide space for reflection around it, just as the white space in the original version suggests that we pay a different kind of attention to it.

All these nuances are attributable to the visual identity of the words on the page, which in a poem are designed to convey a musical – or, at least, rhythmical identity. Rhythm is crucial to a poem – almost its identifying characteristic – and conveys the relations in time between the words. In this poem, the rhythm is not reinforced by rhyme, but emerges more subtly through repetition of the structural form (the quatrain) and of the lines 'Nine days out of ten' and 'One day out of ten'. There is more to say about the exact placing of the words in the poem, particularly those at the line endings, but that would be to engage in a full-scale exegesis of the poem. Here, we are concerned with how its visual properties carry meaning. One last visual point: the first stanza has punctuation, but the second one has none except for the closing full-stop. There is something about the flow of the second stanza that is indicated by the lack of punctuation in comparison to the first. So even small punctuation and diacritical marks have significance.

Monomodal writing implies other modes

Before we move on to discuss multimodality, it is important to note that a seemingly monomodal form like the poem can imply other modes. This is particularly true of the poem, because (in general) poems, because of their compression and attention to form, resonate with *suggestion* of experiences beyond the words themselves. In the case above, the poem is a dance in words; that is to say, it is arranged formally in two quatrains. Each quatrain has lines of roughly the same length, and the nature of the poetic lines requires a 'turning' at the end of each one, even though there is also a syntactic flow through the sentences that make up each stanza (particularly noticeable in the second stanza where there is no intervening punctuation). The poem can also be sounded by being read aloud; it can be performed. Above all, it can be visualized: this particular poem is strongly visual in that it evokes contrasting days on Hadrian's Wall in terms of how far one can see. But, like many works of fiction, the imagination is called upon to accept that, on a clear day, 'Rome appears'. There is nothing you can tangibly feel in reading or hearing the poem, though your feelings might be engaged.

In short, dance (movement), sound (specifically speech) and the visual are all implied by the poem. The very compression of the work, along with its disciplined structure, keeps out the other modes though they are suggested by it.

Is this the case also with more prosaic verbal text? Let's take two examples: one from a travel guide and one from a credit card statement. First, the travel guide:

> I like to walk with food in mind: a picnic in my backpack or a restaurant at the end. All the best walks incorporate food – boozy lunches in village squares in Spain, Moroccan picnics on a carpet spread on desert sand, a Cape beach *braaivleis* [meat barbecue], that first glass of red and a *bruschetta* [toasted bread with olive oil, tomatoes etc.] when you've made it to a Tuscan hill-top town.
>
> (Leith 2006: 34)

This extract is deliberately poetic and evocative. Its description of walking in the countryside and food is designed to awaken the senses. Its itinerant, worldwide feel brings to mind a wealthy traveller who has experience of such variety; and the dropping in of two cooking terms, from Afrikaans and Italian – 'braaivleis' and 'bruschetta' – lends an exotic atmosphere to the description. This extract has none of the choreographic formality of the poem, but it does evoke the visual ('a carpet spread on desert sand'), the gustatory (because its subject is food, evocatively described) and the physical ('when you've made it to a Tuscan hill-top town'). We might conclude, then, that even plain prose text, albeit 'poetic' in its style, can evoke the other modes and engage the imagination.

The second prose example is from a credit card statement. It is part of the standard rubric in such a statement:

> If you do not pay the full amount outstanding, we will allocate your payment to the outstanding balance in a specific order, which is set out overleaf in the Allocation of Payment section of the Summary Box. The way in which payments are allocated can make a significant difference to the amount of interest you will pay until the balance is cleared completely.
>
> (source: The Cooperative Bank 2010)

What is distinctive and indeed multimodal, if anything, about this extract? It is typical of small print legalese in that it tries to make explicit the consequences of non-payment of the full bill on a monthly basis. It is neither suggestive nor evocative and thus unlike the poem or poetic prose above. It refers to other text, which gives the specific order in which payments are allocated (and which in turn has the caveat: 'The information … summarises the key product features and is not intended to replace any terms and conditions. It is important that you read the terms and conditions carefully.' The terms and conditions are not supplied, but can be accessed via the web. They constitute even smaller print.)

There is thus a great deal of verbal written text underpinning the short extract above, and no attendant imagery or other modes. These texts are part of a highly verbalized world (rights, obligations, law) in which possible *actions* and *consequences* are made clear. The only way in which imagination is engaged is in asking the reader to imagine the scenario in which they do not pay off the bill monthly ('we will allocate your payment to the outstanding balance') and the ways in which such allocation will take place. In this example, we could say that the written verbal text implies action, but not other modes as such, unless we consider that imagined action can be visualized.

Perhaps we can summarize the implying of other modes by written text, based on these examples. Writing can evoke imagined scenarios at the very least; but in more 'poetic' text, like evocative travel writing or poems, the senses are more fully engaged through the act of reading. These can include sight (e.g. more precise imaginings of landscapes), sound (the significance of a read-aloud text, of musical patterning and resonance), movement (e.g. choreographic shape) and touch (the almost tangible *feel* of an evoked experience), smell ('a Cape beach *braaivleis*') and taste ('that first glass of red'). The senses themselves do not map exactly on to modes of communication (speech, writing, the still image, moving images, movement (dance), etc.) but they are closely associated and a principal way in which channels of communication are explored.

Writing alongside other modes

So far in this chapter we have discussed the *visual* nature of writing and writing which *implies* other modes. Now we turn to writing *alongside* other modes. There was no need for a theory of multimodality in a world where writing was assumed to evoke the senses or indeed the other modes. But as part of our exploration of writing development, it is necessary to acknowledge that writing is one mode among several, this has particular affordances, that the other modes interplay with it in various ways, and that – more generally – that we need to place writing and writing development within a theory of multimodality in order to build a new theory and model for it. In order to explore the place of writing, we will use as our points of references one early (1997) and one more recent (2010) account by Kress: *Before Writing: Rethinking the Paths to Literacy* and *Multimodality: A Social Semiotic Approach to Contemporary Communication* respectively.

In what is avowedly '*not* a book about the development of writing' (Kress 1997: xvii) *Before Writing* sets out its stall early on: it is a book about meaning-making, about form as meaning rather than as formalism, about composition as design. 'Above all, this book tries to look freshly at children's engagement with print by treating this as just one of a plethora of ways in which they make meaning before they come to school' (p. xix). From such a perspective, we would not see writing as the central mode of communication in schooling (see the discussion earlier in the present chapter and in the previous one) but as one among several. It is a sign system, a particular sub-branch of the 'study of the meaning of systems of signs' (p. 6) – semiotics. So, in pre-school as well as in the early years of schooling (and beyond), writing sits alongside other modes of meaning-making.

The relationship between writing and other modes varies according to purpose and intention, but also according to the preference of the reader. Let us take writing and the still image, in all its forms. In some cases, writing is foregrounded and the image – say an illustration in a children's book – remains literally *illustrative* of something in the verbal written text. In a recipe book, too, the writing is crucial (the photographs, on the whole, do not tell you the steps you have to take to make the dish) and is illustrated by accompanying photographs. But even if the intention and purpose of the composer of the book is to foreground the writing, it may be the case that the reader operates by giving attention first to the images, and only then to the written verbal text. The images can stand on their own, and as a way into the text.

In other cases, the image may be foregounded and the written text is supplementary. An example would be a catalogue (of art, of shopping) where both the intention and the attention are given first to the images, and then to the accompanying verbal text which acts to give more information, sometimes of an explanatory nature, and which cannot be given by the image itself.

Thirdly, there are the interesting cases where neither written text nor image is in the ascendancy, but they both sit alongside each other in a complementary fashion or in tension. In such cases, the reader's attention moves as they wish it, back and forth between the two modes, making connections, looking for points of comparison. This is a highly productive state of attention in which the mind is asked to shift between the two modes, and thus must gain meta-modal perspective on the kinds of communication that are taking place. Kress's argument in *Before Writing* is that the child draws on their range of meaning-making practices in a range of modes in order to make sense of the written system. The social semiotic theory 'insists that all signs and messages are always multimodal. That is, no sign or message ever exists in just one single mode' (p. 10), as we have explored above in the section on the implications of the seemingly monomodal written system. But Kress adds something more: that all writing takes place in some form of material state; that the medium in which it finds itself inscribed (e.g. on a scrap of paper, on a computer screen) has further physical, cultural and symbolic association; and that modality is influenced by medium and the wider environments of physical/economic resource (and its distribution) as well as by accompanying modes.

What about writing in relation to sound, moving image, gesture and broader categories of physicality, like movement, dance – even something as simple and everyday as moving from A to B, either in a wheelchair or on foot or via transport of some kind? These questions may seem strange in relation to the developing writer, but we will address them briefly here as they shed more light on what it means to learn to write.

Kress (1997, Chapter 4) has written at length and with insight into the difficulties and pleasures of linking sounds to the alphabetic scripts of English (and by implication, other languages that use the alphabet) – he has also touched on the different transitions that are required in moving between the sounds of Chinese or Japanese and the written forms of Chinese characters or *kanji*. We will take a slightly different perspective on the speaking/writing relationship here, seeing them both as productive skills in the development of literacy (and thus widening the notion of literacy to include speaking and listening as well as the narrower definition of reading and writing competence). What speaking can 'offer' writing is a number of correspondences: one of them is the production of meaning. One of the difficulties facing young people, and many older ones, is how to begin to utter what one wants to say, or commit to paper or screen what one wants to 'say'. Filling a blank page is one of the terrors that faces many such people, at times. Once that first hurdle is jumped, either by means of a first draft that will need a good deal of work on it, or by committing to saying something that can at least be seen as a starting point for discussion or narrative development, the rest of the composition may flow more freely. The dialogic nature of speech offers a model for writers to follow, if they see that their own writing (cf. Bakhtin) is a response to existing communication: part of a dialogue rather than a solitary voice in the wilderness. That dialogism can manifest itself in play writing, in dialogic essay writing, in question-and-answer formats.

A second way in which speech and writing can interact is in each acting as a rehearsal for the other. It is often thought that speaking comes first, and that we can rehearse in discussion what later we will write down. That transition is underestimated in terms of difficulty, because often the job is to capture what was multi-voiced, fast, dynamic and interactive into something in print that is monologic, deliberate and reflective. But writing can also precede speech, as in the making of notes for a speech, the scripting of a play, or the making of a list of points that one wants to raise in an agenda – a spoken meeting.

Thirdly, we do not use transcription of speech as often as we might in demonstrating to developing writers that what they say can appear in a written version. The written conventions can become clear when they are compared to how speech looks when it is written down: the hesitations, the repetitions and other features of speech disappear, and written and transcribed versions can make for fascinating comparisons in the writing classroom. Particularly for people who find writing difficult, the transcription of their speech can be a revelation.

Let us finish this section with a consideration of moving image and physical movement: modes of communication that are often not associated in any way with writing. We think of writing as still and fixed, but in electronic billboards, on television and via other media we can see writing moving, changing shape (in the hands of graphic artists), flying into sight in powerpoint presentations, emerging as in a developing tray in cloze exercises, flashing in neon displays; even flying past on the side of a bus or taxi. So the first point to make is that writing itself can be kinetic, dynamic and fleeting. When it is associated with film, or in choreography, or in the simple transportation with the body from A to B, it takes on a different kind of multimodality: when used in a film, for example, it can signify layers of complexity and time (in, for example, the reading by voice-over of a letter in the hands of an actor). In this case it provides otherness, the importation of a different world and time into the moment of the film. Polanski's film *The Ghost* (2010), for example, uses a draft manuscript of memoirs by a failed British prime minister as a core text in the action of the film: the text is read aloud, edited, transported physically, and is ultimately decoded to provide a written note to the dead prime minister's wife at a book launch for the book itself. Not only is the palimpsest of the draft book a metaphor for multi-layered and many-leaved complexity of memory; it physically is strewn across a street in the final frames of the film, suggesting that secrets held in the manuscript are lost – or found again – in fragments of meaning across an urban landscape (see also the book by Robert Harris, *The Ghost* – an interesting comparison is possible, as in all book/film adaptations, of the two modes at work; Harris 2007). In another very different example, the Taiwanese dance company Cloud Gate use calligraphy as the inspiration for a piece called Wild Cursive – a particularly free-form style of the Chinese character. Dance movements are shaped by a wild cursive style, while banners are draped from the flies with Chinese characters on them to suggest the origin of the dance movements. Earlier in this chapter, in the discussion of the poem, reference was made to its choreographic nature. Such correspondences of rhythm, shape and form are at the heart of learning to write, whether with the Chinese character or in the alphabetic script.

The affordances of writing

From a multimodal perspective, what can writing do that other modes cannot? We have already set out what we see as the particular qualities of writing, but the term used by Kress and others is affordances: what does writing *allow* us to do?

Through a process of transformation (including translation from one written language to another, transduction from one mode to another), writing appears to have the following affordances that we have not yet explored in detail: it is low cost, and therefore can be used in situations where cost is at a premium. Unlike the image or any mode which requires expensive means of communication, writing is eminently transportable. Its function in telegrams and handwritten letters in the days when electronic transfer of bits of information was undreamt of indicate its clear affordance; but in a digital age, writing can be transported as easily as sound or image, and vice-versa. The advantage of writing, in that sense, has been diminished. But what writing can do that the other modes cannot is provide a permanent, explicit message to convey a mix of feeling, abstraction, particularity and metaphor (because of its multi-levelled operational capacity). Or, perhaps it is more accurate to say that other modes (the still image, moving image, sound, music) can convey these features, but in a different way. Writing has the affordance of sequence, multi-levelled logical connections through linguistic hierarchies, explicit argumentation as well as narrative drive. It can convey nuances of abstract meaning.

In terms of translation, something is always lost in translation when written texts are moved from one language to another. This is because each language charts experience in different ways. Images, music and physical movement do not need such translation, though there are aspects of each mode that do need, if not translation, then at least explication: not all gestures mean the same thing in different cultures, and an image or sound may be read differently by different people from dissimilar backgrounds. Nevertheless, the process of written translation raises the question about cultural and linguistic difference, and sensitizes the reader to the particular characteristics of each language.

We can see the differences between writing and other modes in the following extended example. One of us had to write [sic] instructions on how to get to particularly remote place in the Adirondack Mountains of New York State. We knew most people – Europeans, anyway – would come from the south or east via New York or Boston, so the directions were written with that orientation in mind.

Here are the written instructions:

1. **From Burlington, Vermont**

   Head south on Route 7 through Shelburne (the Ethan Allen Highway) and on for a few miles until you reach a crossroads with traffic lights.

   Take a right turn (west), signposted to Charlotte for ferry to NY state.

   Continue to Charlotte. Take ferry to Essex, New York, across Lake Champlain.

   Once off the ferry, turn left, then right and out of town on route 22/9N, following signs to Highway 87 the whole time. You go through Whallonsburg, then Wadhams. In Wadhams, continue to look carefully for the signs to Highway 87. (In Wadhams, you cross a river then turn right and 200 yards on, at the top of the hill, turn left.)

   Continue for a few miles until you come to a t-junction. Turn right. You'll see Highway 87 in front of you. Go under the bridge, then turn left to join the southbound carriageway of route 87. Go south for ten miles or so to Exit 30 signposted for Keene Valley. Take this exit. Then follow 'The last mile' instructions below.

2. **From Middlebury, Vermont**

   Take 125 West all the way to the Crown Point ferry on Lake Champlain (there's a dog-leg junction about half way). The bridge at Crown Point was demolished in December 2009. There is a replacement ferry.

   Take the ferry from Addison, Vermont to Crown Point, New York state.

   Follow the road for two miles or so to a t-junction. Turn right to Port Henry.

   In middle of Port Henry, take a left turn. At the top of the hill you pass a school, then turn right and go to Moriah Center (about 2 miles).

   At crossroads/traffic lights in middle of Moriah Center, turn right. Very soon (about 200 yards or less) take the left fork to Mineville-Witherbee and probably signposted to Highway 87.

   Follow road for two miles or so to Mineville-Witherbee, and look for signposts to travel west on the Tracy Road (again, signposted Highway 87). The Tracy Road meanders for eight miles or so. Don't give up. It ends at a t-junction. Turn right on to route 9 north, go under Highway 87, then follow 'The last mile' instructions below.

3. **From New York/Albany on Highway 87 (the Adirondack Northway)**
   Take Exit 30.

   As you come off ramp, turn left on to route 9 north. Then follow 'The last mile' instructions below.

('The last mile directions' have been left off for privacy purposes.)

What is distinctive about this set of directions? As well as indicating the main routes and turnings, it has some helpful hints for drivers and their navigators, e.g. 'In Wadhams, continue to look carefully for the signs to Highway 87. (In Wadhams, you cross a river then turn right and 200 yards on, at the top of the hill, turn left.)' or 'The bridge at Crown Point was demolished in December 2009. There is a replacement ferry.' These are the kind of details that a map might not tell you; indeed, a map does not 'tell' you what to do at all.

The map is shown in Figure 7.1. The difference between the written instructions one the one hand, and the map on the other, are clear: the writing is detailed, sequential and written very much from the point of

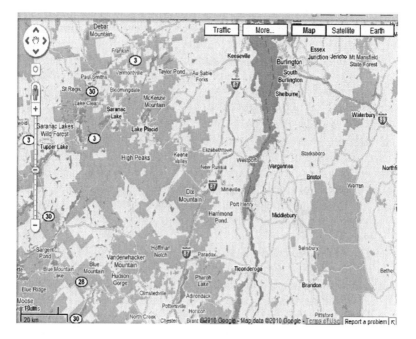

Figure 7.1 Map of Adirondack High Peak region and Highway 87
© Google 2010

view of the travellers making their way from the east or south towards this destination. The map covers a greater area, indicates the main roads and towns, gives a fairly precise location to aim for, and then lets the driver/navigator do most of the interpretive work. The annotation provides more information – and, admittedly, a larger scale map of the local area would have been better for the detailed navigation needed at the end of the journey.

Another way to get people from A to B is a satellite navigation device ('satnav' in the UK) into which you simply key in the zip- or post-code and follow the directions, given to you in computer graphic form and additionally in a human voice. Again, like the writing, the directions are from the point of view of the driver, rather than map-like. It is not uncommon to see people reading a map who turn it so that the road they are travelling *on the map* is the same as the direction in which they are heading. This is one way of bringing the map in line with one's own point of view.

Once directions to a particular place are used and taken on board, after two or three visits there is no longer any need for directions. The driver simply uses cues from their memory to make the journey successfully: an exit number, a roadside fence, a break in the trees – anything that will remind them where to turn. These cues become fewer in number until it becomes 'second nature' to make the journey (of course, cues are still needed, but they are merely point markers rather than conscious orientation points).

Our extended discussion of different ways of getting from A to B is intended to draw out the affordances of the different modes of communication. Note that the written version implies visual engagement with the landscape; that the visual map requires written annotation; and that the satnav requires a zip- or post-code and a willingness to listen to instructions. Each text is very different, but these use more than one mode to operate successfully.

Finally, it is worth noting that as Maun and Myhill (2005: 9) suggest, writing needs to be designed too: 'It is important that the notion of designing embraces not only visual and presentation choices, but the linguistic choices too'. Elements of writing design can be seen to be at play at every level from the shaping of a text in its context, through the positioning of the text as a whole on a page or screen or in the sand, to the way parts of text are related to each other.

Does writing as a multimodal activity determine our view of the world?

In this section we address one of the questions asked by Kress (2010: 76) in his own consideration of two modes of representation in a child's accounts of a visit to a museum. One of the accounts was visual, the other a written transcription of speech. Kress's initial discussion is of the questions posed by the two modes, and then of their affordances and different logics. But then he asks the question: 'whether a habituation to representing in one *mode* or the other could come to organize and shape our engagement with the world prior even to any request from outside or need to make a representation' (p. 76).

We think, from our experience as teachers of writing, that the mode of written verbal text *does* habituate its users to a certain way of seeing the world. We have recited these affordances above and elsewhere in the book: a predilection for logical sequencing, a narrative drive, a categorization facility, a proximity to speech. Catalogue systems, search engines and keywords, classifications in science and other fields, all depend on the written word for making sense of and archiving the world. In short, the production of knowledge and its storage depend heavily on the written verbal language. Because words are also highly sensitive to changes in culture (they reflect such changes) the history of cultures is carried in the verbal language. Speech, and in its transcribed form, written language act as the glue in social relations: we could say that social relations are constituted in verbal language. For all these reasons, writing is a powerful mode of representation and communication.

Does such habituation preclude other ways of representing and communicating? No, as long as the learner is aware that there are limits to seeing the world through a lens of verbal spoken or written language. We perhaps take for granted that sports activity, some of the performing arts (mime, dance), music and mathematics operate without or 'beyond' words, partly because words often accompany these activities as means of explaining, directing or bringing about such action. When activity happens without words, it can be arresting. Imagine a theatre performance without words (e.g. Beckett's *Act without Words*) in which there is also no programme, no mediation of any kind from the written verbal mode to 'introduce' one to the experience. Such activities are not only stunning in themselves; they remind us that verbal language is not everywhere. So, too the experience of uninscribed landscape can be liberating as well as terrifying. Words, it seems, belong to and tie us back into the world of human, social culture.

In schooling terms, the prevalence of the word in the day-to-day business of schooling and in the curriculum – and especially in assessment – makes it a dominant mode in that environment. The tendency we see in schooling from a synaesthetic use of a range of modes in the early years (associated with the senses) through to an increasingly stripped down 'monomodal' set of discourses in the secondary or high school years (associated with abstraction) needs to be understood, so that balances can be restored where appropriate, and the other modes can be used both separately and in combination with words to express, represent and communicate a developing understanding of the fast-changing world of knowledge. The prevalence of the word, and its increasing influence, is a mark of the belief in *abstraction* – highly valued in academic circles, but counter-balanced by tangible and practical activities in the arts, engineering, technology, sport – and in generalization. It is thus likely that the written verbal language will continue to hold its place within schooling and education – hopefully alongside other modes rather than dominating them, and in combinations with other modes to bring out the creativity latent in young and older people by offering them more outlets for representation and expression.

Conclusion: what implications does a multimodal approach to writing have for development?

Finally, in this chapter that addresses some of the multimodal considerations associated with writing, we turn our attention again to the overarching theme of the book: writing development. What implications does a multimodal perspective have for writing development?

First we need to distinguish between what we might characterize as the logical developmental sequence in the refinement of a writing system on the one hand; and the development of individual writers on the other (as we have discussed in Chapter 6). The former is an 'idealized' systemic sequence extrapolated from observation of various studies of early writing development, including the separation of letter forms from the visual nexus, the build up of not only the mechanical side of gaining command of the pen, pencil, brush and (currently) keyboard but also the conceptual demands of composition. The latter charts the individualistic ways in which writers must be allowed to develop, including drawing on other modes to complement and sit in a variety of positions in relation to writing. Moving between modes, and engaging in transduction (changes from one mode to another) is an essential part of finding one's way in writing and seeing it as part of a larger meaning-making and communicative activity. When we re-connect writing with speech as well, we realize that writing has particular affordances but that these are highlighted and strengthened when we see them in the light of a multimodal perspective.

We now move on to a different consideration: the nature of writing in the digital age. While digitization and the advent of the personal computer have had a galvanizing effect on writing processes and possibilities, it is always useful to separate the multimodal from the digital: they overlap considerably, but are not the same.

8 Writing in the Digital Age

Introduction

What is different about composing digitally in writing, compared to composing with a pen and paper, a typewriter or other 'pre-digital' medium? And what are the implications of this difference for writing and its development? Such questions guide this chapter. Let's begin by considering what writing in the digital age has in common with writing in the pre-digital age. First, we are still operating with written languages that have developed over centuries. Whichever language we use, there are component parts that make up larger components, and these in themselves are combined with other components to create meaningful utterances or statements. The written systems allow for such communications to be stored, in draft form or in more formalized, finished form for future use. Writing allows for reflection and revision before a thought is committed, i.e. before it is given to the receiver. Furthermore, what cannot be conveyed by gesture or movement, voice or tone, must be conveyed via the conventions of writing as fully as possible, even if part of the writing is to say 'Call me' or 'Look at this picture' or 'Turn right at the next junction'. Writing has been and will continue to be embedded in a particular situation for a particular purpose and imagined audience, all within a broader cultural context. Writing, as one of the principal and most enduring means of communication, is a powerful, conceptual, beautiful mode in which to work.

There have been at least three phases of an emerging relationship between advances in new technologies and writing curricula. These phases can be framed in decades: the 1980s and the arrival of the personal computer; the 1990s and the advent of networked communication and the worldwide web; the 2000s and the phenomenon of Web 2.0 with its more interactive engagement with composition on screen, and the ubiquity of digitized text, making it part of the fabric of communication. With each phase we can trace slight shifts in the nature of composing, yet still embedded in each new wave of technology are the characteristics of previous technologies and writing practices. Taking time to understand the history of digitization allows us to better understand the current landscape of writing and begin to project into the future. Looking back helps us imagine forward.

Phase one: wordprocessing and the collapse of processes

In the first phase, the 1980s and early 1990s, 'information technology' was assumed separate from the business of learning to write, and indeed from English and literacy studies in general. Computers, computer studies and the school subject itself of 'IT' in the secondary curriculum operated as though they were disconnected from the world of communication. Often, stand-alone computers in laboratories were visited for specialized work via what now look like primitive software programs. For developing writers, we did use computer interfaces for one major activity: wordprocessing. With the exception of isolated programs written by reading enthusiasts, like 'Developing Tray' created by Bob Moy, in which texts were completed using a cloze procedure (and thus encourage projection and interpretation in the making of meaning through print), wordprocessing seemed the natural progression from keyboard typing. Indeed, the keyboard remains a key interface between the writer's intentions and the finished piece of writing. Like the pen, once its physical use is mastered at a young age, its role as an interface is often forgotten.

Concomitant with the rise of computing in schools in the early 1980s, drafting and editing became more prevalent in the writing classroom, both in the work of Graves (1983) in the USA and in the UK (e.g. Andrews and Noble 1982). In the hands of the best teachers, drafting and re-drafting became part of the understanding of the writing process and how it could be used in the classroom to help students improve the quality and rhetorical direction and purpose of their work; in the worst cases, it became a matter of tedious ritual for students who were asked to draft and re-draft in the same way in all their writing. Wordprocessing, it was thought, would allow for more developed writing. Computers would help free students from extensive and laborious re-writing, and in ideal circumstances, enable them to focus on composition. But it is not that simple. In a critical review of studies regarding wordprocessing and writing, Cochran-Smith (1991) set forth several propositions emerging from the previous decade of composing on computers – with contrasting research results. For instance, it had been reported that young people make more revisions while composing online, but other studies showed that no significant revisions were made between sittings. Haas (1989) reported that composing on wordprocessing actually decreased planning as defined by Flower and Hayes (1981). Cochran-Smith reasoned that this was because when children and teens are composing on the computer, they attend to the text right before them – to the visible typos and the immediate next paragraph. With paper and pencil writing often resulted in linear process – a sequence of rewritten distinguishable drafts or products that could be compared side-by-side, rather than what occurs on the computer with revisions or edits at the microlevel at any time in the process. Depending on when and what the researchers counted as revisions, computers were either seen as a tool that impacted the writing process in a significant way or not. When composing with wordprocessing programs, lines between stages of writing were blurred and collapsed, leaving us with a markedly different writing process than was seen before.

In terms of products, Cochran-Smith (1991) also reported that word-processing on computers did not improve writing in terms of quality. Taking a different approach to products, Snyder (1994), noticed in her research in Melbourne that when using computers in the teaching of different written genres, wordprocessing seemed more beneficial when writing arguments than when writing narratives, because the structural re-arranging that is helpful in argument writing was facilitated by word-processing packages. In narrative, the accretive method of building a text that took its bearing from chronological patterns was often best suited to pen and paper rather than the computer.

Phase two: orientation to communicating on the screen

The second phase of the relationship between computers and writing saw the insertion of the term 'communication' in 'information and com-munication technologies' (ICT, or C&IT). 'Information' here meant both digital coding of data and information in the sense of news, material and text. 'Communication' indicates that computers were seen as vehi-cles for connecting people, with writing as the principal mode for such communication. Thus, with email, and their drafted and re-drafted texts, and with text messaging in later portable third generation phones, the written word assumed a new position in everyday communication.

What is significant about this phase, which took place in the 1990s, is that it enabled a re-definition of what it means to be literate. To be literate in the late twentieth and early twenty-first century means, among other things, that you must be able to compose and read text on screen as well as in printed format. Alongside the re-establishment of written text in what had seemed to be an increasingly oral and visual world, the arrival of the Internet and worldwide web by the early 1990s meant that reading, at least, gained new significance and range worldwide.

The educational research community has attempted to keep up with changing technologies in order to explain the corresponding changes to reading process and products, and their pedagogical implications. The Internet, at that time, served as a repository of information uploaded from persons or groups with programming expertise and access to the necessary hardware, such as server space. The information was organized in a hierarchy of linked pages from a front page, all of which is designed and presented by a limited set of producers – often unknown to the consumers. Many websites currently are still organized and produced in this manner (Cormode and Krishnamurthy 2008). Search engines allowed the search of content through these pages using a matching hierarchal Boolean logic. Searching through the indexed terms, readers of the Internet were offered snippets of content linked to the source page. Reading the Internet involved (and still involves) heightened inferential decision making resulting in a 'choose your own adventure' style of reading path through content. With all web content available through such searches, searching skills and logic, credibility of producers, and reliability of information became prime pedagogical concerns in the 1990s. Coiro and Dobler (2007) extended these concerns with findings from their studies with sixth grade students. They concluded that not only was finding and evaluating content important, but as students used Internet search engines to locate and retrieve information, they were actually engaging in a new reading phenomenon – self-directed text construction. The young people were not just finding 'the answer' to their question or following an idiosyncratic reading path. By choosing the content they deemed relevant to their inquiry, they were actually constructing 'the answer' itself. Seen in this way, reading the Internet is not just an issue of conscientious consumerism, but of text construction – and thus knowledge construction.

Phase three: Web 2.0 and the digital age

By the mid-2000s, the advent of Web 2.0 meant that writing and composing for reception online became more possible for ordinary users (and developing writers) rather than just for programmers. The digital space of the Internet became one of interactive writing, not just reading consumerism. Consider, for instance, the advancements of digital archiving and mining of text, which previously established the web as a repository for consumers. Printed material can not only be scanned and digitised; with text recognition and handwriting recognition software, text that previously was scanned and existed as a fixed picture, can now be edited and reformatted. This text can be transported, re-purposed and communicated in ways that were unimaginable even ten years previously. No longer is it only short texts that can be searched and retrieved; whole books could be placed on the web in repositories and on websites for public consumption and re-purposing. Writers even developed networks and associations like Creative Commons (see http://creativecommons.org), which promoted the free distribution and access to works in a relatively copyright-free space.

Social groups built up around accessible, user-created, free content are a defining characteristic of Web 2.0. In an extensive comparative review, Cormode and Krishnamurthy (2008) examined the changing landscape of the Internet, and posited changes that made the user the central component of the Internet experience. This has had important implications for the nature of composing digitally. The user has become central to the way websites themselves and their content is organized. Users can tag – or label for categorization – and set links to outside digital information themselves, which affects among other things, search engine results. In fact, many websites now feature a personalized front page, determined by a user's use, typical use patterns, or the user's choice. Users also have options to create robust online profiles, including screen names, avatars, and links to other social networking or personal websites. Instead of just linking people by providing contact information, such as an email address, Web 2.0 encourages user interaction with the site content through threaded conversations and public feedback forums, as well as with other users by 'friending' or otherwise managing the various ways that others have access to their public profile and written digital communication. Whereas Web 1.0 was organized in a hierarchal form with front page and subpages, navigated by clicking on creator-determined links, now users can also determine the format in which they receive a website's information, such as in an RSS feed by email. This results in an ecological or evolving site organization centred on the user.

Cormode and Krishnamurthy explained that though much of the Worldwide Web still operates with Web 1.0 structures, technological aids, changing structures and social interaction have levelled the content creation and distribution playing field, and shifted usage of the Internet from one that was repository-consumer oriented to one that is collaboratively innovative and productive:

> The democratic nature of Web 2.0 is exemplified by creations of large number of niche groups (collections of friends) who can exchange content of any kind (text, audio, video) and tag, comment, and link to both intra-group and extra-group 'pages'. A popular innovation in Web 2.0 is 'mashups,' which combine or render content in novel forms.
>
> (Cormode and Krishnamurthy 2008: 2)

Communal composing spaces such as blogs and wikis are created by people coming together around common interests like a political event, a new medical procedure or a musical group. Tumblr, a short-form blog, is one such platform for these groups to come together. Its selling point is the ease with which creators and submitters can gather and embed existing content, pictures, music, quotes from outside digital sources into a post with written comment. Creators and submitters to a Tumblr site are given user-friendly embedding design options, such as font style, size, colour, and page placement of images and quotes, making multimodal, multimedia posts with reappropriated and re-purposed media the norm. Users are relieved from re-typing content or needing to know complicated HTML code to effect the same ends. Within each Tumblr site, patterns in the compositions and design choices develop as members of the community post. Persons on one site may position an image at the top and in the centre of the post, and write just a one-line quote as a comment. In another Tumblr site, creators and submitters may frame the viewing of a video with a short paragraph and then discuss the video in depth after positioning it between the introduction and discussion. Composing together on these platforms means that writers not only have new formats and genres within which to work, but also must contend with a constant landscape of invented formats.

In the present decade, networked digitization is so much the norm, at least in the developed world, that it almost has become a non-issue. Networked digital composition is similarly ubiquitous. On behalf of the United States Department of Education, Wells and Lewis (2006) reported that from 1994 to 2005, the number of school classrooms with computer and Internet access increased from 3 per cent to 94 per cent. At the same time, the number of students per computer with Internet access in the classroom decreased from 12:1 to 3.8:1. Such dramatic increase in access has not been seen with older technologies (i.e. television, telephones), and such increases while slightly lower, hold for households. According to the US Census Bureau (Cheeseman Day et al. 2005), 61.8 per cent of all households in the US had a personal computer, up from 8.2 per cent in 1984. Starting in 2007, householders were only asked regarding Internet connection, as computer and Internet access were seen as synonymous. In 2009, 68.7 per cent of householders in the US reported having Internet connection (US Census Bureau 2010).

Use of computers for school and personal writing among teens is inversely related to their access in school and at home. In a nationwide interview study of 700 12–17-year-olds, 65 per cent of teens reported completing schoolwork by hand rather than computer, and 72 per cent of youth, who reported writing outside of school for personal reasons, do the same (Lenhart et al. 2008). In the same study 48 per cent of youth reported accessing the Internet weekly to help complete homework including looking up pictures, definitions and asking others about assignment criteria. That just about half of students surveyed reported using the computer to complete schoolwork is actually quite surprising, considering the page and print-centric modes of teaching and learning in schools. With nearly 100 per cent of schools having access to computers – even networked computers – we still see printed pages, books, worksheets, etc. dominating lessons and assigned compositions. Lenhart et al. (2008) explained that teens do not consider digital communication, such as emails, text messaging, Internet searches or text messages, as writing – even when used to complete schoolwork. In Moje et al.'s (2008) survey, observation and interview study in the United States on adolescent literacy preferences and practices in and outside of school, 82 per cent of the teens reported writing three or four times a week. In observation, the researchers saw far more writing and varied writing practices than students self-reported, leading the research team to conclude that the definition of writing is over-determined by the genres taught in school. Writing outside those genres, even extended pieces of writing, are not considered writing because they do not fit the schooled genres.

In her work with youth in South Africa, Walton (2009) reminds us that digital capability and Internet connectivity are not limited to computers. In fact, she asks us to question the assumed dominance of the computer in the digital age. In her studies of the use and composition practices of youth, she found that not only do teens have more access to cell phones than to computers, they have a 'mobile-centric' use of digital media, explaining that youth have a '"delinked" mode of interacting with media driven by downloading, saving and sharing media via bluetooth, rather than "surfing" or browsing media online' (p. v). The International Telecommunication Union (2010) has reported that in both developed and developing countries worldwide, there are now more mobile broadband subscriptions than fixed or household broadband subscriptions. Because of this, Horrigan (2008) describes the nature of digital communication as fast and mobile, reporting 62 per cent of all Americans participate in non-voice activities on mobile devices away from home and work, and 32 per cent of these write this way every day. Non-voice activities include sending or receiving text messages, instant messages, or emails. In other words, phones are interfaces of content creation, not just devices to communicate previously instated content or for voice exchanges.

Cell phones are one of several types of mobile possibilities. Flash drives, iPods, MP3 players, all data storage devices contribute to the mobility of digital composition, not to mention several travel-ready computers, laptops, tablets and iPads. Networked or not, digital composition is mobile, and though a networked digital divide exists, it is fast closing, worldwide. Internet users worldwide have doubled in the last five years (International Telecommunication Union 2010), making the adoption of the networked digital communication one of the fastest adopted electronic technologies (Horrigan 2005).

Looking back to project forward

The implications for writing, writing development and the teaching of writing are manifold. First, writing is potentially ubiquitous, as it has always been, but now has the added dimension of writers being able to broadcast it from wherever they can get access to the web and/or to a wireless telephone signal. Secondly, organizations can go 'completely digital' by never committing anything to print, but always digitizing incoming messages and documents, working on them, and sending them out digitally/electronically without passing across paper. Thirdly, for the young developing writer, and indeed for any developing writer, movement between handwritten notes and drafts on the one hand, and digital versions on the other, is increasingly seamless. Many people compose straight on to a computer interface, whether the medium is a mobile/cell phone, laptop, desktop or other device. Spell- and grammar-checkers can ensure, if well used, a relatively error-free composition. Finally, the rate of development in technologies is exponential. Not only do we need to have capacity to take advantage of the leveraging of current technologies, we need to develop adaptability for future possibilities. Google recently rolled out its newest version of a search engine called Google Instant. In its present form, as a term is searched the rest of the predicted search term is displayed along with links to websites that pertain to the predicted search term. In this way, not only is Google claiming searches will be faster, but that these predictions are feedback from the technology to the user. In the same way a listener provides feedback to a speaker by their reactions to what is being said, this predictive interactive technology promises to shift the search itself. Google claims, 'Even when you don't know exactly what you're looking for, predictions help guide your search . . . Now results appear instantly as you type, helping you see where you're headed, every step of the way' (para. 2). Not only does this type of software change the experience of researching on the Internet, it also leads to responsive and predictive possible technologies. Imagine a wordprocessing tool that includes predictive text, beyond predictive such as T9 software on cell phones, but one that provides the endings to phrases and sentences. Such a product could be marketed for use for when 'you don't know exactly what you want to say'. Or imagine a tool that translates sentences from one tone to another, predicting how it would sound in academia versus in a blog or on Facebook. Or imagine instant predictive feedback according to the community or rhetorical expectations. The possibilities are endless with just this one type of Web 2.0 technology. Clearly our need to adapt to the changing landscape is paramount.

How do we characterize composition in current digital landscapes?

Digital communication is often thought of as 'free space' – the ultimate informal non-school writing scenario. Compared to the monitored and conventional nature of school-based literacy, digital space offers room for innovative composition and relationships. However, writing is never 'free' in the sense that it does not exist outside a rhetorical frame – a writer with a purpose for an audience. Instead of imagining a freeform writing condition, frameless and freewheeling, the nature of writing in the digital age can be imagined as writing within a shape-shifting rhetorical frame. To explore this phenomenon, let us consider Engeström et al.'s (1999) description of the nature of human activity in the present era as an increasingly co-configured existence. Instead of only acting within pre-established groups with pre-established rules and resources, increasingly, we cross groups in our daily lives. In so doing, we configure momentary groups, rules and resources. Kell (2009) researches transcontextual writing practices and explains how 'the meaning' of a text or a person's 'message' morphs as texts and people move in and out of settings – each with their own configurations of people, rules and resources. This transcontexual writing occurs both off and online. Smith's (2011) research studies the changes in what, how, why and when teens write as they literally move across multiple contexts. Once on a train between a workshop and a performance a few of the teens were practising pieces of writing they would perform. As one boy finished his piece, a woman began applauding and another commented on a line in the piece that she thought was powerful. She then began to tell a short story about a similar experience. Several on the train nodded as she spoke. Strangers on a train established a community, one with shared roles of performer and audience, and not just any, silent typical audience, but an audience rather like a family gathering where story weaves to another story. The teens thanked the women and turned to each other to discuss how to perform lines in their pieces to get similar reactions at the later official performance. They also decided they would start performing on trains to make a few extra dollars as they travelled, establishing a literacy practice they have continued based on their experience in this momentary community. Speaking of this type of phenomenon, Engeström et al. (1999) explained, 'They literally constructed the collaborative relations on the spot as the task demanded' (p. 346).

Engeström et al. (1999) refer to this tying and untying of people, re-sources and social activity as 'knotworking'. Fraiberg (2010) applied the concept of 'knotworking' to describe the landscape of networked digital communication. Written pieces are shaped by a writer to fit particular digital contexts with their particular forms, purposes and audiences. These messages (with linked and delinked profile of the writer) then wind through digital communities and websites. They are commented on in blogs by 'friends' and strangers, quoted in newscasts, and parodied in video or argued about in a podcast – creating new knotted combinations of people, rules and resources as they go. 'Going viral' is only one way a text moves in networked digital communication. Pieces of composed text stall in one rhetorical frame, then are linked or tagged by another composer, and sent off again. Sometimes the text from one writer is re-appropriated by another in a quotation, or re-purposed and designed next to a visual. The writer moves along these unpredictable routes as well, encountering new combinations of text types and people.

Leander and Lovvorn (2006) explain that online and offline, a person is involved in an idiosyncratic and constantly fluctuating literacy network. Literacy networks are created by the patterned movement of people and their texts. One person's literacy network may include several 'knots' and differs in ways writing process and written products circulate and are valued or positioned. In this landscape, a person's literacy networks and movements are of interest to understanding their development. Additionally, in a digital landscape, a person's ability to cross spaces successfully is of interest. In other words, these young people's development is not only influenced by their participation in formal school and non-school settings, but learning extends across settings and in and through these varied configurations or knots, ever shifting the rhetorical frame.

Thomas et al. (2007) propose transliteracy as the targeted ability for writers in the twenty-first century, explaining that the nature of written movement necessitates 'the ability to read, write and interact across a range of platforms, tools and media from signing and orality through handwriting, print, TV, radio and film, to digital social networks' (abstract). Digital space is not one 'free space', but several instantly created and disbanded spaces that people and text cross and create. In such spaces, we are afforded the opportunity to explore communication in its pluralist sense – multilingual, multimodal and multichannel in multiple communities and with multiple identities.

What are the affordances of digital written composition in the current landscape?

In digital written composition, the first thing to note is the re-surfacing of the word 'composition'. While the composing of parts of a whole text, and of attendant images, sounds and other modes is possible in 'pre-digital' formats, it is easier in digital media. We could not have predicted the over-abundant proliferation of computers themselves or the myriad of software that makes multimodal design and representation in one location with one person possible. Modes that have been out of reach for production, and thus, representation have been levelled by such technology (Kress and van Leeuwen 2001). Not only are there larger free clip art and sound effect libraries, but people can now redesign images with offline and online software. Voice recording is similarly available with most digital devices, and music mixing software, such as Garage Band, are open for free use. Because composition is potentially more fluent, the invitation to combine modes is greater. This means that the habitual meta-genres of the conventional written mode – narrative, argument, description – are challenged by digital composition, where boundaries are crossed, hybrid genres are more common, and 'originality' takes the form of compositional originality rather than more purely expressive originality in a (seemingly) single mode. The abilities of interpreting and designing visual and multimodal texts are critical as we move into an age where it is not only prevalent, but possible and expected for the layman to create such pieces.

The second point to note is that writing is more easily shared. It is self-publishable. There is no need for peer review, lengthy editorial commentary and review, or approval by higher authorities. Writing can be published at will on the net. This does not mean that it need be any less accurate or beautifully worded. Black (2009) researched English language learners' activity on fan fiction sites. Fan fiction sites are communities in which participants write alternative stories, borrowing elements of the fiction piece or pieces the site pays homage to. In these settings, quality is paramount to the writers. Rather than a traditional power structure in which the more experienced and trained correct the products written by novices, standards and expectations are enforced through distributed power in mentor-mentee relationships that come into existence through virtual experiences of reading and commenting on each other's work. On the web now, what writers share and what audiences see may be what previously had been considered mere 'drafts'. For the individual writer, this means a collapse to the writing process. Pre-writing may be done publicly within social networking, in notes or linked sites on a Delicious site or a series of responses to sites on Tumblr. Drafts may be posted in blog form – open for public comment and feedback. Writing shifts from a 'private act with a public result' to one that is possibly completely public and collaborative.

In Web 2.0, texts can be shared and created collaboratively, for example via Google Docs or wikis, so that co-writers can work remotely and still create a single text between them. Working in collaboration with colleagues, Croxall (2008), an advocate for technology in humanities research and pedagogy, provided instructors a user-friendly version of an open source timeline tool, provided for free from MIT, which utilizes a Google Docs spreadsheet to create an interactive, multimodal timeline that is synchronously and collaboratively written. Throughout courses, students create and flesh out the class's timeline by inserting video, artefacts, primary and secondary documents and notes. No longer is all writing a solitary activity done alone to 'discover meaning', but communities create meaning together.

Writing is also potentially more ephemeral. That may seem a contradiction in terms. But throughout history, the notion of a palimpsest has intrigued writers. This is a working document: one which can be written and re-written. The latest device which allows such a facility is the iPad: it emulates the writing pad or notebook, but is a digital A4 or standard paper-sized screen which can be used for notes, fully-fledged works, watching films, engaging with the net and virtually every other sign-based communicational activity. Although writers may archive their written material in external hard drives, on CDRoms or in cloud-based technologies, the assumption must be that these technologies – and the devices via which they are accessible – may not be around in ten years' time. Libraries, which deal with archiving, often resort to paper-based backup copies of digital texts for exactly this reason.

In these many ways, time and space between writer and audience is collapsed, making digital communication, at times, even preferred over speaking. Through multichannel communication while composing and with finished products, people have more experience and access to audience and audience *en masse* than ever before. Edwards (2010), president of the International Reading Association, urged that students 'must be able to adapt and reinvent the ways that we will read and write the world' (p. 22). The devices, software, interfaces and platforms discussed in this chapter may be irrelevant in a number of years. Definitions of a literate person now include being a composer, and qualities of adaptability and reinvention are central to this new definition.

Affordances beyond technology: self and other

The complicated paths of the 'knotwork' and the speed at which even personal messages become common on the Internet, can promote a feeling of anonymity online. Digital communication is sometimes described as virtual, unreal, and ironically disconnected. Kirkland (2008, 2009) paints a different picture. He tells us about youth like Derrick and Raymond who utilized digital resources to create, manage and re-imagine their identities.

Connected, intentional and real, digital communication straddles social communities – the official space of schooling, the formal spaces of community-based organizations, and unofficial spaces of youth culture. Kirkland (2009) explained that negotiating multiple communities using digital resources affords varied language use – standard and nonstandard – and makes multimodal representations of the self available. These characteristics of digital communication allow youth to play with identity, making sense of the self as writer and person. Using digital recording technology, computers and MySpace (a social networking site popular with music aficionados), Derrick, an otherwise struggling reader and writer, built a robust literate self in his MySpace page with autobiographical explorations in rap and poem. Derrick was intentional in his compositions and interactions on MySpace. He explained that his use of these digital tools has offered him the ability to write his autobiography to the world, and this, explained Derrick, 'changed the game for me' (2008: 4). Another youth, Raymond, who, after enduring bullying at school, and unusually violent experiences in his neighbourhood, created an alter-ego female character in SecondLife (a virtual world in which participants interact through digital avatars) to distance himself from current conditions and try on an existence he desired as a popular youth in a stable home situation.

Such identity work is available to the masses. Lenhart et al. (2005) reported that 60 per cent of teen Instant Messaging (IM) users create profile icons and make intentional choices about font, colour, style and size. Not only are actual photographs of the users used for these icons, but youth modify their representation of self in various ways, including images of popular movie or sports stars, video-looped animations, and scanned images which were drawn by hand or produced through a graphic design program. In addition to modifying profiles, which accompany the majority of messages in Web 2.0 (Cormode and Krishnamurthy 2008), exploring the personal publicly has become a norm. Most obviously, blogs are a site of 'personal diary' or extended thoughts written in response to lived experiences and world events. Black (2009) explained that these explorations are done in creative ways in fan fiction sites, wherein writers of alternative stories play with existing storylines and characters by inserting themselves as a character or writing into the plot of an existing character a very real issue from the contributor's own life and exploring how the fictional character handles the issue.

Hull's recent work (Hull and Stornaiuolo 2010; Hull et al. 2010) reminds us that writing in the digital age involves more than technological changes with affordances for the exploration of identity. As communication in the twenty-first century extends past the local and one-directional exchange of ideas, meaning-making is now global, multimodal and multidirectional in ways previously unavailable to the masses. Digital communication is now a site for cosmopolitan practice (Hull and Stornaiuolo 2010) – the work of identity through rhetorical and semiotic choices in relation to audience, but audience in a twenty-first century sense – still particular audiences local or distant, but also audience as *possible, en masse* and global. Considering the nature of Web 2.0 communication and the state of a widely distributed access to the technological means necessary for this communication, Hull proposes that Thomas et al.'s (2007) concept of 'transliteracies' be expanded to include the 'critical and hospitable' dispositions necessary for self and other-work (cf. Hansen 2010) – the eloquent negotiation and co-existence with unknown but imagined others (Hull and Stornaiuolo 2010).

With examples from the global social networking site for youth in four different countries, Space2Cre8, Hull and Stornaiuolo (2010) characterize this concept of cosmopolitan practice: 'As youth interacted with one another around these self-representations, whether profile pictures, background images videos or blogs, they negotiated differences in beliefs, aesthetics, cultural norms, and communicative practices as they searched for commonality' (p. 91). Hull et al. (2010) tell of one particular group of young girls in India who attend a community-based school after working each morning to support their families. In the Space2Cre8 portion of the school, youth explore their sense of self and others both online and offline – through writing, dancing, role-playing and composing multimodal artefacts. In one particular interaction within the social network site, the girls were able to exchange experiences of poverty with youth in the USA. At first the girls did not believe Americans could be poor, but through exchanges of youth-composed digital stories (Hull and Nelson 2005), blog posts and on discussion boards, they came to reframe their understanding of poverty, youth in other countries and the world in general.

One youth, Shushma, whose parents wished would stop her education and get married, explored her passion for continuing her education through several iterations of symbolic work that resulted in a multimodal composition using a reappropriated poem which she translated into two languages and a picture of a woman with open arms, reaching upward. The result was a multilingual and multimodal message previously impossible to create and present to the world. Hull et al. (2010) explained that after she composed this piece, she increased in her sensitivity to the rhetorical and semiotic choices other youth made in their choice of images, blog posts and videos. She had only met these youth virtually, but she infused her readings of others' compositions with the best intentions and possibilities – what Hull et al. (2010) call 'hospitable' reading. In the interactions on Space2Cre8, Hull and Stornaiuolo (2010) found that youth apprenticed each other in such critical and hospitable practices by responding to comments posted on the site with comments that included suggestions for how to interact in these ways.

Conclusion: what is of interest to writing development?

What does this discussion infer about writing development? The immediacy that characterizes the digitized environment can easily affect one's view of how a writer becomes a better writer. No longer does the writer have to wait for feedback to their writing, and no longer is the feedback necessarily evaluative, but participatory in nature with a public audience, unknown in many cases. Process and products are collapsed, as composing and publication become one and the same, and not always by choice. The writer's audience in this new communicative setting is often the public, others unknown, imagined severally and singly. Texts and identities move and change as they circulate through newly established networks. A necessary adaptability to new digital tools fosters innovation, creativity and hybridity as the writer finds themself an expert in one community one day and a novice in a different writing situation the next. The development of the writer is anything but linear and predictable, and more akin to the process of playing an instrument – improvising and responding – in a jazz session.

9 A New Theory and Model of Writing Development

Introduction

Before we set out our theory and model for writing development, we need to re-state briefly the case for a theory and a model, discuss how these two levels of abstraction are related, and argue the case for a *new* theory and model. The exposition of the theory and model takes places over two chapters. The present chapter sets out the basics. The following chapter looks from the perspective of writing in the digital and multimodal age. There are, therefore, a number of principles and generalities to establish before we go into detail.

The first of these deals with why we need a theory and model at all. If, as others before us (e.g. Smith 1982/1994) have argued (and a view that is not incompatible with ours) that everyone *learns to write by writing*, there would appear to be no need for theory. We would simply pick up the practical skill and craft of writing by being part of a community or communities that correspond; we might learn by imitation and the needs of response; and no one would need to talk or think *about* what we do – we would simply do it. However, the shortcomings of such an approach are many. One is that the act of writing is a cognitive/conceptual, emotional and/or political act as well as a physical one. It is part of social networking and has specific social functions. Another is that the choice to *write* rather than draw, speak or use some other mode of communication is a deliberate choice from a repertoire of possibilities. For example, in a community, a person has died. Friends rally around the members of the family who have suffered the loss. They may call by telephone, write a card or letter of condolence, and perhaps cook a meal that can be easily used by the grieving family as they will be preoccupied with arrangements for the funeral. It is unlikely that the gesture of sympathy would be a text or a drawing. Writing in this case is a deliberate choice that the writer thinks is appropriate for the occasion.

A theory and model are needed, therefore, to position the act of writing in its social and political contexts, and also to justify why writing (and particular genres or hybrid forms of writing) is used on a particular occasion. Theories allow a coherence to a field of practice and a repertoire of choice. Pedagogically, we need as teachers of writing to know why we are writing, know the range of forms we are teaching, and know how these can be applied in particular situations.

Furthermore, we need as teachers of writing a *theory of the development of writing* (see Beard et al. 2009) so that we can intervene to help young writers develop into better writers.

A theory and model

Theories tend to be the overarching and unifying rationale for a field of practice and enquiry; models tend to be schematic representations of those theories, simplified for practical application and for ease of recall. It so happens in the field of writing practice and research that a theory is likely to take verbal form (an account in words, like this and the following chapter) and a model is likely to take diagrammatic form, as a distillation of the theory. There is a large number of models of writing and writing development, as we have demonstrated in the present book; but there are fewer theories of writing development. A surfeit of models can be confusing, as each seems to have its own perspective and justification. Our aim in the book remains to make sense of most of the theories and models of writing development and to create a new theory and model that will be fit for purpose in the contemporary world. Our theory, and its model, should be able to 'explain' a range of different writing practices.

Figure 9.1 could be re-drawn with the writing practices at the top and the model and theory below, suggesting that the theory *supports* the model, and the model in turn *supports* the range of writing practices.

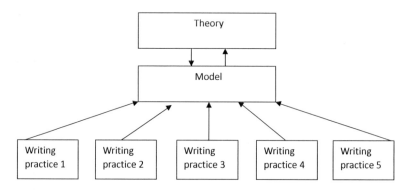

Figure 9.1 The position of a theory and model in relation to writing practices

The conventional depiction in the figure merely uses the metaphor of the theory and model being 'higher' and more abstract than practice, thus informing practice.

Our theory and model assume a range of writing practices. These vary in function and form (including whether they form part of a multimodal array) according to social situations and needs. There is a vast number of writing practices, and they change and develop in time according to social and political situation and need. The reason we need a new theory and model in the contemporary age is, as we have argued in the book so far, that the current theories and models do not only not account for the range of writing practices that are extant; they also do not account for writing development in the current environment.

A new theory of writing development: the constituent elements

Like any theory, our theory of writing development is made from a number of key elements or concepts. These are the rhetorical context, framing, multimodal choice, composition and development.

The rhetorical context

Any act of communication is a question of who is communicating with whom, why, what is the substance of the communication, when is it taking place, where and how. These seemingly simple questions cover the range of what *rhetoric* is interested in. Whereas classical rhetoric was designed for the particular functions of persuasion, largely within public forums in pre-Athenian and Athenian democracies, contemporary rhetoric covers the full range of functions and forms of communication. Whether writing is being used to set down a formal constitution for a nation; for correspondence with a newspaper; for more informal reasons like a personal letter or email or text; or merely for a note on a Post-it sticker, left for someone who will act upon and then throw it away, writing has a rhetorical function.

The first consideration in a rhetorical view of writing or any kind of composition is *who is communicating with whom*? The 'who' could be a single person or a group of people (for example a group composing a manifesto or a memo of agreement between themselves or with others). Similarly, the 'whom' (the 'addressee') could be a single person (even the composer him- or herself, as in the writing of a private diary) or a group of people or a very large audience (for example, a speech written for a large public gathering). Whatever the dynamic of the addresser and addressee – and we will use these technical terms sparingly as we want the theory to be accessible and close to functional everyday use – there is always a power relation between the sender and the receiver of the message. The power factor changes the nature of the language used in the exchange, and the outcome (if any) of the exchange. It fundamentally affects the choices made by the writer, especially if the writer is in the less powerful position. They have to choose a language that will persuade the powerful to listen and to move towards the less powerful person. At the same time, the discourses and diction of the exchange are probably determined by the powerful. For example, a lecturer bidding for a grant from a research foundation will need to follow the rubric and use the language that is appropriate for that particular foundation. If they fail to use the appropriate language, it is likely that the bid will be seen in an unfavourable light from the start. To use a more everyday example, asking a scaffolder for a quotation for the erection of scaffolding outside a house in order to paint a window requires not only politeness in the approach, but precision: how high is the window, and what width of scaffolding is required?

Secondly, the 'why' of a rhetorical approach takes into account the *function* of the communication, whether that function is mundane and brief and ephemeral, or – at the other end of the spectrum – whether it concerns the creation of a major artwork. The function partly determines the choice of language. If writing is to be used in the communication, the circumstances determine the decision to use it and the kinds of written language that will be employed.

Thirdly, the *substance* of the message is important, not only for itself but also because it is affected by and affects the way in which the message is conveyed. This seeming truism is not the same as 'the medium is the message'. In rhetoric, it is essential to think of the function and substance, along with who is addressing whom, in the first instance, so that the 'social is prior'. Rhetoric therefore reflects the creation and development of language, rather than being seen as a self-justifying communication system in its own right. It seems to us that the mistake made by rhetoric in the past has been when it reifies itself into a system that is self-perpetuating, as in manuals and guides to communication, rather than letting itself be driven by the social requirements of communication. Rhetoric gains its strength as a discipline through the driving momentum of need and substance.

The 'when' and 'where' of writing place it in time and space. To approach these aspects of rhetorical propriety through negative examples: it is inappropriate to send a letter to someone who has just had a delightful or devastating personal experience with a request for money (at least in most cultures). The request for money, if it is an invoice, for example, could follow later. Lest it seem, however, that a rhetorical approach is too concerned with 'propriety', it is important to say that rhetoric does not only deal with the 'appropriate': humour, resistance, political activism and other kinds of communication that require a subversion of the norm or some kind of contrapuntal statement do not tread a careful line of compliance. They intervene when it is inappropriate, if necessary. Decisions about when and where to communicate can be as much about upsetting received assumptions and conventions as they are about using 'appropriate' forms of communication.

Finally, the 'how' of a rhetorical approach to communication concerns exactly the questions that we will address in the following sub-sections: how to frame communication; when to use writing as opposed to other modes; how to use writing in a multimodal context; and how to shape and compose it.

Framing

Andrews (2011) sets out the advantages of rethinking approaches to literacy in terms of *framing* rather than frames. Without repeating the argument here, the essential points are that frames, which derive from genre theory that sees genres as text-types rather than as social action, tend to become fossilized. These in turn are taught as scaffolds for writing, often constraining the act of composition and reverting to a box-filling exercise. The commodification of writing in this way puts emphasis on the *product* rather the process of writing. This commodification leads to imitation of models of text-types themselves, or of an assumed 'structure' to the text-type. In other words, students are forced into the same position as those in the Renaissance in Europe who learnt the various text-types from *progymnasmata* or exercises in which a model was provided which they had to imitate. This is a clear example of the *form* of the communication gaining dominance in pedagogical terms over the function and substance. Ultimately it leads to enervation on the part of the communicators.

Framing, on the other hand, retains the power of shaping the communicative act in the hands of the composer or rhetor. They choose the genre (as social act rather than as text-type) or hybrid genre or new form in which to couch the message that is to be sent. The act of framing is a creative and critical act in that it draws a line around the parameters of the communication; it creates an 'inside' and 'outside' to the communicative act; it invites transgression of the boundaries or frame; and yet at the same time it gives meaning to the transaction through the very creation of the frame. The point is that the frame must be created by the person making the communication, and must be understood by the person receiving the message. If the frame is not clear, the message that is being conveyed may well not be understood. Receivers of messages bring framing to the understanding of communication, just as composers create frames (or use existing ones). If the two sets of frames do not match up – at least roughly speaking – there will be non- or mis-communication.

Multimodal choice

Kress (2010) sets out perhaps the clearest statement yet as the case for a multimodal perspective on contemporary communication. The essence of such an approach is that communication cannot be conceived of merely in terms of writing or, for that matter, any other mode. It is always multimodal in that more than one mode – speech, writing, still or moving images, physical presence, spatial considerations, etc. – is present in an act of communication. This is a different matter from multimedia, which describe the vehicles via which communication is carried: via computer screen, television screen, mobile phone, paper and pen, in sound waves through the air, etc. As far as the present book is concerned, we have addressed the question of writing within multimodality in more depth in Chapter 7. Here the point is that within an emergent theory and model of writing development, we need to ask and answer the question: what role does multimodality have within our theory and model?

The answer is partly economic, partly communicational and partly aesthetic. From an economic point of view, the person who wishes to communicate something must ask themselves: what resources do I have to make such communication? Is it a question of inscribing something on a piece of paper and sending it to the addressee somehow; or do I have wireless connectivity and a laptop or third generation mobile phone at hand? These question of resource are questions of the *media* that are available, but they play an important part in determining which modes of communication are possible or desirable for the act of communication. The communicational dimension asks the question: what are the affordances of the particular modes that I could use, and what will work best for the situation I find myself in and the message I want to convey? Do I use a single or (seemingly) monomodal form of communication, or do I deliberately go for a multimodal combination? From an aesthetic point of view, the question that will be raised is: what is the most elegant or beautiful means of representation I can use in this particular circumstance?

A key issue with regard to writing and the development of writing within a multimodal framework is whether the writing is foregrounded or backgrounded; or whether it assumes equal status with other modes in the act of communication. The issue is not necessarily always one of which comes first in the composing process. It is possible to design a page in which the ultimate intention is for writing to be foregrounded, but to start with issues of design: what font will I use? where will the writing appear? what images shall I place and where in order to complement the writing? etc. Once the design and composing process is complete, however, and the message is ready and attains the status of a product, it is usually clear which mode is foregrounded and which is or are backgrounded. In the eye of the reader, where the attention is first attracted will most often be the area of foregrounding. But one of the most interesting aspects of multimodality is the dynamic interrelationship between the various modes that make up the message.

Lastly, *affordance* is a key factor. The affordances of writing include its capacity to capture abstract concepts; its close relationship with speech; its capacity to contain conceptual and narrative sequences; its regularity (in relation to speech). But disadvantages include its embodiment in a particular language (English, Mandarin, Spanish, etc.); and its second order symbolic system (based on the first order system of speech) which requires learning and apprenticeship.

Writing benefits from a position within multimodality because we become more aware of its affordances and can deploy it more effectively when we know its strengths and weaknesses as a mode of communication.

Composition

Much of what has been said above about writing has implied that learning to write is learning to compose; that rather than 'write' something that is an act of 'writing' and, in due course, becomes the product 'writing' itself, it is better to see writing as an act of *composition* that produces a composition. The advantage of the term 'composition' is that is literally means 'with' and 'put' or 'put in place'. In other words, composition is an act of putting elements with other elements – a collage-like act. In writing, we put parts of words together to make up words; words together to make up clauses, phrases and sentences; sentences together to make up paragraphs and other sub-textual units of meaning; and all these parts together to make up whole texts operating in particular contexts. The process is not just bottom-up, as described. It is also top-down, so that the contexts and environments for writing determine the texts we create (see the section on rhetoric above), and these texts in turn determine their parts, and so on.

Another advantage of seeing writing as composing is that we can align it more readily with acts of composition in other fields, like music, architecture, engineering, art and sculpture, etc. In all these fields, and in others, makers put together works that are *com-positions*. The creative act is the act of composing.

By changing the emphasis to composing rather than writing, the pressure is taken off writing as a medium of instruction and as a system to be learnt. There is no doubt that it still has to be learnt. But when writing is seen as composition, the wider aperture brings meaning and colour to the act of writing. Images, sounds and other forms of communication can help the interpretation as well as the composition of writing, by providing cues, supporting information and other means by which the writing – and writing development – is highlighted.

Development

What place, then, does *development* have among the constituent elements of writing that include rhetorical context, framing, multimodality and composition? As our concern is with the emerging writer of whatever age who is trying to improve their grasp of the written language (in whichever language), the principal form of development we are interested in is individual development that combines cognitive, emotional, experiential, formal and (to sum up the four constituents described so far) communicational elements. We cannot separate these developmental concerns from social or indeed political and economic factors: the person who is learning to write is part of a society and of a global community where resources are unequally distributed; where learning is an effect of the community and communities (including electronic communities) in which they operate; and where power relations obtain.

Development, then, is a matter of progression for the individual within these parameters. *Writing development* traces the progression in command of the writing system in any particular language, taking into account the elements described immediately above and the dimension of writing in the digital age, which is the subject of the following chapter. We wish to note here that we do not see development as either lagging behind teaching and learning (which, to put it crudely, is a Vygotskian position) or as preceding them (the more Piagetian position). Rather, we see development as a matter for the individual in their social and political *milieu*, measurable in terms of progression and intimately linked to learning in the sense of transformation from one state of knowledge and being to another.

In the next section, we set out the lineaments of the theory of writing development itself, followed by a model of writing development which distils the main elements of the theory.

A theory of writing development

So far in the book, and specifically in the present chapter, we have laid the ground for a new theory of writing development. Here we use the background (which includes references to existing models) to help us design and develop our theory.

In essence, every writing act is an act of communication, even if the communication is with oneself as writer (as in, for instance, writing that is personal and private, like a diary that is not for public consumption or notes to help record and/or clarify thinking). As such, the rhetorical context for writing is an important first consideration. As stated above, such consideration includes deciding the what, why, where, who, to whom, when and how of the communication. In many cases, it will be decided that writing is *not* the preferred or appropriate means of communication, and others will be used. But when and where writing *is* chosen as a principal or secondary mode of communication, the next stage in the theory will be triggered.

This is the stage of framing, in which the parameters of the communicative situation will be judged and set; without such framing there can be no communicable meaning as both parties need to be able to locate the utterance in some kind of interpretive frame. If the frames do not coincide, there could be mis-communication. The act of framing may choose pre-set frames (text-types) to convey the message, or it may adapt existing frames into new hybrids. It may define its own new frames by using a meta-language to alert us to those frames, derived from the need to draw attention to the frame itself. (For example, we want to convey meaning to a group of people at a conference. Instead of conventionally addressing them with powerpoint or from a lectern, we decide to place an envelope with a comment about our topic inside it. We imagine that most of the attendees will open the envelope and possibly start to talk with each other about its content. They will naturally question the conventional format of the presentation, using a meta-language.) Whichever approach is taken, an act of framing has taken place. Mostly, frames are invisible in the world of writing in that they surround a written text with space; it is a way of separating the writing from its immediate physical context. Such creation of a space around writing is most obviously seen around poems, which 'do not go up to the right-hand edge of the page' and which often finish with white space below them. (There are other ways in which poems distinguish themselves from other forms, but that is not the main focus of the present book.) But these spaces are there also in less formal or less consciously rhythmical text-types, like novels, reports, manuals, letters and so on.

Once the rhetorical setting and its agent, framing, have determined the nature of the written communication (driven by the writer), issues of composition come into play. Composition is not only a matter of 'putting things together' in words; it is also usually a matter of choosing whether to use only written words, or whether to use other modes of communication too. In a sense, other modes are always there, as words have a visual identity defined by the spaces around and between them. But there is a more complicated arrangement when words interact with other specific modes like still images, moving images and sound. The full range of these other modes is depicted in the model which follows the explication of the theory, as are the specific aspects of each mode (e.g. the integration of whole text, sub-sections of text, sentences, phrases, clauses, words, parts of words and spelling in writing). Composition, then, is the act of making; it includes, within each of the modes that are possible, further refinement through 'shaping' (e.g. drafting and editing words, digitally changing images, etc.).

Development in writing adds a temporal dimension to the above. Such development can take place within an individual over a period of time, within each element in the theory, and within each sub-element (e.g. the specific sub-elements of the written code). Thus, to make a complex issue more simple: if a parent asks of a teacher 'How has my child developed as a writer since we last met a year ago?' the answer must be much more detailed than the general observation that 'he or she has improved'. The answer must also certainly move well beyond the notion that his or her grades have improved, as these are abstractions that are calibrated each school term or year for reasons other than to indicate progress in writing. Rather, the answer – to really reflect the development that has taken place – must be something like 'She has strengthened her command of sentence structure and widened her vocabulary, and has also become more aware of how writing changes when it sits alongside other modes' or 'He has achieved a better sense of relating text to audience'. In Chapter 11, we present some ways in which the assessment of writing development and its communication to learners and others can be improved.

Essentially, our theory locates writing in the real world, embracing through a rhetorical perspective both fiction and 'non-fiction'. It brings meaning to writing, acknowledging that writing is one of the modes that seeks to communicate. And it posits a way of understanding development in writing, from the micro-level of the development of individual elements of writing to the macro-level of personal development of the writing repertoire over a period of time.

A model for writing development

In this section we convert the proposed theory of writing into a model, by distilling its constituent parts. We then explicate the model further. Once the design is complete, we interrogate the theory and model in the rest of the present chapter, subjecting it to criticism in order to strengthen it.

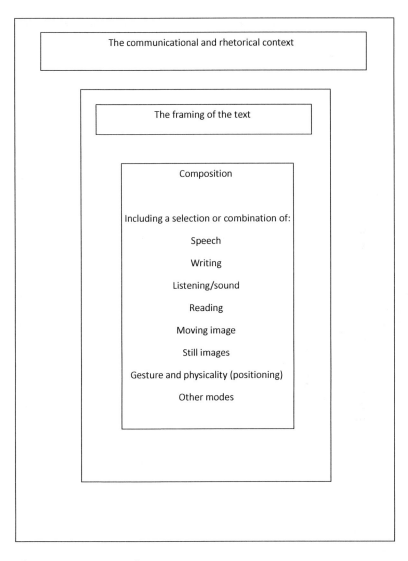

Figure 9.2 A model for writing

The theory can be depicted in a series of frames leading to the central aspect of writing: making and composition (see Figure 9.2). Framing theory will help us explicate the model. The definition of the communication and rhetorical context at the outer limits of the model indicate that this is the frame within which acts of writing take place. Beyond that outer frame are other worlds, not mediated by rhetoric. These would be worlds in which there is no signification, no semiotics, no ostensible communication (there are plenty of these worlds, like landscapes, the sea, animal life itself – these operate with signs and semiotic systems, but they also have a life of their own beyond the world of signs and rhetoric). Some believe that philosophy, logic and thought operate beyond the world of signification, but clearly they do not, as the first two at least would not be possible within some form of communication.

Within the frame of the rhetorical context is the act of framing itself. This level has been well documented above and in *Re-framing Literacy* (Andrews 2011). Suffice it to say at this point that framing is the creative and critical act that determines the extent, scope and broad shape of the message to be conveyed, drawing a frame that acts as 'common ground' on which the writer and their audience can meet.

Within the boundaries created by framing, the writer-as-composer chooses to make writing the primary and sole mode of communication; or combines it with other modes, still in the primary position (e.g. with illustrations in a reading book that operates largely through words); or puts writing in the secondary position in relation to other modes that carry the main burden of communication (as in a reading book that operates largely through images). Writing itself operates according to the combination of language units that have already been described: whole texts, sentences, phrases, clauses, etc. But it also operates in relation to the other modes. These modes can be variously placed in relation to the written verbal code. Our depiction in Figure 9.2 is just one way in which the configuration can take place. It can equally be rearranged to place other modes next to writing. So, rather like an iPhone screen, the individual applications' icons can be moved around into different configurations according to purpose. What the icon of writing appears next to suggests particularly close reciprocities and relationships – like the reciprocity between reading and writing, or the close relationship between word and image, or the dynamic relationship between speech and writing. But other modes of communication can also operate in close proximity to writing.

Rhetoric, framing and composition can be depicted in a single plane. But development, because it operates in time and at the micro- and macrolevels, needs a second dimension in order to depict it. Hence, our model to date needs to be extended to take into account that dimension (see Figure 9.3). This model begins to look like a Battenburg cake, a stick of rock, or sushi. As in sushi, to take the healthier of the three metaphors, the dried seaweed and packed rice contain the different ingredients that make up compositions; so, too, in our writing model, rhetoric and framing 'contain' and 'enclose' the ingredients of communication. Development will happen maturationally, cognitively, emotionally, morally along that

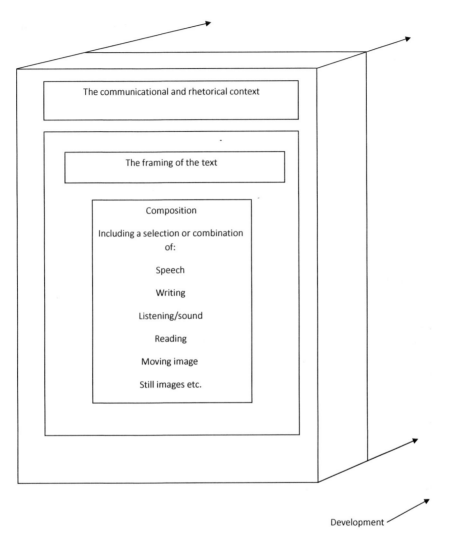

The communicational and rhetorical context

The framing of the text

Composition

Including a selection or combination of:

Speech

Writing

Listening/sound

Reading

Moving image

Still images etc.

Development

Figure 9.3 A model for writing development

axis; but it will also happen in relation to writing. The development in writing will not be steady; it is partly dependent on how the elements within writing develop, and how the other communicational elements outside and near to writing develop too. Along the developmental plane, there is also the phenomenon of a widening range of genres and hybrid texts that is possible as command of the field increases. Such widening of the scope of communication is sometimes accompanied by specialization within each of the modes; at the same time, it can still be accompanied by multimodal choices and combinations that enrich the acts of communication.

Objections to the theory and model

In the next chapter we consider the application of this theory and model in the multimodal and digital age. But first, we subject both theory and model to critique in order to test its strengths and weaknesses.

The theory and model are too simple

Objections could be made that the theory and model are too simple; that they over-simplify what is, in fact, a highly complex set of relationships and practices that cannot easily be unravelled, let alone depicted, in distilled form. Furthermore, such over-simplification masks the huge variety of writing practices that exist in the world and the differences in approaches to writing that exist between individuals. We could respond in a number of ways. At the most general level we have to reiterate the claim that theories and models are useful in that they provide generalized patterns that describe how phenomena operate and interact. Their very aim is to simplify, and many theories (like good designs) are quite simple. They are the identification of pattern which is then realized in words and in the diagrammatic form of the model. At a more specific level, we could say that the art of theorizing and modelling is to find the right balance between complexity and simplicity: to be able to express the complex in a relatively simple set of terms and their relations. Yet further, we could point to other theories and models and say that they are too complex; their complexity defeats the purpose of a theory/model in that cannot be applied in the learning or teaching of writing.

The theory and model do not sufficiently distinguish between process and product

This objection can less easily be rebuffed. Whereas we have identified models in the past that tend to either describe products or processes, our theory and model does not distinguish particularly between the two. This can be seen as a weakness, as it is not always clear whether we are talking about the process of composition or the actual compositions that are created. Our rejoinder is that through choosing the term 'composition' to sit at the heart of our theory and model of writing development, we have chosen a term that embraces both product and process. Like the term 'writing', 'composition' is one that denotes both. But whereas 'writing' as a term has the imprint of the physical act of putting pen to paper, or keyboard strokes to screen; 'composition' is more to do with the act of 'putting things together' – not just words, but words and images, words and sounds, and so on. For us, then, 'composition' is the element of our theory and model that captures the essence of the act of making, but at the same time describes the products that are made.

'Development' is insufficiently theorized

There is still a static feel to our theory and model. It does not seem to have the dynamism that might be depicted in a more fluid medium than the printed page. Such dynamism would reflect the human characteristics of development which are tied in closely with physical, emotional, moral, imaginative and other types of 'naturally occuring' maturation. It might also be objected that the theory and model do not fit every individual. That would be a difficult challenge, as individual developmental characteristics cannot always be predicted. What we have tried to convey is a broad framework for understanding writing development: one that is sufficiently applicable to be useful, at the very least in providing a model *against which* as well as by which individual development could be charted. It is also possible to say that we have not resolved in the theory and model the relationship between the learning situation, in all its social and political characters, with the individual take on that situation. Our answer to that objection is that we have taken rhetoric to be our point of reference and *primum mobile*. Because the nature of rhetoric is to embody the social and political in its deliberations about the function and form of the communicative act, we have implied a consideration of the social and political context in each act of writing.

We do not need another theory and model of writing

Objections might be forthcoming that there are already too many theories and models of writing, and that what we need is good practice or best practice disseminated more widely. We are fully in accord with the dissemination of good and best practice. What we think is useful about a theory and model of writing development is that it provides a framework against which good and best practice can be evaluated; and a starting point for the generation of new practices. In time we expect our own theory and model to be superseded by more appropriate identifications of patterns in writing development; that is because the nature and also the environments of writing will change, just as they have changed since the 1960s. In addition, a theory and model of writing development provides a foundation on which pedagogies and assessment systems can be built. Without such a foundation, fashions will dictate what is taught and how. There is no evidence to date that research or even systematic research reviews and experimental studies can determine what works in the teaching and learning of writing. Rather, writing practices have developed according to underlying paradigms and theories that have not always been articulated. Where they have been articulated, such theories and models have helped teachers and curriculum and assessment designers to build better and thus longer-lasting structures upon them – structures which can be justified because there is an underlying or overarching theory.

In the following chapter, we apply and test out our theory and model further by subjecting it to questions that arise from contemporary communication inside and outside the classroom. In particular, we explore, in more depth, questions of multimodality; and also consider what role writing takes in a world of digital transformation and representation.

Conclusion

This chapter has proposed a new theory and model of writing development. Its constituent parts are contemporary rhetoric, framing, composition, multimodality and a notion of development that constitutes progression from one state of writing capability to another. Such a new prototypical theory needs to be tested in practice, with curriculum design and assessment being conceived, applied and evaluated; and with pedagogical approaches being created to teach writing more effectively and with more concern for the rhetorical context that is currently the case. If found to be useful, this theory and model can apply equally to writing in digital formats as well as with a pen and paper, because its focus is not on the media in which writing takes place, but on the modes that surround it in the contemporary world. Seeing writing as one (very powerful and flexible) mode among others is a way of liberating the teaching of writing from too narrow a focus on the mechanics of writing as a system. Rather, the new emphasis is on the rhetorical functions of communication, writing's affordances, and the relation of writing to other modes that can be used to ensure that communication is effective, appropriate to intention and engaging. Once the teaching of writing is matched to its real world and fictional practices, it is likely that developing writers of any age will find the mode of writing more relevant, powerful and closer to their own communicational needs.

10 A New Theory and Model of Writing Development: the Digital and Multimodal Age

Introduction

In the previous chapter, we presented the initial workings of a new theory and model of writing development. In that theory, we articulated a number of key elements that address both the mezzo-level aspects of writing, such as *composing with multiple modes* and *framing*, and the macro-level issues of writing, such as the *rhetorical context*. These elements of writing are set in motion as we consider the final element of the model – *development*. Development in this model is concerned with both the dynamic development of the elements, as they develop concurrently, yet dissimilarly, as well as development as the whole – the writer who is developing a repertoire of experiences, skills, dispositions, facility with tools, interests and so forth, over time. In this chapter we aim to continue to flesh out the elements of this theory as they are shaped in the digital age – an age of almost constant multimodal communication. We also will continue exploring how to account for dynamic, nonlinear, holistic development.

Elements in the digital age

The element most obviously influenced by the digital media of the twenty-first century is *composing with multiple modes*. We will begin with an exploration of this mezzo-level element of composing. However, each element of the model is shaped by the current state of communication in the digital age, and thus we will then move to the macro-level elements of the model – *rhetoric* and its practical, creative device, *framing*.

Composing with multiple modes

As discussed in Chapter 8, composing in the digital age involves multiple shifts from previously held notions of composing with the written word – not only the technology used to compose the written word, but in terms of the constantly widening range of text types and formats of written products, and the sociality of composing – with whom and for whom we write in the twenty-first century. In this element of the model, we see that developing writers are engaging in several aspects of composing that can be considered as expanding and growing:

- negotiating and controlling writing processes that are collapsed, including the immediacy of publication;
- constant innovation, creativity and hybridity in terms of inter-preting and composing with multiple forms and types of net-worked digital messages;
- facility with and adaptability to new digital tools;
- transliteracy – crossing devices, platforms, tools and media.

Additionally, as discussed in Chapter 7, written words communicate not only through linguistic, but also through visual and (in sound) aural com-ponents. With digital composition in particular, the visual components of writing, such as font, size, colour and white space can be easily exe-cuted and revised. Developmentally, in this element of the model, we see that developing writers grow in their experiences using and navigating multiple modes:

- understanding the affordances, and the communicative and inter-pretive possibilities of various modes, e.g. writing, video, sound, diagram, artistic rendering;
- facility with and adaptability to tools for creating multiple modes;
- telescoping in to compose within a single mode and expanding out to compose, position and layer several modes together;
- drawing on modes other than linguistic to complement in a vari-ety of positions in relation to the written word;
- transduction – engaging in decisive changes from one mode to another;
- remixing and appropriating existing communicative messages in multiple modes, i.e. using an image within a film or a section of a speech in a song.

Composition has always been multimodal, but the twenty-first century with its digital tools and changing social landscape is a time of new pos-sibilities in which the digital and multimodal have converged to a greater degree. Digital composition on the screen affords the assembling of ad-ditional modes of communication, such as sound, video, animation and linked sources of other pieces of written or drawn text, that otherwise – on a page – would not be available. But youth in the digital age do not only compose for a screen. They are still asked, and sometimes find it necessary themselves, to compose on the page for the page. More often they use digital screen devices to compose for the page. Navigating these different forms of production and distribution is yet another dimension of developing in the multimodal and digital nexus.

We will begin our consideration of the development of composing in the digital and multimodal nexus by comparing composing on the screen for the screen, to composing on the screen for the page, and on the page, for the page. The question, 'How does it look?' is increasingly meaningful when composing for the screen, as reading a screen affords the use of sound, image, colour and animation not available in other forms of dissemination. On the screen, colour becomes a particularly meaningful composing tool, especially compared to previous uses of colour as relegated to decoration or illumination on a printed page (especially because of its printing costs). On the printed page, words could be emphasized by underlining. When composed digitally for the printed page, the same words could also be set in bold or formatted in italics. These forms of emphasis, however, have alternative meanings in print, usually signifying titles or when a word is being discussed rather than being used to discuss. On the screen, colour can visually emphasize words and phrases without the added grammatical signification of title or focus. Developing writers need to learn how colours work with words and behind words for emphasis. Additionally, they need to learn how colours work in concert to complement or counter the intended, aesthetic response of the reading audience. With each mode, it is in the experience of composing and interpreting that youth develop such sensibilities.

Typically, screens on which we compose provide a horizontal plane, which influences our choices of visual elements. On the page, ideas in written form are set apart by paragraphs or line breaks which provide breaks for the reader through white space on the page that surrounds or frames ideas. These paragraphs array themselves on the typically vertical page, and the pace of reading can be interpreted visually by glancing at the page and seeing how the author has separated ideas. On the horizontal screen, there is less room, at first glance, for a series of paragraphs in linear fashion. Instead, written text is often shortened into sections set apart, sometimes to the side or offset down the page. Not only do developing writers need to consider paragraphing, but other forms of grouping of ideas and the relations that are possible in layout. Composing with the written word changes as transitions between ideas are communicated graphically, or through placement of text, instead of transitional phrases. Ideas that may have been expanded for a vertical page may be shortened into a one word summary or a phrase and linked to images, text or other messages in other modes and media, moving the reader away from the current visual screen to another combination of modes. In these ways, new meaning is made possible as the content in the text is placed in different positions in relation to other content. Kress and van Leeuwen (1996) provide a helpful and extensive review of logics of layout and visual design. Their theory would be too much to review for our present purposes, but suffice it to say that just as words are used in relation to each other and made meaningful through a grammar or set of patterned rules, so are visual images. Composers should consider what is implicitly communicated in the layout – when placing images in a row or stacking them vertically, or expanding one image, or making it more dominant than the rest by setting it centrally and in the top half of a composition.

As multiple modes are increasingly used on the screen, a sound clip, a video segment or another communication medium in addition to visual elements of text, can be placed laterally or offset to add another dimension of meaning. No longer do writers need to stick with the original settings on any composing software, such as in wordprocessing or website templates; rather they must learn to manipulate the software in order to produce the intended message. Formatting can no longer be considered a final stage of composition before presentation to an audience, or separate from the composing process all together. In planning and composing a product on the screen, a writer may begin with formatting existing messages in multiple modes appropriated for the product, and then move to composing text. For instance, they may compose a blog post by embedding an existing video, then change the background of the post with a colour treatment, and then publish, waiting for written responses from a self-selected community before composing written text that they will decide to place to the side of the video as a parallel statement for the reader to consider, simultaneously, with the video images and sound.

In the mobile sense, screens of several sizes exist and on many types of devices. Writers need to also consider how a composition will be viewed within the limits of screens other than the computer, as well as when multiple screens might be used (such as two computer monitors or a phone and a television screen). Several devices, such as laptop tablets, smart phones and iPads, make the flipping of a screen from horizontal to vertical and vice versa possible. Developing writers need experience in composing text that is 'readable' horizontally and vertically, and also to consider the possibilities in flipping the screen.

When composing on the screen for the page, which for many youth is the current main mode for composing in schools, the skills of transduction are highlighted. When going from screen to page, writers must consider the limits of printing capability, changing colour to black and white, and reformatting to communicate emphasis in other ways. Modes that utilize other media, such as sound and video, must be transduced into written word or image. Horizontal printing is possible, but the typical orientation for the page is vertical, and the composer must take conventions of reading into consideration, and cannot ask the reader to flip the image to another orientation on the page. The stable essence of text on a page also limits the reading paths a composer could design with links on a digital networked screen. Linear composition, as in this chapter, implies a logic that is sometimes unintended – that one idea builds to the next or is an illustration of the previous paragraph. When text is positioned differently, using visual and multimodal logics, new meanings are possible. Nonlinear reading is possible on the page, utilizing layout and white space, but as with the vertical or horizontal orientation, it is not expected by the reader. Sensitivity to the expectations of the audience for the screen or on the page, as well as the communities that form around variations of text types on the screen and on the page, are critical in composing in the digital and multimodal nexus.

The vocabulary used to describe these elements or components of design, such as sensitivity to communities and global audiences, transduction from mode to mode, and appropriating images and layering with another mode, may initially make them sound like skills, abilities and experiences for teen or adult composers only. However, young children are highly practised in these very skills. When a child picks up a crayon and visually represents their last adventure with Dad and then represents this adventure by writing on lines beneath 'I lv mi Dad!!!', or cuts pictures from a magazine with safety scissors and with a glue stick places the pictures together in concert with a star sticker and then posts it on a bulletin board next to another composition that received a star sticker from a teacher, the child is being sensitive to audience, transducing from one mode to another, positioning text, and appropriating images. Children at a very young age compose text on the computer as well, learning to manipulate the mouse or touch pad often with the same facility as the pen or pencil. They ask to hear about responses to their posted videos or ask to write an email after a Skype conversation is cut off because of a bad Internet connection. With young children in mind, it becomes apparent that the development of composition in the digital age is not an issue of introducing particular tools or genres or processes at particular ages or stages of development. Rather, as we will explore more in depth in Chapter 11, teaching the developing writer requires sensitivity and responsiveness to the writer's existing range of experiences, abilities and repertoire of strategies.

Rhetorical context

As a cultural and communicative act, writing is situated in a rhetorical context – the what, why, where, who, to whom, when, where and how that evolves as a writer composes a text. In Chapter 9, we proposed the rhetorical context as a central element in our model of writing. We discussed the influence that the power relations between writer and audience – the who and to whom – have on the choices a writer makes; the shaping influence and constraints the particular purposes and circumstances of the communicative act have on determining the function – the how – of a text; and how these social dimensions – audience and function – impact the resulting substance – the what or content – of a written product. In the digital age, each of these rhetorical concerns is shaped not only by the technological changes in production and distribution (though these play an influential role that we will discuss), but also by the contextual factors of the digital environment – the people, relations, interactions and exchanges of text that characterize writing in the twenty-first century. In this section, we will review the new rhetorical possibilities for experience and growth starting with substance, then function, and finally audience.

Though far from equitable, the general access of digital tools – both hardware and software – has levelled the playing field in terms of possible modes and media that composers can use in forming the *substance* of their written compositions. As discussed in Chapter 8, more than any other technological advancement in recent history, globally, people have access to mobile digital devices, such as cell phones and PDAs. These devices have multiple media capabilities – video, sound, image – making the production of multiple types of media available. Software to edit, splice, layer and remix the media is also accessible both in terms of that which is installed in widely distributed computers in schools, homes, and community centres, and also on networked devices online. Online, free, and user-friendly sites and open source software such as Picnik or GarageBand make the editing of media self-created or appropriated and available to the masses. As simply as typing on a keyboard or moving a mouse, a person can edit multiple types of media. With the drag of the mouse to highlight a URL and the click of the button to copy and paste, media can be appropriated and remixed with text. Such tools make the creation of products in new media and with multimodal designs possible as never before. And these can be used for daily communicative purposes – not just for major formal occasions. All of these change the possibilities of the substance of a written composition.

For understanding a developing writer's experiences with rhetorical context, not only is their sensitivity to the requirements of the function of a text and the needs of the audience of critical import, but we need to know how the child is developing their meaning-making across tools and media. We should ask to what extent are they taking full advantage of the range of mode, media, screen, community in their choices of substance to meet the needs of the audience or the purpose of a piece. It also becomes clear that knowledge of, access to and experience with the constantly advancing production and distribution tools and various hardware and software enables and constrains possible development. It is necessary to account for access and experience in understanding a child's development in the rhetorical context.

The *function* of a given piece of writing – to persuade, to entertain, to inform – influences the choices of substance or content, such as the language that will be used or the sections and type of content that will be included. In the digital age the circumstances within which and purposes for which we write have shifted in ways that make purposes previously available to a select few, available to the masses. Texts that had previously been available only to those with monetary resources and social capital, such as social commentary and critique, poetry chapbooks and online publication of novellas, songs and musical scores, are now widely available. Radio shows, which mix commentary, sound effects, interviews with experts, and function as a hybrid product that informs, entertains and subtly persuades the listeners to a particular viewpoint, were only available to radio hosts and broadcasting companies. Produced and planned ahead, but performed and produced live, they only existed for a moment on the air to those tuned in and in range of the broadcasting tower. In the digital age, similar productions, podcasts, are options for any person with a networked mobile device – written, recorded, mixed with music and sound, and disseminated with relative ease. Once distributed, podcasts can be listened to repeatedly, fast forwarded, rewound, saved and passed on, changing the uses of listeners. Such complicated and hybrid functions were not available to the masses, especially youth, in the era when Britton et al. (1976) studied the functions of the texts written by 11–17-year-olds in school. Compositions with multiple modes and media rarely have one dominant purpose and function.

Not only are the functions of texts in the digital environment more complex and hybrid, formats and types are constantly being invented and then remain in flux. Messages once composed under particular circumstances for intended purposes are set off in socially networked digital landscapes in undetermined and unpredictable paths in which their functions actually shift. Take, for example, the seemingly simple function of the 'status message' in Facebook or the 140-character 'tweet' on Twitter. At face value both seem similar in form and function – both are brief, one-line statements often referencing the activities and emotions of the author. However, how these messages function continually shifts. Facebook has added the 'like' button and the possibility to comment on posted statuses of 'friends,' which make the status messages conversation starters rather than shouts into the ether. Tweets are distributed to the general public and show up on feeds of those who 'follow' a particular author. Twitter has recently added new one-click options that followers can use to 'retweet' or 'quote tweet'. These functions were initially created by the users of Twitter who would begin tweets with phrases such as 'RT @[original author]' to indicate a 'retweet'. Additionally, companion websites have created the possibility of shortening website addresses so that addresses can fit within the parameters of the 140-character limit. In these ways, what once could have remained as 140-character statuses, now serve several functions from advertising and publicizing to linking people around common interests. To compare the functions in one more way, if a person tries to post a link in a Facebook status message, it immediately turns into a linked post with a small picture and is present in the person's activity feed, rather than showing up in the status. This constrains the function that the status message can serve. However, users of Facebook still find ways to quickly delete characters at the end of posted links or post links in the status from their phones in order to have linked websites in their status messages.

With just one example of the malleable nature of text functions in the digital environment, we can see that predetermined circumstances, purposes, forms and functions do not make sense in this era. Rather, the era is marked by inventiveness and creative repurposing of text types and technology itself to create messages which function in complex ways. Developing writers will need sensitivity to a changing landscape of possibilities, and must know how to appropriate and repurpose existing messages for new functions that suddenly exist. Writers also need to develop an understanding of how their messages will be used by others, appropriated and remixed for different purposes previously unnecessary with other combinations of people and interests.

In terms of *audience* – the who and to whom of a written piece – several shifts have occurred. Writers in the digital age have increased access to a wider variety of social groups with possible global reach. With multiple modes at their disposal, writers can communicate across language, age range and educational experience in ways impossible with just the written word – particularly in one language. Audiences in the digital age are also known, local and near. Youth exchange digital and multimodal compositions – from short text messages on cell/mobile phones or more expanded notes on Facebook. And, as with the functions of texts, once the communicative message is set out digitally, audiences are unpredictable and varied. Compositions are forwarded, copied and pasted, saved on flash drives, posted and downloaded. The typical question of a rhetorical approach – whether a composition is suitable to the intended audience, or whether it could be effected in a different way – is no longer adequate. We must not only evaluate our writing from the perspective of the imagined and intended audience, but from the multiple possible audiences and perspectives that will also see it, use it and set it in further motion. As Hull and Stornaiuolo (2010) suggested, the skill of transliteracy does not just include facility transferring between devices, platforms, tools and media, but also includes developing cosmopolitan sensitivities and hospitable dispositions toward possible audiences, both close and far.

The role of audience, itself, has shifted in the digital age. Audiences see and expect to see what might have been considered first drafts or just brainstorming, and expect to give and respond to feedback. Whereas audiences were once relegated to receiving and interpreting, and at times responding to written pieces, their role was often at a distance and disconnected from the composer. Now, it is much more often the case that the intended audience is engaged in the creation of the composition from the co-creation of the social space and purpose for the written piece to shaping the content or substance of a piece through constant, immediate feedback loops. With synchronous technology, collaborative relations can truly exist to co-author a piece. The rhetorical concern of audience in the twenty-first century takes on a relational dimension. Composers establish online identities that travel with written pieces and meet other composers in collaboration. Developing writers need to not only learn to consider the needs of the intended audience as they compose, but need experience:

- in communicating about writing for and with particular audiences who are also immediately multiple, public, unknown, imagined and several;
- in shaping identities through writing for and with texts, and setting these in circulation;
- of establishing and responding to changing social networks, and participatory composition, responding to mentorships and feedback;
- of transliteracy, crossing communities in which 'self- and other-work' is done publicly;
- in developing sensitivity to audience and community established expectations.

Framing

With the rhetorical context – the concerns of audience, function and substance – in mind, and with a growing repertoire and facility with the tools of multiple compositional elements, such as language, image, animation and sound, the writer begins to shape the text, framing and re-framing the scope of the composition. Framing and re-framing are devices which operate in the service of rhetoric. They empower the composer to make meaning and communicate it in distinctive ways, sometimes using existing frames ('genres'), sometimes using hybrid forms, and sometimes creating new frames. In concrete ways, such as deciding which elements to include and exclude, and abstract ways, such as positioning the text in a particular interpretive community, the writer is 'framing' a text. For example, the same scripted love poem that is recorded and layered in a video with images of kittens and soft music will have different interpretations if positioned as a submission to funnyordie.com, a satirical political commentary website, or posted on a YouTube.com channel dedicated to people who love cats.

Just as a picture is framed by what is included in the boundaries of the viewfinder of the camera, a composition has boundaries or parameters. A photograph of a sunset typically includes a mountain range, the sun peeking out and a portion of the sky ablaze with colour. Written texts have similar typical boundaries, such as a story which includes a setting, characters and conflict. Text types have been traditionally presented as having a predetermined form and boundaries. In classical rhetoric, we learn of particular forms of persuasive argument. From nineteenth-century rhetoric, we have a larger set of forms, and students learn particular forms of essays that satisfy the demands of the functions of writing, such as the definition essay, the compare and contrast essay, the persuasive essay. Genre study was the next wave of defining text types and form. Though it includes a wider range of text types than previous approaches to rhetoric, genre study includes the study of static forms of written text. In the digital age, genre study of existing, pre-set forms is not sufficient to meet the demands of a constantly shifting rhetorical context. Inventiveness with existing genres and playing with the boundaries of what is included in text types is expected in and across digital communities. That is why the emphasis must be on 'framing' as a verb, rather than the more static 'frames' where the power is invested not in the writer and audience, but in the existing conventions and patterns of communication. Re-framing existing compositions is also a common practice, and an expectation in the digital environment (see Andrews 2011 for a full account of framing and re-framing).

In the co-configured spaces of the digital environment, communication with a varied and participatory readership is the norm. The social dynamics of written composition are heightened. Developing writers build their awareness of the social impact of their compositions, how they frame those compositions and how they position their communicative epistles to the world. Framing decisions are intentional, deliberate, and cognizant. Writers should ask themselves what existing frames – social and textual – they are drawing from to form their ideas and shape their compositions; how their choices are being made about what existing media they are appropriating or what modes they are choosing to use under which social conditions and for which social groups; what they consider to cohere in a text and what is extraneous – that with a shift in framing could be included to affect a different end; and how they decide the text is completed, ready for public, or if co-authored and already public, how they decide it is ready for distribution to additional audiences. In a digital and thus global audience, communicating positioning, shaping and framing is often necessary through meta-language about intention and acknowledgement of breaking and bending existing forms. Youth need to develop a vocabulary to talk about their choices, to become articulate regarding the framing decisions they are making. Our question of product quality also shifts: not only do we wonder how the product fits the frame but how sensitive the young composer is to the range of choice in framing and then shaping their rhetorical choices. Furthermore, how sensitive and aware is the writer to the linguistic and aesthetic modal choices in the light of framing and re-framing possibilities?

Finally, framing allows the consideration of power. Who is doing the framing or re-framing? Is the composer in control, or does the audience have the upper hand? How are the dynamics of power in a conversation, mixed-mode digital composition or film played out? When we become aware of the way a message has been or is being framed, we can begin to see the rhetorical choices more clearly. It is also the case that without framing, there is no meaning – so understanding the frames that are being created and deployed is essential not only to good communication, but to the very nature of communication itself.

Development in the digital age

In our proposed theory and model, an individual develops through experience with each element – rhetorical context, framing and composition – and with each component of each element, such as with layout with multiple modes and communication with others. In this chapter we explored how the nature of writing has shifted in significant ways in the twenty-first century, evolving these elements in new ways and dimensions. To summarize what typifies development in the digital dimensions of the twenty-first century, we add our voice to the many others who describe development as an expanding repertoire that writers draw from to design their compositions. Myhill (2009) who studied just over seven hundred compositions of young children, concluded that existing scales for linguistic and multimodal development are insufficient, explaining, 'Development . . . is thus about acquiring the possibilities of choice, about having a design repertoire to draw upon, and about crafting sentences and texts to satisfy the rhetorical demands of the task' (p. 413). Additionally, youth are developing in their dispositions (e.g. being cosmopolitan and/or hospitable [Hull and Stornaiuolo 2010], toward text – its nature and social functions – and the people with whom they are collaborating, and with whom their texts and online identities may potentially interact). Online and offline, a person is involved in an idiosyncratic and constantly fluctuating literacy network (Leander and Lovvorn 2006). Finally, a person's ability to cross spaces successfully, or their transliteracy, is of interest (Thomas et al. 2007). Youth develop in facility and adaptability with tools, resources and the endless possibilities of form, function, audience, framing, substance and modes in Web 2.0 and beyond.

At this point, one may ask: 'What end-goal are young writers developing toward?' or its companion question, 'When will a writer be developed?' Many of the theories reviewed in Chapters 4 and 5 left this end-goal unstated, as the typical target for most theories of development is adult competence. With Arnold (1980), the core self was developing in interaction with different discourses of adults until their products were similar to those of adults. With Flower and Hayes (1981), young children's processes were most often compared to that of older more experienced writer. Although through the years the modelling of development has shifted from straight linear lines (Hunt 1970), to flow charts (Bereiter and Scardamalia 1987), to spirals (Arnold 1980), 'developed' writing is still conceptualized as a linear regression scale, using adult competence as the marker of maturity and working backward to determine what to expect for children. Kress (1997) is the only theory of writing development that we could locate that posed an alternative to adult competence as the goal. Kress argued that the differences in writing between the ages are more like a difference in 'dialects' than a question of development.

In our theory and model of writing development in the digital age, adult competence is not the end-goal. For one, adults are often not as skilled with digital tools. They often do not have the developed facility and adaptability and have less experience composing with multiple modes, or balancing writing with other modes of communication. Finally, though adults may have experience negotiating social networks and texts online, there is no guarantee that they have developed dispositions for communicating in a global and constantly shifting space. In another sense, it is also a fallacy to assume that adults are more successful in their framing and composing of text than youth. Are adults less susceptible to unsuccessful attempts at writing in the traditional expressive, poetic, transactional discourses? With even more functions and forms available, attempts to compose for particular rhetorical contexts by both adults and children will vary in quality dependent on several factors, the least of which is age. Adults are just as vulnerable and limited by experience.

What then is the goal? Instead of positing the goal as a product, in this theory, the goal is the activity of growth itself. Instead of asking if the writer is developed, we ask if the writer is engaged in developing their range of choices and repertoire of designs, their dispositions and sensitivities to text and audience, and their facility and adaptability to tools and the landscape of writing in the digital age. In this sense, the writer cannot only be tasked to write in these particular dimensions, but must become an agent of development themselves. Their awareness of rhetorical possibilities and desire for growth in a wide repertoire are principal gauges of their development.

Modelling development in the digital age

As development is not linear progression toward one type of adult communication or composing practice, we are aware of the limits of modelling tentative and shifting development of young writers on the printed page. We are limited by the mode of lines, vectors and boxes in composing our model in chapter 9 for the printed page in a published book. The result is a framed model that visually can be shown to grow in its depth, but cannot be visually modelled as in progress or in growth. On the screen, we would be able to animate the elements of composing, framing and rhetorical context. They would be set into motion, changing and shifting as the writer is developing a repertoire of possible modes and tools, and gaining experience with differing communities, and interaction with others collaborating while composing. Items outside the current developmental frame – as possibilities in technology, sociality and genre continue to change – could also be modelled.

We leave the reader, at this time, with our best unanimated visual to represent the developmental element of our model of writing development in the digital age. As suggested in Chapter 6, symbolic modelling or visual metaphors of development help to reframe our existing notions of development (Kress and van Leeuwen 2001). One such visual metaphor would be the Mandelbrot[1] or Julian sets from complexity science, as seen in Figure 10.1. These intricate patterned designs are created by running particular simple mathematical equations that result in individual points on the graph. Where these points will show up is unpredictable, but related to the 'initial conditions' or the initial input variable. With several iterations over time, patterns develop. In the Julian set in Figure 10.1, these are spiralling patterns of various sizes and set in different angles to each other.

This visual metaphor is appropriate for the type of development we are proposing and aligns to the theory of writing development we are proposing. This visual metaphor highlights the trends or patterns of growth

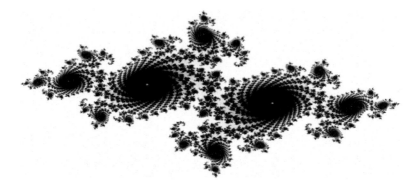

Figure 10.1 Symbolic model of idiosyncratic yet patterned development using a Julian set.
Source: MacGill, V. (2009) *Complexity pages.* Available: http://complexity. orconhosting.net.nz. Used with permission from the author.

that occur across age groups as connected with the 'initial conditions' or experiences afforded to an individual student or groups of students, such as experience with particular digital tools and devices or experiences communicating with others local and globally. Each point, or writing experience, will have unpredictable results for each child, but over time, the student's idiosyncratic growth as to the elements of composing in the digital age will be seen to develop in several directions and dimensions, but still in patterned ways, such as in the spirals above. In this visual metaphor, the reader can imagine development in motion as a writer draws from existing experiences, forms and practices, expanding their facility with and adaptability to new tools and audiences, resulting in a pattern of development unique to each individual writer.

11 Implications for Practice and Assessment

Introduction

We have devoted much of our attention in this book to developing a theory and model of writing development for the digital age. We turn now to the practical matters of teaching and assessing as informed by the model we have proposed. This brings us full circle, back to the problem of writing performance presented in the first chapter of this book. To address performance of our students, in this chapter, we ask: What practices can be implemented and should be sustained to encourage development of writing in the digital age? How can we measure the expansive list of skills, abilities and dispositions necessary for communicating effectively in the twenty-first century?

We begin this chapter by inviting you to reflect on your own current writing and teaching practices in light of existing product- and process-related theories that may guide your current work. Through reflection we can ask what adjustments, if any, we need to make in our perspectives on writing development in order to take on a new model. After this reflective exercise, we will turn to the issue of teaching practices that align with the theory presented and encourage our students' development. Then, we will turn our attention to assessment. Students are being assessed increasingly frequently (annually and sometimes by term or by semester). We will be advocating a formative model of assessment that is 'owned' by the writer, but which also uses benchmarks to enable comparisons with peer groups.

The theory/practice nexus

Explicit theories – the ones we are conscious of and can articulate – do not always directly align with our working theories, or the tacit theories that guide the way we engage in the world. Based on our day-to-day experiences, our working theories are always in flux. Say, for example, a school administrator is adamant that 'all kids can learn'. She can articulate this saying and even passionately encourage others to take it up as a school motto. Over time the administrator may begin to support the quick removal of students with behavioural outbursts by transfer to an alternative high school or even expulsion. She may say that the students will be better served in another environment, thus rationalizing her actions to align with the theory about children and learning that she has explicitly learned and can articulate. However, in essence the theory in vivo is more nuanced than the articulated one. Her working theory is more accurately 'all kids can learn, but not in this school,' or 'we aren't equipped to teach all students, especially ones who behave differently than we'd like'.

Theory and practice are not at odds in this example, but rather are intricately related: our working theories of how the world works or how it should work stem from our experiences. Likewise, the assumptions teachers have about learning are influenced more by the working theories they have formed from their own experience with students and less by the explicit theories that have been explained to them in training they have attended or in books they have read. Guskey (1986) explained that contrary to previous ideas about professional development, teachers must actually make a change, however small, in their teaching practice and see its impact in student learning, before they will typically change their attitudes and beliefs.

Realizing the great influence your experiences will have on the extent to which the theory we have posed in this book will be taken up and used to guide your everyday practice, we invite you, with the following activity, to reflect on your experience, theories and assumptions – those that form the basis of your own writing, teaching and researching practices. You are encouraged to then locate your practices and personal theories within those offered by researchers and theorists. Consider which approaches seem most logical, practical or insightful to you. You may find one theory that is closely aligned – explicitly and articulated – to your experiences of writing development, but we also hope that through this reflective activity you can discover tensions between explicit theories and your working theories. When our working theories – the implicit theories of our everyday practice – become clear, we can see which theories guide our work and what, if any, adjustments we might need to make to take on a new model.

Writing practices

Even more than lesson guides or curriculum, the National Writing Project, a US-based professional development organization, points to teachers' own writing experiences as the prominent source of knowledge that guides writing instruction and classroom decisions, along with theory, research and curriculum guides. Like the National Writing Project, we invite you to begin by reflecting on your own writing practices

Exercise

Gather two of your own written products, one recent and one older. Set the products side by side on a table or desk and ask the following questions:

1. What do you initially notice is different between the two products? What is similar? Is the more recent product more developed? What do you take into account to make this judgement?
2. Consider linguistics
   (a) Count the length and note the complexity of the sentences. If you notice a significant difference, what accounts for this difference – your age difference, your experience of writing or the topic, audience and purpose of the written piece?
3. Consider function and audience
   (a) What function does each piece of writing serve? Is the later product's function more advanced, in your opinion?
   (b) What audience(s) were you writing for and to? Were the audiences more distant in the later piece than those in the earlier piece?
   (c) Has your ability to write to the designated audience for the particular function improved?
4. Consider changes in morality and affect
   (a) Is there evidence of changes in your personal emotional or moral states? Is the later piece more mature in this sense?

Now sit back and consider your findings. Were you able to satisfactorily assess your personal development from one product to the next? Which foci – linguistic, function and audience, or moral/affect – did you most attend to in your initial comparison? If you were drawn to the differences in audience and function, your working theories about development may align currently to Britton et al.'s (1976) writing theory that functions become more abstract and audiences become more distant the longer we write in schools, or to Arnold's (1980) theory that the more we write in a particular community, the closer our written products will adhere to the expectations of that community.

If you do not feel like you see much arguable development from one document to the other, your working theories of development may adhere more to a process model of development. As we learned in Chapter 5, process-related models can help explain problem-solving and the order that pieces typically come together for you. Review the more recent product. Annotate the draft with three categories:

1. Sticking points
   (a) Which sticking points were you aware of as you were writing? Which ones are you only noticing in hindsight?
2. Compositional decisions
   (a) What linguistic, rhetorical or formatting choices did you consider? How long did these decisions take? How easy were the decisions to make?
3. Order of print on the page
   (a) What did you do before, while and after print went on the page? Did you start in the middle of what ended up as the product? Did you outline or write a different version first?
   (b) Did you repeat words in your head before writing them on the page? Did you think of entire passages or word by word?
   (c) Did you think about the writing task while doing other things? Did you talk about the topic or the piece to others?
4. Reflect on the annotations you have made, asking the following three questions:
   (a) Was this experience of writing typical for you?
   (b) When has writing been different for you?
   (c) What contributed to the sticking points, decisions and order of print?

Finally, looking back on your notes about your written products and writing processes, do you recognize any changes that you would consider a regression (as opposed to an improvement)? Did you stall in any characteristic of your written products or overuse a certain writing strategy over time? Have you had the same kinds of problems or sticking points when writing different pieces? Have you developed in ways that aren't 'better', but in ways you might call 'richer' or 'more nuanced' or 'more sensitive'? These questions point to the nature of development we have proposed in Chapters 6, 9 and 10. In previous theories, these types of growth would not have been considered development, and thus not included on the radar of your development. Once they are considered, we have a better picture or map of your development to date.

Additionally, we have suggested in Chapters 9 and 10 areas beyond product and process in which you can map your development. Consider the repertoire of modes, tools and experiences from which you drew to create the products in front of you. Ask yourself how you imagined the audiences to whom you directed the pieces, and if you considered other possible audiences. Did you collaborate with others? How cordial and effective were those interactions? Where did these pieces fit within your literacy network? If you attempted to shift the writing from one audience, community, mode or tool, how successful were you? Finally, consider the ease with which you physically composed the text. What tools did you use and did you struggle with these tools in any way?

Teaching practices

Now that your own development is a little clearer, let us consider how your teaching practices are guided by existing theories and what adjustments may need to be made to take on a new theory.

Exercise

Consider the last time you observed students writing in class:

1. How was the writing task explained? What aspects of composing were given emphasis?
2. What composing activities were given classroom time, e.g. idea germination, generating text, editing?
3. When did the composing time come in relation to learning new content? Was writing used as a means to come to understanding about the content? Were ideas expected to be formed first and then written out on the page? What amount of creativity and choice did the students have?
4. Who made decisions about pacing, criteria and product characteristics? Who gave advice about meeting these expectations?
5. How was progress monitored? Who kept track? What was measured? How was it measured?

Take a product and make note of how you assess it. Ask yourself the questions that follow:

1. What attributes of the written product did you look for?
   (a) What counts as evidence of those attributes?
2. What does good writing look like?
   (a) What is different between a good and poor product?
   (b) What factors influence the quality of a written product?
3. How do students' written products differ from adults' written products?

The concerns posed in these questions stem from the existing product- and process-related theories presented in Chapters 4 and 5. However, many of these questions would be the same in the current study, but with different emphasis. For instance, the punctuation in a written composition remains important, but not as an issue of overall correctness. Rather, students need to punctuate similarly to those with whom they wish to place their writing. We would also be interested in finding out if the child can transpose punctuation from one community's standards to another's. Similar to the final list of questions we asked you to pose to yourself in regards to your own writing practise, ask the students you have observed about the repertoire and range of student experiences and skills, their consciousness of the sociality of text and networked communication, their literacy network, and so forth.

Implications for practice

There are at least three ways digital multimodal composition might be used in our classrooms today. First, the teacher might use it for delivery of content. A teacher using a Smartboard for instruction is an example of this application. Second, a teacher may plan to integrate digital technology into the activities students will do to learn content. We see this when students provide feedback to peers on their writing in a writing lab. Third, we can teach the use of digital technology directly, such as learning how to manipulate an image in PhotoShop. All three of these applications are applicable and necessary to teaching writing in the digital age. Many resources are available to teachers interested in these three applications of digital multimodal composition in the classroom. Recently the National Writing Project published a companion to their statement *Because Writing Matters* (Nagin 2003). The companion, *Because Digital Writing Matters* (DeVoss et al. 2010), outlines areas of interest to classroom teachers as well as administration and policy-makers, including how teachers can help students juggle digital tools and the quantity of information available on the Internet; what school environment factors can support writing in the digital age; and implications for curriculum design and assessment in relation to new technologies. They also include several suggestions of classroom activities. In concert with this release, the National Writing Project went live with a website 'Digital Is' (digitialis.nwp.org). In true Web 2.0 style, this is not a resource website, but a growing compilation of resources under these areas with interactive discussion boards and threads.

Several out-of-school, after school and community-based organizations are focused on twenty-first century literacy and digital technologies. In such programmes students are using digital devices and tools, gaining facility and adaptability with them, finding out how to stay on top of the most recent advances in technology, trying on collaborative dispositions towards others, learning how to be sensitive in their framing of compositions, and learning to be flexible in framing for varied rhetorical concerns.

These types of non-school organizations can be great sources for learning how to guide students in their development of writing in the digital age.

No single classroom activity, teaching tool or assessment from the resources listed above is the golden ticket to improved writing or supporting a developing writer. Rather, to foster development of writing, teachers must consider a much bigger picture of the student and the context in which their writing is developing. Through direct observation and conversation with the student a teacher can begin to appreciate and understand the student's idiosyncratic developmental patterns.

In response to the ever-increasing complexity of schools and their societies, which seek to control the chaos of human systems through standards and scripted lessons, Schultz (2003) proposed 'listening' as an alternative conceptual framework for understanding the work of teachers in their attempts to support students' development. She suggested that listening closely to the patterns of growth and challenges posed to each child can lead to more responsive teaching and action with better results than trying to control the ecosystem-nature of learning systems. Teachers, she explained, must listen to particular students, to the rhythms of the classroom, to the social, cultural and communal aspects of students' lives, as well as the silences and inactivity in those spaces. 'Listening', she proposed, is a receptive and responsive orientation toward students in the classroom:

> In place of silencing the cacophony of a classroom and imposing order on top of it, I suggest that teaching involves improvisation. Jazz musicians draw on multifaceted knowledge in order to improvise ... Like teaching, playing jazz involves moment-to-moment decisions, interpretations and improvisations ... [and] takes many years of playing and listening [to learn].
>
> (Schultz 2003: 171–2)

Taking such a stance with students in the classroom is the first step in implementing the proposed theory of writing development. Rather than curriculum guides or standardized mandates, which are often based on outdated theories or arbitrary decisions for administrative purposes, teachers must centre the writer as the source of information regarding their development to date – the experiences that the student has been afforded and the areas that have been sticking points. Like practices derived from previous theories, we need to collect writing samples and have students think aloud as they compose, but we do these things not only to evaluate them against a benchmark or to see immediate changes after a lesson. Rather we want to take the receptive and curious stance to see what is happening in their writing practices and then respond accordingly.

The conferring or conferencing method is a straightforward approach that we can put into our teaching practice to enact this conceptual framework. In a conference a student and a teacher sit down together and have a conversation. Anderson (2000) suggested that this conversation has two parts: discussion about the work the child is presently doing and conversation about how the child can develop as a writer. In the first part, the student is the source of information, sharing their products and drafts, the tools they are using, and the sticking points or areas of excitement about a piece. The teacher listens closely, receptive to the developmental possibilities they may hear. With the theory of writing development in mind, the teacher asks themselves several questions as they listen closely.

Regarding the rhetorical context:

1. Audiences—How is this child considering audience and considering audiences that may follow? Who are they engaged with in composing collaboratively? Who are they seeking feedback from? How are they accepting the feedback and what is he/she doing with it? To whom is the student presenting himself/herself online and offline?
2. Functions—How is this student sensitive to expectations and possibilities in this setting? Are they inventive to meet the complex purposes?
3. Substance—Is the student taking full advantage of possibilities in tools, resources, distribution, production?

Regarding framing:

1. How is the student shaping and positioning the piece of writing? Can the student articulate their choices?
2. What existing genres are they drawing from? Which adjustments to genre are they making to meet a need?

Regarding composing:

1. How is the student negotiating and controlling collapsed writing processes?
2. What tools does the student have facility with? How flexible and adaptable is the student to new digital tools? How easily does the student cross devices, platforms, tools and media?
3. How well does the student understand the affordances, and the communicative and interpretive possibilities of various modes, e.g. writing, video, sound, diagram, artistic rendering?
4. How is the student at composing in a single mode and then with modes together? Does the student draw on modes other than linguistic to complement the written word?

5. Does the student make decisive changes from one mode to another depending on the resources, audience? Does the student take advantage of remixing and appropriating existing communicative messages in multiple modes?

Responding to developmental patterns:

1. Is the student regressing in any element (as opposed to an improvement)?
2. Are they stalling in terms of any characteristic of their written products or do they overuse a certain writing strategy over time?
3. Have they had the same kinds of problems over several drafts?

Most likely the child or teenager will not know the areas of interest to the teacher. In this case, you may need to draw more information from the student. Anderson (2000) suggested that for youth who are talking only about the substance of the piece and not about the writing of it, you could say something like, 'That is really interesting. So what are you doing as a writer today?' For students who don't know how to begin talking about writing, a teacher could say, 'I'm going to take a look at your draft, and describe what I think you're doing as a writer today' (p. 97). One way to keep key issues in mind is to use sticky notes to jot key phrases that have become salient in the student's composing processes. For instance, if a student was overusing the word processor's thesaurus in her attempts to sound highly educated for a piece she wanted to publish in the school newspaper, the teacher might write 'thesaurus overused/needs newspaper tone'. These notes could be made during these conferences, but also during any short conversation or observation. They are then transferable from the draft, to be placed in a folder with other notes for the child for later reflection.

The second portion of the conference is when the teacher responds to 1) the next step the student could take in the current piece; and 2) the next step for the student in terms of their larger development as a writer (beyond the particular piece). While still in conversation, the student now shifts to listening as the teacher shares knowledge and experience in reflection on the model of growth. The teacher can begin with statements, such as: 'I think your piece needs X. Maybe you could ...' or 'Have you considered X? If not, here's what I'd like you to try ...' Students will benefit the most when the teacher is transparent, clear and concise. To review for the student, after sharing a strategy, framing option, or concern about rhetoric, they can conclude with two statements, 'I think what's next for this piece is ....' and 'I think what's next for you as a writer is ...'

After the conference is the time for the teacher to reflect on the notes from conferences with this and the other students in the class, noting individual trends or patterns and patterns that extend across the class. For instance, students in one class may not be using dialogue in their stories. A small group of students may not be working well with others in collaborating to design a brochure. Another student may be reframing older pieces of writing for new audiences and not be aware of the sophisticated and sensitive tactics they are using.

How a student's writing develops depends on their experiences and the resources available to them, the tasks they are faced with and the audiences they are aware of. All of these things make up the context in which writing occurs and yet context rarely gets our attention. Conferencing makes us more attentive to the contextual situation that surrounds the activity of writing. In conferring with the student, we can get to know them better and become more aware of the context in which they write. It allows us to understand a piece in process within particular surroundings. We can see which lessons have influenced the student's decisions, audiences, technology use and demonstration of skills. We should ask two questions of the information we learn in conferences: 1) What has been constrained? and 2) What has been enabled? With these thoughts in mind, the teacher can then design responsive instruction to fit students' patterns of growth in multiple dimensions and in light of the contextual constraints on learning. This instruction could come in many forms including: mini-lessons, whole class lessons, guided writing groups, additional conferences or partnering students together to learn specific skills from one another.

In an age of increased communication, ironically, many of the assignments and classroom 'writing' activities that have characterized today's classrooms can actually separate writing from direct communication and make the connection between writing and communication vague. Our teaching practices have tremendous shaping influence on developing writers. Worksheets on discrete skills and writing for fake audiences can create a disconnect so pronounced as to cause some students to deny that their day-to-day writing with technology, for example, is writing at all (Lenhart et al. 2008). If we are to learn from our past experiences we must let go of the security of 'assign and assess'. Conferencing emphasizes the relational dynamic of teaching and learning and puts writing instruction back within the communicational frame. In these many ways, the conference method orients the teacher as an observer of multiple components of writing, and positions the student as central as they reflect and articulate their writing experiences. When faced with teaching in an era of fast-paced changes and shifts in the landscape of composition, we must talk to our students like never before.

Implications for assessment

Writing, assessment and digital technology have had a long history with implications pertinent for our theory. Penrod's (2010) analysis of this history is illuminating. Like many in compositions studies, she begins the history of writing and assessment in 1874 when Harvard introduced a college-entrance essay exam. Most colleges have writing portions of their entrance exams today. The first multiple-choice tests for college entrance in 1919, and the beginnings of standardized testing and test-scoring machines in the 1920s have set precedence for what is considered practical, valid and reliable in testing. When the other assessment methods are too costly, the machine-scored, multiple-choice questions are often the fall-back. However, these multiple-choice tests are limited to testing discrete knowledge of particular rules in application to examples. In 1966, the first computerized or automatic scoring of a written product was created and counted such things as the number of words per sentence and the length of words to determine text quality. Computerized assessment of written passages has since evolved. Today several companies have developed computer programs that automatically produce scores and feedback to students, which they claim is similar to that which would come from a teacher. These computer programs are able to 'score' a paper by comparing linguistic patterns of the product in question against the results of the evaluation of hundreds of similar products by humans that were entered into the computer. Linguistic patterns do differ based on topic, discipline and formality, and this automated information could be valuable, but just like multiple-choice tests, the mechanism is a scoring machine, and its use is based on the assumption that there is one set standard for writing quality.

Concurrently with the emergence of computerized scoring, two other paths of assessment have been introduced: portfolio assessment and criterion-referenced rubrics. We first see portfolios in the 1980s and electronic portfolios in the 1990s. Portfolios are primarily collections of student work from a range of writing samples composed under varied circumstances. Portfolios are offered as an authentic assessment of writing (Murphy and Yancey 2008). Portfolios have been criticized for several reasons, including: 1) the varied ways they are implemented; 2) the administrative time it takes to maintain the collections; and 3) the overwhelming amount of raw data provided. In 1977, the first rubric-like scoring method was developed, ushering in criterion-referenced testing rather than norm-referenced testing (as in standardized testing). Primary-trait (one criterion) and analytic (multiple criteria) rubrics made interrater reliability possible: the more specific the grading tool, the more often raters scored pieces of writing similarly. In the current era, the large-scale, high-stakes writing assessments in the UK and the USA (e.g. National Assessment of Educational Progress 2007; Jeffery 2009) are based on samples of products that students write in single, timed sessions under strict parameters such as the topic, audience, format and length. Rubrics are used in the evaluation of these pieces, and are similarly controlled with pre-determined criteria and benchmarks. As these assessments have become the centrepiece of school reform efforts, assessments, in general, have gained a negative connotation. Designed to provide comparative data from one geographic area to another, large-scale assessments do not inform us about individual students. At best, we can gauge a sense of a group's collective performance. It is no wonder then that large-scale, high-stakes assessments that have taken large portions of instructional time, and become the primary means to judge teaching and learning, have been criticized.

This history carries with it several problematic assumptions about what defines writing and its development. For instance, other than the discrete multiple-choice style assessments, all assessments are focused on written products. The act of measuring written products, Neal (2010) argued, assumes that writing is 'stable, static and measurable' (p. 175). It also assumes that successful communication can be predetermined by those outside of the intended audience. Even more basic, it is assumed that these single pieces – or in the case of portfolios, a set of written products – can determine writing ability. Performance on one task is assumed to be representative of typical current performance, as well as predictive of future performances. It is also assumed that writing ability can be measured by a written sample decontextualized from the place, situation and communicative purpose for which it was written. It is also assumed that individuals can and should be assessed in isolation from others, and that writing is always a solitary activity. Finally, when these isolated performances or measurements of discrete skills are compared against each other by age group, they are described as if they measure development of writing – not just performance. Comparisons are simply not development.

Possibilities with portfolios

Considering the established forms of writing assessments reviewed here, portfolios are the most aligned with the present theory of writing development in the digital age. Portfolios have the potential to measure development, because they sample each student's performance over time. The following issues will need to be addressed, however, in order to fully align to the theory: 1) portfolios are generally limited to final written products—leaving processes, practices, dispositions and skills unaccounted for; 2) portfolios are often either teacher selected or student selected – either way the selection process results in a loss of the necessary ecological snapshot; 3) the reflective responses that accompany some portfolios are a start, but they are not sufficient to account for the social, cultural, instructional and contextual factors that enable and constrain development; and finally, 4) portfolios, even current electronic portfolios, do not take full advantage of the networked, multimodal capacities of the communicative digital age. We will address each of these concerns as we share one current electronic portfolio – The Learning Record – that addresses a few of these concerns, and then overview a conceptual frame for 'deep assessment' (Penrod 2010) with which we will make our final recommendations for assessment systems.

Developed from an earlier version from the UK Centre for Language in Primary Education, Margaret Syverson and a large team of teachers developed an electronic portfolio, The Learning Record, and made it available online (learningrecord.org). As one of the first entries in The Learning Record, students are invited to interview a person outside of school who knows them and their development well. This type of data collection is a radical departure from traditional writing assessments, even the typical portfolio. Information from summaries of these interviews is used in concert with a series of observation notes, samples of written products with student reflections, and teachers' assessments of products, during a 'moderation process'. The moderation process is a session in which two teachers (other than the classroom teacher) read the learning record and decide on a level of achievement for the student. These sessions are open to the public, and stakeholders (i.e. students, teachers, parents, counsellors) are invited to observe the session. Moderation sessions are held to ensure equity and reliability of the classroom teacher's assessment. In this way, the assessment meets the demands of quality assessments, i.e. validity and reliability.

As noted, written products are assessed by teachers using rubrics. In contrast, the Learning Record assessments uses rubrics, but instead of using arbitrary, preset standards, the rubrics are developed locally with those involved in the creation of the writing tasks. The assessment of individual products in this way is situated in the communicative exchange. And as described, the quality of written products is just one component of The Learning Record, which Syverson (2006) explained comes from a holistic frame of reference:

> The conceptual work indicated by this model involves rethinking our whole approach to literacy education, requiring, in this case, close observation of naturally occurring activities, a regular practice of recording observations, summary interpretations of the meaning of the observations in terms of literacy development, and open sharing of those interpretations with the participants in the situation, who also contribute their perspectives.

Like Schultz's (2003) 'listening' stance and in conferencing, with an assessment such as The Learning Record, assessors take a receptive stance looking across varied data to see patterns of growth. Instead of single performances, which are neither predictive of future performances nor necessarily representative of current performance, we can begin to see patterns and habits of writing across the performances. So, we are looking at the qualities of the written products and the record of the processes that were observed in the creation of those products – not as an assessment in and of itself – but to see the patterns that cut across them. With a shift in stance from evaluating to understanding, development can begin to be identified. Though not capitalized in The Learning Record itself, the use of interviews, observations and document gathering (and local rubrics for those products), keeps possibilities open for the recording of multimodal compositions and networked digital communication.

'Deep assessment' and portfolios

Penrod (2010) presented steps to 'deep assessment', an assessment approach developed in response to the challenges of writing in the digital age. Her model includes five steps. We will overview and describe the ways each of these steps can further adapt electronic portfolios, like The Learning Record, to align with the theory of writing development we have presented.

Collect data from numerous sources

In addition to written products, in an electronic portfolio, or simply on a flash drive, multimedia projects, email exchanges, videos, letters, websites, and any number of drafts and ideas can be collected. The wider the variety the better, as we are looking to capture a student's range and repertoire. Often performance outside of school differs from that which is demonstrated in school. For an actual snapshot of development, documents, communication logs, IM chats, blogs and such from both in and out of school should be solicited.

Data regarding the contexts in which the child is developing should also be collected and taken into consideration to assess development. In a digital sense, the possibilities are quite broad: notes from teachers' study groups and professional development sessions, interviews with members in and out of school, school assessments and accreditation reports, writing samples of others who are communicating in the same space, surveys of stakeholder satisfaction, course materials and resources.

Develop an audit trail

Just as The Learning Record called for 'regular practice' in recording observations, Penrod (2010), too, argued for consistent procedures in data gathering, explaining that audit trails ensure validity of assessment procedure. Mobile digital devices that teachers could carry would increase the ease with which they could gather data – by taking pictures of products in process or recording sections of writing conferences – and ensure consistency in record keeping. Such devices could also be programmed with reminders and one-touch linking of data with student.

Conduct member checks

In member checks, teachers discuss the student's development with the student. In a networked digital community, member checks can become a standard component of daily interaction. Like The Learning Record, many electronic portfolios are just written pages in digital form, either in text boxes on a webpage or in wordprocessing documents on the computer. To fit in the digital age, portfolios need their own Web 2.0 revolution. With Portfolio 2.0, in addition to member checks, the whole community – students, teachers, parents and other stakeholders – could be in constant communication and exchange.

Develop an assessment team

Like the moderation sessions described above, Penrod (2010) suggests teams of assessors meet to assess work together. We would add that instead of working as a team to judge the quality of the written products, the group would work together to identify developmental patterns. This would mean that the group would do the work of 'deep viewing' described in the next step.

Apply deep viewing approach to the data

'Deep viewing' is an approach to the data that is less concerned with categorizing writing on a rubric or judging its qualities, and more interested in its several components, especially in light of its context to find patterns. Together the assessment team could identify aspects of each piece of data that have particular saliency. One piece of data, a lesson plan, for instance, might have been designed to help students read their pieces from a new perspective, and to do this, the teacher asked students to role play with a partner. This lesson could be coded 'rhetorical – audience' and 'disposition – collaboration' (because of the practice of working well

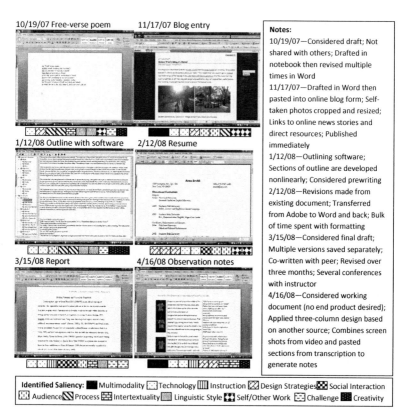

Figure 11.1 Uses of coded multiples to map writing development

with a partner). In deep viewing, the data could be sorted and rearranged to help highlight differing aspects of development. The group could also ask of the data the same questions we suggested teachers ask themselves while listening during a conference.

Harnessing the semiotic power of multimodal texts for portfolios

An electronic portfolio, even after sorting through in deep viewing, would still be a loaded digital file of information difficult to digest. Our last recommendation for assessment – the use of multiples – would make portfolios more comprehensible and comparable. In arguing for the benefits of multiples, Tufte (1997) used the example of medical patient files as one site of personal histories that could be more effectively used in practice if represented by multiples rather than as a collection of test results and notes. He provided an example of a series of one-inch squares of data (i.e.

chart, X-ray, notes) that summarized each medical interaction arranged in chronological order. In one glance, medical staff could see the numerous and varied tests conducted, as well as the patterns and confounding results across the patient's history. Such use of multiples, particularly digitized multiples from screen shots of the data gathered or thumbnails that are linked to the documents themselves, could be an approach to mapping the development of student writers that both shifts attention away from single product measures of writing assessment, as well as honing the portfolio approach (much like medical files) to a targeted mapping of qualities and attributes demonstrated in portfolio pieces. The thumbnails could be coded for each of the salient features of the data source that were identified in the deep viewing portion of the assessment, with notes regarding the rhetorical context, framing and compositional choices of the student. One example of how this could work is fashioned in Figure 11.1. The use of multiples to focus the portfolio approach has many possibilities for use in the classroom, as well as the possibility of clarifying assessment goals for larger groups of students.

12 Implications for Research and Policy

Introduction

We have suggested that there needs to be a new theory of writing development, and we have gone some way to proposing a new theory and model. In the previous chapter we have looked at some of the practical implications of such a new approach, including teaching and assessment issues. In this final chapter we turn to the implications for research and policy, including issues of curricular design.

Research

Multimodality and digitization provide two interrelated challenges for researchers on writing development. Let us repeat that the two share common ground: the advent of high speed and portable digital computing has meant that word, image and sound can be composed and 'read' in combination. However, multimodality and digitization are separate entities. Multimodality can operate, and has operated, in the pre-digital world; and similarly, digitization does not necessarily imply multimodality: it is possible to digitize a (seemingly) single mode like the written verbal code.

Multimodality and related issues

As far as multimodality goes, the principal questions for future research on writing development can be grouped under a number of headings. The first set of questions concerns matters outside the mode of writing itself: issues that we might characterize as to do with the politics or economics of writing. For example, it is often claimed that the image has replaced writing as the central mode of communication. This claim needs to be researched, because it is not always evident that it *is* the case that there has been a 'turn to the visual'. Writing seems as prevalent now as it was several decades ago; in fact, in has seemed to permeate more aspects of working life (regulations, health and safety guidance, audit culture) in an increasingly bureaucratic society. Even the very evident turn to electronic billing, the access to information systems through passwords and usernames, and the social networking sites use words as well as images. It may appear that the visual has become more prominent, but it does not mean that the written word is any less prominent or significant. As the economy of modes of communication shakes down, writing finds and renews/consolidates its place.

A second aspect of research that is related to multimodality is the rise in interest in framing theory as applied to writing. Andrews (2011) charts the key points in the history of framing theory since 1945, suggesting that framing and re-framing offer helpful ways of thinking about the language curriculum in schools and beyond. Essentially, communication is framed socially and also aesthetically and functionally (in print, in speech and more formally in art forms like theatre, sculpture and painting). Such framing and re-framing, especially when modes are changed ('transduced') and/or combined with other modes within certain frames, provide a fertile field for research. In fact, it is hard to conceive of writing research that does not take into account such framing and positioning in relation to other modes.

Third, writing itself is multimodal in that it has a visual dimension. It is not just a monomodal phenomenon. Scripts and printed type in all languages are visual: they have shape, form, character. Different fonts and type sizes are further variations on printed type (whether it appears printed on a page or 'in print' on a computer screen).

Fourth, and more obviously multimodally, writing sits alongside other modes in popular and other forms of communication. In fact, this is the most common incidence of writing in culture. The dynamics of the relations, the kinds of meanings that are conveyed, the relative prominence of the various modes, the aesthetics of the relationship – all these aspects of writing in a multimodal context are important areas for research.

Lest this catalogue of possibilities seem unduly list-like and scientific, here is an example of where new forms of research might be necessary. A child's writing development in the years from, say, 3 to 6, is a rich area for research. Indeed, it has been researched by Kress (1997), Andrews (1998; reprinted and revised in Andrews 2011: 109–34) and others, largely using a case study approach. All four of the suggested areas for research above can be included in such a study. Such studies are central to writing development research, because they set out the parameters and possibilities for research. They need to be complemented by larger scale studies, not only in pre-school and in the first years of schooling, but with developing writers at any stage of the lifecourse.

It goes without saying that any research that attempts to capture and analyse the visual (or aural) as well as the written form needs to finds a methodological approach and methods for representing such work. At the very least, in non-digital form, illustrations of examples of text and image must be included in theses and dissertations – in the main body of the text as well as in appendices.

The second set of questions is to do with the writing system itself. For the moment, let us take English as the language on which we are focussing. Gaining command of the core elements of the English writing system is a long and complex task. It requires understanding of the correspondence between sounds and alphabetic letters forms (the grapho-phonemic interface); learning the various ways in which spelling can be understood and practised, including morphological conventions and etymologies of root-words; widening experience of the semantics of words; skills in using dictionaries, spell-checkers and thesauri; artistry and knowledge in the rules of syntax and the combination of phrases, clauses and sentences in larger units of meaningful communication; deployment of register and tone to suit particular rhetorical needs; and a sense of the cohesive properties and elements of whole texts. This multi-levelled operation can take years, and understanding some aspects of the system, like judgements of spelling variations, can take a lifetime. Writing research often focusses on just one or two of the levels mentioned here (two are often needed because a higher level – say morphology – informs the level below – say phonology), whereas we wish to suggest that research needs to take into account most if not all of the levels in order to be able to describe the writing system adequately. When it comes to *development* of writers in using such a system, further issues of uneven development, tensions in the learning of a system, and actual longitudinal development in gaining increasing command of the system need to be taken into account. The lack of longitudinal studies in writing research is common knowledge; small-scale longitudinal studies at Masters or doctoral level (e.g. Bodger 2011) can play an important role in understanding how writing develops over time. The model of development for writers in the digital age that we proposed toward the end of Chapter 10 has implications for research, and suggests that more case studies are needed of individual writers' development so that new theory can be built.

The third set of questions moves beyond multimodality and the writing system of English itself into the area of writing in a range of languages. It is not the same to learn to write in Modern Standard Written Chinese or classical Arabic as it is in English. Writing systems may move from the top of the page to the bottom and operate on the principle of a box within a grid, as in Chinese; or move from right to left, as in Arabic. Furthermore, variations of written English – like American or Indian English – need to be addressed, as they do in other languages. The ideographic nature of the Chinese character has its roots in the visual representation of meaning, whereas the alphabet is based on phonetic principles. These fundamental differences in the writing system have implications for learning and for the pedagogies that are used to encourage and aid learning. In addition to research into the different systems that languages use, studies of bi- and multilingual writing development are needed. These will cover not only naturally occurring multilingualism, but also the learning of second languages in the formal schooling system – especially global languages such as English, Mandarin and Spanish.

Digital and related issues

The digitization of print has had a huge impact on the practices of writing. Many aspects of these changes have been researched, usually in small scale case studies and by practitioners and course designers. The results of these studies are almost inevitably positive, fired by enthusiasm for embracing new technologies around old practices (writing). A smaller number of studies suggests there is 'no difference' to the quality or length of writing; and hardly any such studies suggest there is a negative effect or that writing via digital means is a distraction.

Many studies are set up to compare and contrast writing by hand with writing via the keyboard – or, more rarely, writing via speech recognition technologies. We find this a false comparison, because writing by hand and writing via wordprocessors are two different means of making meaning on paper or on screens. They each have their own affordances. More productive is an approach which looks at a wider economy of writing practices in school and society.

Some of the issues that require further research, then, include how access to wordprocessing can influence writing development from an early age; whether the QWERTY keyboard in English, or other forms of keyboard arrangement in other languages, hinder or help writing development; what portable devices and their (verbal) textual interfaces mean for writing, especially for brief interchanges in writing like emails, Twitter messages, texts and form-filling. For longer texts, drafting and editing are commonplace stages in the writing process that can be researched in relation to digital versions of texts. For example, what are the practices of poets, short story writers, dramatists and novelists in moving through the stages of drafting: do they compose directly on to the screen, or at what point do they make the move from handwritten notes and drafts to a typewritten version? What differences does it make to their composing? Equally, in the commercial and 'real world' contexts and environments for writing – like the composition of a report or a prospectus – what are the practices in relation to digital composition? Is it the case, for example, that design issues are more to the fore from the start?

Digitization also has implications for research in the storage, archiving and accessing of writing. At first look, this issue may seem to have more to do with *reading* than writing, but on a closer look, there are implications for the writer/composer, and for the developing writer. We take as an example here academic writing at advanced levels, for publication. Universities are increasingly creating their own 'repositories' for the storage of works by their lecturers and professors: these are digital archives that allow access to 'final versions' of works. These final versions are either works that are in the public domain in finished form, like articles in journals that are more than two years old and thus slightly freer of copyright; or final versions of 'manuscripts' (the term is vestigial) that formed the basis for a submission to a publisher. Repositories are bound by copyright and other constraints, but they remain a useful point of access for students and others who wish to access material freely. The implications for research are considerable, however. First, readers will want to know what version of the work it is that they are accessing: is it a definitive 'final' version, or is it a final draft that has been adjusted somewhat as it moves to publication? The onus is on the writer to specify exactly what the nature of the draft is. To summarize, we are in a position where the versions of works could be in a number of different states and bound by a number of different rules on copyright. The temptation for writers is that they will update work, and that even the 'final' version in published (say, book) form will not represent the latest version of the work. To complicate the picture yet further, movements like Creative Commons, which has as its founding principle the idea that work should be freely accessible, have bypassed print publication altogether and relied on digital communication to make such work available. A writer who chooses to go down the Creative Commons pathway for a particular work, or for all their works, will 'release' compositions into the public domain at points where they feel they are ready, irrespective of editorial practices and conventions (unless these are carried out by the writer him- or herself).

What is clear about research into one aspect of the digitization of writing – the relationship between the development of new technologies and the development of writing – is that studies that work in a simple causal paradigm and that look at effect sizes cannot account for the complexity of writing processes and products. Andrews (2004) looks at a number of research studies in the period from 1990 to the early 2000s and concludes that when studies compared handwritten practices to wordprocessing, they almost always showed a positive effect for the latter in terms of quantity of writing, and less so for quality. However, most of these studies saw new technologies (digitization) as an intervention on an existing set of practices rather than a new technological innovation in its own right (and finding its place in an economy of practices alongside older technologies, like pen and paper). The questioning of the causal paradigm led to a new model for the relationship between literacy development and new technologies, set out in the Introduction to Andrews and Haythornthwaite (2007). The model suggests that the relationship between the two is not simply causal. Nor is it merely symbiotic (a relationship that encourages co-dependence and stasis). Rather, the relationship can best be described as a reciprocal co-evolutionary one. That is to say, as new information and communication technologies develop, so too does literacy change and develop. What is means to be literate in 1990 is not the same as what it means to be literate in 2010 or 2020; and advances in technologies may have residual effects on literacy (in our case, in the present book, writing) development. Equally, advances in compositional practice, drafting, editing, multimodal composition, collaborative writing and other forms of making meaning in words, may have a direct or residual effect on new technologies. If the latter idea in particular seems fanciful, we need to think about how Word, as a wordprocessing package, has continued to update its drafting and editing tools to reflect current writing practice and possibilities.

These reflections on digital and other issues in relation to writing development lead us on to a further area of writing development research: the question of methodologies and method.

Methodologies and methods

Conventional methodologies and methods continue to be possible in research in writing and writing development, largely because writing offers a tangible object for research: examples of writing by children, young people and adult learners. For the whole spectrum of methodologies, from ethnographic study to library-based studies; from single case studies to large scale surveys; and from comparative studies to comparisons between control groups and experimental groups – writing is grist to the mill, as well as to action research approaches. At the level of methods, there are few that cannot be used to investigate writing. Again, written products lend themselves to document analysis and categorization (and thus to theory-building); and writing processes lend themselves to discussion in focus groups, think-aloud protocols, interviews of various kinds, observation and self-report. What is lacking from conventional writing research is much on *development*. This is partly because time and resource are needed to track writing development, other than through single case studies or small scale cohort studies; and there are few if any archives of children's writing (this latter lacuna is being addressed in work at the Institute of Education, University of London).

Longitudinality is important in research design if writing development is to be addressed. Whether the design is pre-test and post-test; or taking snapshots of practice over time; or genuinely and fully tracing progress in writers over time – the longitudinal dimension needs careful planning. Perhaps the best models of longitudinal design are the Millennium Cohort studies, the most recent and large-scale of which in the UK is the Millennium Cohort Study (MCS), started at the Centre for Longitudinal Studies at the Institute of Education, London. The most recent results from the study (October 2010) suggest that in reading in the UK, white Caucasian children are losing their early lead over young ethnic minority children in reading. By the age of 7, ethnic minority children read English at least as well as white pupils. The best readers, on average, are Indian children who are significantly ahead of white pupils by the second year of primary school even though they had a poorer vocabulary at age 5. Other longitudinal cohort studies housed at the Centre include the 1958 National Child Development Study and the 1970 British Cohort Study. There is little, however, in any of the studies about writing development *per se*, despite a focus on cognitive development and other factors which may affect writing development.

Another major longitudinal study of language development is the Bristol Language Development Research Programme, led by Gordon Wells from its inception in 1972. The project focused largely on spoken interaction and to a certain extent on reading – but with little on writing development. See Wells (1985) for a rich account of the results of the study.

In fact, none of the large-scale longitudinal projects appear to focus on writing and writing development. The long-running Effective Pre-School and Primary Education project, also based at the Institute of Education, has little on writing development – again, in terms of literacy, it focusses on reading. There are exceptions, like Beard and Burrell's (2010) investigation of narrative writing in 9–11-year-olds, but this is a concurrent study of Year 5 and 6 pupils rather than a developmental study *per se*.

Given what has been already said in this chapter about multimodality and digitization of writing, what are the implications of these developments for research design, methodology and methods? At a simple level, new methods can be used that do not in any way alter the methodological approach to writing research. These include, for example, email interviewing. Whereas conventional interviewing by phone or in person is conducted in speech, and thus benefits from the affordances of speech, email interviewing is conducted in writing by email exchange. So, in practice, a set of questions may be sent in advance to an interviewee; or could be sent one by one. The interviewee replies in writing at a time of their own choosing. The asynchronous nature of the exchange gives space for reflection. One of the advantages of such exchanges in email is that there is no need for transcription from speech to writing: the data is already in written form.

More complex is when the writing itself, as the topic for research, is multimodal and/or digitized. At their simplest, research methods will want to capture the products and processes of writing via video, still photographs and other visual means. These can be stored in the appendices of theses and research reports, but it is increasingly more satisfactory and proper that they are integrated into the fabric of the report (article, thesis, book) itself. To take some examples: first, consider a piece of writing that has been worked on collaboratively, e.g. a wiki or blog. Issues of the development of such a work – of its temporality, its provisionality, its co-authorship, its authenticity – are all important for writing research to consider. Second, an example of a highly multimodal text like a page from a magazine or graphic novel or manga, will need consideration of its provenance, its design features and choices, its composition and its collaborative composition (if this is the case). *The Sage Handbook of Digital Dissertations and Theses* (Andrews et al. 2012) tries to address some of these problems and possibilities in advanced institution-based research.

Policy

Curriculum, standards

We are writing at a time of world recession where policy matters are ever more subject to financial constraints. The danger is that writing will again be squeezed to the margin by an overemphasis on reading measures. If we look at large-scale curriculum reform – for example in the UK and USA – the high stakes testing and accountability regimes that have been brought in to monitor and 'raise standards' have tended to make the curriculum assessment driven rather than developmentally driven. Even though the very inception of the National Curriculum in England and Wales was based upon a felt need for a clearer sense of *progression* from ages 5–16, such progression (as measured by the system) is only tenuously related to *development*.

There is a double-edged sword as far as the assessment of writing goes. Within a high-stakes testing regime, is it preferable to have writing remain on the edge of the testing radar and thus free teachers to help young writers develop (perhaps measured in coursework); or is it better to have writing come under the radar and for periodic (end of year or end of stage) tests, alongside reading? Although initially, reports of literacy progress in the USA under the No Child Left Behind initiative have concentrated on reading and mathematics scores, Sainsbury (2009) cites Hillocks (2002) who found that at around the time of the No Child Left Behind initiative, 37 states out of 50 included assessments of writing, though not all of these were high stakes' (Sainsbury 2009: 546). Since the mid-2000s, writing has been included in national testing programmes; as it has been in England since the start of the National Curriculum in the early 1990s. Problems in the validity of writing assessment tasks in both the USA and England are explored in Sainsbury (2009). Her chapter is recommended reading in terms of policy development in relation to the testing of writing within high-stakes accountability systems. As far as the present book is concerned, there are considerable implications for the teaching and development of writing, not least because testing regimes have backwash effects on what is taught and what is learnt.

Without rehearsing further the arguments against high-stakes testing and assessment-driven approaches to education, what are the constituent features of a curriculum that is genuinely interested in writing development?

Moving outside the USA and UK, work at the Institute of Education has focused on national curriculum and standards in collaboration with a Ministry of Education (Scott et al. 2010). As far as the development of writing is concerned, thought has been given to the standards and exemplification of such standards in a changing curriculum. From the outset, it should be said that writing is seen as reciprocally related to reading; that, nevertheless, it has its own heading, its own curriculum area; and that it is also joined by headings devoted to multimodality; knowledge about language and communication; language and communication dispositions; and speaking and listening. Writing (development) is thus embedded in a rich nexus of competences in the development of language and communication. Connections are made across these headings wherever possible so that the possibility of a 'silo' effect of seeing writing as a totally separate skill – or, on the other hand, of it being subsumed and lost under the canopy of reading – are minimized.

Without going into detail on the proposed standards, it is possible to indicate in broad terms the development that is expected in writing at key points in the education system: after three years of primary schooling, at the end of primary schooling, and after three years of middle of secondary schooling.

General principles

The focus on reading, writing, speaking and listening in any language curriculum is uncontroversial. However, it is important to establish that each of these four language skills is important in its own right, as well as being closely related to each other. All too often, reading gets preference over writing, and speaking over listening. In the present set of standards, each of the four language skills is given equal status; though speaking and listening are combined for the purposes of emphasizing the close connections between them.

At the same time, all four skills are related. Reading and writing are reciprocal, and a curriculum should ensure that such reciprocity is exploited in teaching and learning. Similarly, speaking and listening go together. From the perspective of the productive language skills, speaking and writing can be closely linked; just as reading and listening are both receptive skills (though they both require a good deal of active reading and active listening). It is also possible to exploit the connections between reading and speaking (as in reading out loud) and writing and listening (for example, attending to the process of writing in groups, or listening to each other's drafts).

After three years of primary schooling (age – about 8)

This stage of development aims to consolidate the progress made since the start of formal schooling, and also to recognize the advances made in cognitive development, self-awareness and the identification of different modes of communication. Young children at this stage are more aware of themselves and their position in families and in relation to the rest of the world. They begin to take an interest in the wider world and in moral issues that arise. Their awareness that thought and imagination operate internally, whereas much communication is social and external, is an important step forward in understanding the importance, function and range of communication. It is important to encourage writing as a means of communication. It is best linked to reading (so that they are seen as reciprocal), speech and other modes of communication (particularly the visual).

At the end of primary schooling (age – about 11)

The range of writing includes various forms of literary composition and sub-forms, such as haiku, rhymed and unrhymed verse and ballads in poetry; and autobiography and biography in narrative writing. Documentary writing will continue to expand, differentiating between information-writing and argument-writing. Examples of writing at this stage include the composition of biographies of people they admire, as well as autobiographical writing that draws upon memory and imaginative re-creation. The skills of drafting and editing come more to the fore as writing is tested out with audiences (peers, teachers and others) before completion.

After three years of secondary schooling (age – about 14)

Students will explore more specialized texts during this phase, and use writing to reflect more deeply on matters that arise from social experience and from their reading of literary and documentary texts. During this phase, there is the opportunity to embrace the written world of discourse as manifested in all aspects of society. For example, students should be exposed to the role writing plays in the creation of scripts for performance on TV, radio, film and in the theatre, as well as in public forums. They should be taught advanced word-processing skills in order to improve their capacities as writers of a wide range of texts.

None of these proposals is controversial, but as a collection they do emphasize the social construction of capability and competence in writing development, as well as the connectedness of writing to other modes. They are also broad enough to encompass a wide range of written genres (there is more detail in the full document) and to ensure that documentary types of writing (sometimes rather negatively called 'non-fiction') stand alongside fictive and autobiographical writing. Furthermore, although they are intended for the development of writing in a particular language (not English, as it happens), the implications are that they are transferable to other languages in terms of writing.

The notion of linear *development*, however, that is implicit in such curricular documents, must bear in mind what we suggested at the end of Chapter 10: that development is recursive, unpredictable, multidimensional and organic. To impose a strict sense or expectation of progression upon it, as curriculum documents and assessment regimes do, is unrealistic and creates tensions between what actually develops and what is assumed to progress.

Professional development

Sainsbury (2009) makes an important point towards the end of her chapter on developing writing in a high-stakes environment. She suggests that one of the implications of better testing (assuming it can be designed) is that it is less likely 'that good teaching will be impeded by the testing regime. Alongside this, it is essential to strengthen teachers' capacity to teach writing well and their confidence in their own ability to understand what this means when confronted with high-stakes assessment. Professional development is key in this' (p. 557).

Andrews (2008c) puts the case for a national writing project for the UK, based on the work of the National Writing Project in the USA since 1974. Similar cases have been put in New Zealand, where initial developments have occurred, and South Africa. The National Writing Project in the USA was set up in the early 1970s in California in response to concerns about the state of writing pedagogy – concerns that have not gone away. The growth of this largely grassroots movement in the USA in the last quarter of the twentieth century was remarkable, with more than two hundred centres being established and a national network formed, creating one of the most sustained and successful professional development projects for teachers worldwide. With the advent of No Child Left Behind and in-creasing federal interest with the USA, came a demand from the National Writing Project to show how its professional development of teachers im-pacted on children's development in writing. A series of independent and internal evaluation studies has subsequently proved the efficacy of the National Writing Project approach for writing standards across the USA.

Essentially, the National Writing Project approach consists of a num-ber of key elements: in order to teach writing, teachers must become writers themselves; they discover through their own writing the processes and pedagogical moves that are necessary in order to learn to write well. Structurally, as teachers develop themselves as writers, they help other teachers to write through peer review and support. Those teachers who wish to take on training roles at a local, state or national level do so by researching their own practice, running courses, acting as mentors to beginning teachers, and generally taking more responsibility within the specific professional development system. They have found that in-creased professional commitment and enjoyment of the subject and of their career have resulted.

The best attempts to re-make such a system in the UK have come, again, from the grassroots level. In 2009/10, Simon Wrigley and Jeni Smith, from Buckinghamshire County Council and the University of East Anglia respectively, set up a Teachers as Writers group, crossing primary and secondary school boundaries, which has been successful in building confidence, extending expertise and discussing pedagogical advances that can improve the learning of writing for students. There have also been initiatives from the Open University, National Association for Writers in Education, the Arts Council and others to establish a national network for the development of writing for teachers. Other initiatives have bub-bled up too, usually funded by small amounts of money and from the commitment of headteachers.

Another take on policy development pans out more widely from a fo-cus on writing to the context in which English is seen and supported as a school and university subject. Writing tends to be seen as the province of English teaching, even though it is used in most subjects across the cur-riculum and as a means of mediation and assessment in most disciplines at higher education levels. As suggested earlier in the present book, 'writing' is best seen from this wider perspective as 'composition' because it may include other modes and because of its collage-like putting together of others' voices into a coherent and well-argued or well-told work. The more one sees development in English as a lifelong course, at least from pre-school to university or college level, but preferably beyond those parameters, the more writing and composition are seen as developing over a long period of time. One implication of this perspective is to see writing development as socially as well as institutionally situated, and to acknowledge the influences and framings that shape one's own development as a writer.

Conclusion – and the way forward

Writing development, we have argued, is in need of renewed focus in curricula around the world. The problems in the writing standards of young people may be to do with the difficulty of composing as a generative activity; they may be to do with inappropriate assessment regimes and measures; they may be to do with lack of confidence on the part of writing teachers; and/or they may be to do with pedagogies that need improving. Whatever the problems are, one key element needs further development so that discussions about writing development can progress: the building of a theory and model for the digital and multimodal age.

We have suggested that such a theory and model must build on existing sociocognitive theories of development, adding to existing notions of transformation. They must also take into account that learning is an effect of communities – families, schools, classrooms, but also street communities, clubs and other social groupings, and e-communities. The interfaces between these various communities ('transliteracies') are also crucial to learning as people of any age navigate their ways through and across the communities every day of their lives. At the same time, models of writing development that are informed by these theories must embrace both the processes and the products of composition. Such models must be fit-for-purpose for the twenty-first century, which means being up to speed on the multimodal and digital dimensions of writing as well as the integration of writing into the curriculum – not only in relation to speaking, listening and reading, but also with regard to knowledge about language, dispositions towards writing, and the wider functions and uses of writing across the curriculum. To put it succinctly, learning to write involves more than a command of a system in any particular language; it involves the place of writing in a wider sociopolitical and rhetorical environment.

Future research studies in the field will embrace a wide range of topics, methodologies and methods. We are committed to the idea that as writing changes, so too methodologies and methods for researching writing development will change. We see writing in a reciprocal co-evolutionary relationship to new technologies: a relationship that will create new affordances, new economies for writing within an overall fabric of communication. One of the most pressing research needs is to develop ways in which we can be aware of the limitations as well as the possibilities of writing.

In policy terms, there can be nothing as important as designing ways in which communication plays a role in the learning of young people. If the social is prior, and social interaction is a prime way in which the business of the world progresses, then writing plays a large part in that repertoire of communicative skills and practices. There is no sense, from our point of view, that writing is going to fade in significance, even though other modes may come into sharper focus or prominence. Rather, we see writing as taking its place as a flexible, powerful mode of communication alongside other modes – made more powerful by interaction alongside those other modes rather than less so. In global terms, the emergence of three world languages – Mandarin, English, Spanish – in the early part of the century, makes it all the more important to understand writing systems in different languages, and to preserve other languages' writing systems – especially those that are in danger of disappearing.

Finally, we sense the importance of the written word in whichever medium it is presented: book, e-book, film, magazine, newspaper, website. Writing takes on much of its power through its close association with speech. The fluidity of the spoken/written modes, their ability to capture concrete particularities as well as degrees of abstraction; their ubiquity; their adaptability and capacity to renew themselves as new perceptions and concepts emerge; and their relative lightness in electronic terms makes them an essential part of communication. Such fluidity and adaptability is as true in tagging, in keyword searching and in other ways of navigating through information systems as it is in day-to-day communication.

It is therefore likely that a better understanding of writing development will help us in developing better writers – through theory, modelling, research and the application of research in policy and practice. We are conscious that the environments for writing may well be different in ten or twenty years' time; but we are fairly confident that writing will be a tool by which we create and also make sense of the changing environments for communication. As teachers, writers and researchers, we need to keep up to speed by observing the evolutionary nature of writing in our own and other languages.

Notes

Chapter 1   The Problem with Writing

1   This does not mean to say there is not a problem in reading performance, which has fallen behind writing performance at Key Stage 3
in the last three years.

2   Only about half of level 5 pupils go on to a C at GCSE; level 6 is more
likely to secure such a grade at GCSE.

3   See the introduction to Andrews and Haythornthwaite (2007) for an
explication of the notion of reciprocal co-evolution between new
technologies and literacy/learning, as opposed to any notion of 'impact' of one on the other.

4   *Expression* and *articulation* are part and parcel of the current curriculum but both need to be re-emphasized; *framing* derives from sociological and discourse theory (see, for example, Tannen 1993) as a
way of making sense of the demands of meaning-making at text level;
shaping derives from Britton's notion of 'shaping at the point of utterance' (Britton 1980), i.e. giving credit to the fact that much oral
and written communication is not pre-planned, but is shaped as it
happens.

5   According to Hemingway, 'prose is architecture, not interior decoration.' To raise standards of writing, we need to spend more time on
the architecture.

6   See DfEE 2001a, c; 2002a, b and c; and DfES 2003b, for example.

7   The Ofsted Annual Report for 2005/06 states 'In English [imaginative
and enjoyable learning] was achieved through a range of teaching
styles...For some pupils, however, the experience of English had
become narrower in certain years as teachers focussed on tests and
examinations; this affected pupils' achievements in speaking and listening in particular' (2006: 57).

8   The findings of this report are mirrored in a report by the US-based
Alliance for Excellent Education – see Graham and Perin (2006) –
which, based on a meta-analysis of research studies, concludes there
are 11 strategies for improving writing in middle and high schools,
including writing strategies, summarizing, collaborative writing, specific product goals (audiences), wordprocessing, sentence combining

(cf. grammar review by Andrews et al. 2006a), pre-writing (planning), inquiry activities (research) and a process writing approach.

9 'In less effective lessons, teachers often used recommended structures and approaches too mechanistically, with too much emphasis on content rather than the development of conceptual understanding' (Ofsted 2006: 58). One could add after 'content,' *and/or form.*

10 The list is based on anecdotal accounts from teachers, Ofsted reports and document analysis.

11 The draft orders from QCA define creativity as 'using imagination to create settings, moods and characters and convey themes, ideas and arguments; drawing on a rich experience of language and litera-ture to make fresh connections between ideas, experiences, texts and words; using inventive approaches to making meaning, playing with language and using it to make new effects.' This definition confines itself largely to creativity in language; it could add that creativity con-tributes to problem-solving via the projections of scenarios, and that the generation of 'fictional worlds' (Pavel 1986) can apply to both fictional and non-fictional settings.

12 See also previous materials and resources from the strategies that have been influential; and, separately, QCA (1999).

Chapter 2 Thinking About a New Model for the Digital Age

1 Another excellent review of research regarding the in and out of school literacy conundrum is Hull and Schultz (2001, 2002). In this review (2001), they remind us that writing – the process and product – is a literacy act, meaning it is part of a larger way of acting with words. They encourage us to take steps toward:
  1. Decoupling the effects of literacy from the effects of schooling;
  2. Developing the notion of literacy as multiple;
  3. Accounting for school failure and out-of-school success;
  4. Identifying additional [non-school] support mechanisms for children, youth, and adults;
  5. Pushing our notions of learning and development.

Chapter 4 Product-Related Models

1 Britton et al. (1976) noted: 'We are ... familiar with the very bad writ-ing sometimes produced by very experienced and learned writers – bad, that is, when judged for its intelligibility or its consideration of

the reader' (p. 19). Thus, the idea that a more experienced writer consistently produced higher quality products would be faulty.

2 Each of the models generated in the Crediton Project had designated starting and stopping points. However, the researchers noted that: 'There is no "end product": maturity is not a state which is finally attained to: one does not arrive, one is continually arriving' (Wilkinson et al. 1980: 223). This is a note, however, and the positioning of maturity as a target rather than a state is not modelled in the cognitive, stylistic, affective or moral developmental schemes.

Chapter 6   The Question of Writing Development

1 A common misconception and gross generalization of these findings are the kind of polarized implications that characterize research around sex/gender: males write violence and females do not. Newkirk (2002) raised the issue that females do indeed write violence, but that their fascination with horror is often overshadowed by the wider variety of violence written by male writers.

Chapter 10   A New Theory and Model of Writing Development: the Digital and Multimodal Age

1 Mandlebrot, who coined the phrase 'fractal' to describe the patterns found in ecological systems, was a prominent player in making complexity a legitimate study in the sciences. In true nonlinear fashion, he is said to have explained his achievements as: 'If you take the beginning and the end, I have had a conventional career, but it was not a straight line between the beginning and the end. It was a very crooked line.'

Bibliography

Alexander, R. (2006) *Towards Dialogic Teaching*, 3rd edn. Thirsk: Dialogos.

Anderson, C. (2000) *How's it Going? A Practical Guide to Conferring with Student Writers*. Portsmouth, NH: Heinemann.

Andrews, R. (1992) *The Problem with Poetry*. Milton Keynes: Open University Press.

Andrews, R. (1998) The base of a small iceberg: mark-making in the work of a four year old, in C. Woods (ed.) *Image Text Persuasion*. Adelaide: University of South Australia, pp. 5–24.

Andrews, R. (ed.) (2004) *The Impact of ICT on Literacy Education*. London: RoutledgeFalmer.

Andrews, R. (2008a) Shifting writing practice: focusing on the productive skills to improve quality and standards, in *Getting Going: generating, shaping and developing ideas in writing*. London: Department for Children Schools and Families, pp. 4–21. Available via www.teachernet.gov.uk/publications

Andrews, R. (2008b) Ten years of strategies, *Changing English*, 15(1): 77–85.

Andrews, R. (2008c) *The Case for a National Writing Project for Teachers*. Reading: Centre for British Teachers (CfBT) Educational Trust.

Andrews, R. (2011) *Re-framing Literacy: Teaching and Learning English and the Language Arts*. New York: Routledge.

Andrews, R. and Haythornthwaite, C. (eds) (2007) *The Sage Handbook of E-learning Research*. London: Sage.

Andrews, R. and Noble, J. (1982) *From Rough to Best*. London: Ward Lock Educational.

Andrews, R., Borg, E., Boyd Davis, S., Domingo, M. and England, J. (eds) (2012) *The Sage Handbook of Digital Dissertations and Theses*. London: Sage.

Andrews, R., Torgerson, C. and Beverton, S. et al. (2006a) The effect of grammar teaching on writing development, *British Educational Research Journal*, 32(1): 39–55.

Andrews, R., Torgerson, C., Low, G., McGuinn, N. and Robinson, A. (2006b) *Teaching Argumentative Non-Fiction Writing to 7–14 year olds: a systematic review of the evidence of successful practice*. Report in *Research Evidence in Education Library*. London: EPPI-Centre, Social Science Research Unit, Institute of Education, University of London. http://eppi.ioe.ac.uk/reel

Applebee, A. (1984) *Contexts for Learning to Write: Studies of Secondary School Instruction*. New Jersey: Ablex Publishing Corporation.

Applebee, A. (2000) *Alternative Models of Writing Development*. http://cela.albany.edu/publication/article/writing.htm (accessed 24 September 2010).

Arnold, R. (1980) *Writing Development: Magic in the Brain*. Buckingham: Open University Press.

Bazerman, C. (1988) *Shaping Written Knowledge: The Genre and Activity of the Experimental Article in Science*. Madison, WI: University of Wisconsin Press.

Beard, R. and Burrell, A. (2010) Investigating narrative writing by 9–11 year olds, *Journal of Research in Reading*, 33(1): 77–93.

Beard, R., Myhill, D., Riley, J. and Nystrand, M. (eds) (2009) *The Sage Handbook of Writing Development*. London: Sage.

Bereiter, C. and Scardamalia, M. (1987) *The Psychology of Written Composition*. Hillsdale, NJ: Lawrence Erlbaum Associates.

Bereiter, C. (1980) Development in writing, in L. Gregg and E. Steinberg (eds) *Cognitive Processes in Writing*. New Jersey: Lawrence Erlbaum Associates Inc., pp. 73–96.

Black, R. (2009) Online fan fiction, global identities, and imagination, *Research in the Teaching of English*, 43: 397–425.

Bodger, F. (2011) The nature of syntactic and textual transformations in the writing of 9–11 year olds: a longitudinal study. Unpublished PhD thesis: Institute of Education, University of London.

Boscolo, P. (2008) Writing in primary school, in C. Bazerman (ed.) *Handbook of Research on Writing*. New York: Lawrence Erlbaum Associates.

Breuch, L. (2003) Post-process 'pedagogy': a philosophical exercise, in V. Villanueva (ed.) *Cross-talk in Comp Theory*. Urbana, IL: National Council of Teachers of English, pp. 97–126.

Britton, J. (1980) Shaping at the point of utterance, in A. Freedman and I. Pringle (eds) *Reinventing the Rhetorical Tradition*. Las Vegas: Long and Silverman.

Britton, J. (ed.) (1967) *Talking and Writing: A Handbook for English Teachers*. London: Methuen.

Britton, J., Burgess, T., Martin, N., McLeod, A. and Rosen, H. (1976) *The Development of Writing Abilities (11–18)*. London: Schools Council Publication.

Calkins, L. (1983) *Lesson from a Child: On the Teaching and Learning of Writing*. Portsmouth, NH: Heinemann.

Calkins, L. (1994) *The Art of Teaching Writing*. Exeter, NH: Heinemann.

Cameron, D. (2002) Schooling spoken language: beyond 'communication', *New Perspectives on Spoken English in the Classroom: Conference Papers*. London: QCA.

Cazden, C.B. (1983) Adult assistance to language development: scaffolds, models, and direct instruction, in R.P. Parker and F.A. Davis (eds) *Developing literacy: Young Children's Use of Language*, 3–17. Newark, DE: International Reading Association.

Cheeseman Day, J., Janus, A. and Davis, J. (2005) *Computer and Internet Use in the United States: 2003*. U.S. Census Bureau. http://www.census .gov/prod/2005pubs/p23-208.pdf (accessed 1 November 2010).

Christie, F. (2002) *Classroom Discourse Analysis: A Functional Perspective*. London: Continuum.

Clay, M. and Cazden, C. (1990) A Vygotskian interpretation of reading recovery, in L.C. Moll (ed.) *Vygotsky and Education: Instructional Implications and Applications of Socio-historical Psychology*. New York: Cambridge University Press, pp. 206–22.

Cochran-Smith, M. (1991) Word processing and writing in elementary classrooms: a critical review of related literature, *Review of Educational Research*, 61(1): 107–55.

Coiro, J. and Dobler, E. (2007) Exploring the online reading comprehension strategies used by sixth-grade skilled readers to search for and locate information on the internet, *Reading Research Quarterly*, 42(2): 214–57.

Common Core State Standards Initiative (2010) *The Standards*. www .corestandards.org (accessed 24 September 2010).

Connors, R. (2000) The erasure of the sentence, *College Composition and Communciation*, 52(1): 96–128.

Cormode, G. and Krishnamurthy, B. (2008) Key differences between Web 1.0 and Web 2.0, *First Monday*, 13(6). www.uic.edu/htbin/cgiwrap/ bin/ojs/index.php/fm/article/view/2125/1972 (accessed 9 October 2010).

Couture, B. (1999) Modeling and emulating: rethinking agency in the writing process, in T. Kent (ed.) *Post-process Theory: Beyond the Writing-process Paradigm* Illinois: Southern Illinois University, pp. 30–48.

Croxall, B. (2008) *Timelines*. http://briancroxall.net/TimelineTutorial/ TimelineTutorial.html (accessed 1 November 2010).

Czerniewska, P. (1992) *Learning about Writing: The Early Years*. Oxford: Blackwell.

De Saussure, F. (1916/1977) *Course in General Linguistics*. Glasgow: Fontana/Collins.

Dean, D. (2006) *Strategic Writing: The Writing Process and Beyond in the Secondary English Classroom*. Urbana, IL: National Council of Teachers of English.

DeVoss, D., Eidman-Aadahl, E. and Hick, T. (2010) *Because Digital Writing Matters: Improving Student Writing in Online and Multimedia Environments*. San Francisco, CA: Jossey-Bass.

DfEE (1998) *The National Literacy Strategy: Framework for Teaching*. London: Department for Education and Employment Publications.

DfEE (2001a) *A Framework for Teaching English: Years 7, 8 and 9*. London: Department for Education and Employment.

DfEE (2001b) *English Department Training 2001*. London: Department for Education and Employment.

DfEE (2001c) *Year 7 Speaking and Listening Bank*. London: Department for Education and Employment.

DfEE (2002a) *English Department Training Year 7 2002/03*. London: Department for Education and Employment.

DfEE (2002b) *English Department Training Year 8 2002/03*. London: Department for Education and Employment.

DfEE (2002c) *Key Objectives Banks (for Years 7, 8 and 9)*. London: Department for Education and Employment.

DfEE/DCMS (1999) *All Our Futures: Creativity, Culture and Education*, Report of the National Advisory Committee on Creative and Cultural Education. London: Department for Education and Employment/Department for Culture, Media and Sport.

DfES (2003a) *Excellence and Enjoyment - A Strategy for Primary Schools*. London: Department for Education and Science.

DfES (2003b) *Drama Objectives Bank*. London: Department for Education and Science.

DfES (2007) *Teaching Speaking and Listening* (DVD). London: Department for Education and Science.

Dixon, J. (1967) *Growth through English*. Oxford: Oxford University Press for the National Association for the Teaching of English.

Dixon, J. (2010) 'Unfinished business?', personal communication, July 2010.

Domingo, M. (2011a) Multi-sensory design: circulating pliable texts in digital communities, in R. Andrews, E. Borg, D. Boyd, M. Domingo, and J. England (eds) (forthcoming) *Handbook of Digital Dissertations and Theses*. London and Thousand Oaks, CA: Sage.

Domingo, M. (2011b) Migratory practices in e-learning and e-communities research, in R. Andrews and C. Haythornwaite (eds) *E-Learning: Theory and Practice*. London and Thousand Oaks, CA: Sage.

Dornan, R., Rosen, L. and Wilson, M. (2003) *Within and Beyond the Writing Process in the Secondary English Classroom*. New York: Pearson Education Group.

Durkin, D. (1978) What classroom observations reveal about reading comprehension instruction, *Reading Research Quarterly*, 14(4): 481–533.

Dyson, A.H. (1989) *Multiple Worlds of Child Writers: Friends Learning to Write*. New York: Teachers College Press.

Dyson, A.H. (1995) Writing children: reinventing the development of childhood literacy, *Written Communication*, 72(1): 4–46.

Dyson, A.H. (1997) *Writing Superheroes: Contemporary Childhood, Popular Culture, and Classroom Literacy*. New York: Teachers College Press.

Dyson, A.H. (2007) School literacy and the development of a child culture: written remnants of the 'gusto of life', in D. Thiessen and A. Cook-Sather (eds) *International Handbook of Student Experiences in Elementary and Secondary School*. Dordrecht, The Netherlands: Kluwer.

Ede, L. (1994) Reading the writing process, in L. Tobin and T. Newkirk (eds) *Taking Stock: The Writing Process Movement in the 90s*. Portsmouth: Boynton, pp. 31–43.

Edwards, P. (2010) Reconceptualizing literacy, *Reading Today*, 27(6): 22.

Elbow, P. (1973) *Writing without Teachers*. London: Oxford University Press.

Emig, J. (1971) *The Composing Processes of Twelfth Graders*. Urbana, IL: National Council of Teachers of English.

Engeström, Y., Engeström, R. and Vähäaho, T. (1999) When the center does not hold: the importance of knotworking, in S. Chaiklin, M. Hedegaard and U.J. Jensen (eds) *Activity Theory and Social Practice*. Aarhus: Aarhus University Press.

Fairclough, N. (2001) *Language and Power*. London: Pearson Education Limited.

Fisher, W. (1989) *Human Communication as Narration*. Columbia, SC: University of South Carolina Press.

Fitzgerald, J. and Shanahan, T. (2000) Reading and writing relations and their development, *Educational Psychologist*, 35: 39–50.

Flower, L. and Hayes, J. (1981) A cognitive process theory of writing, *College Composition and Communication*, 32(4): 365–87.

Flower, L., Hayes, J., Carey, L., Schriver, K. and Stratman, J. (1986) Detection, diagnosis and the strategies of revision, *College Composition and Communication*, 37(1): 16–55.

Forster, E.M. (1927/1976) *Aspect of the Novel* (ed. O. Stallybrass). Harmondsworth: Penguin.

Fraiberg, S. (2010) Composition 2.0: toward a multilingual and multimodal framework, *College Composition and Communication*, 62(1): 100–26.

Freedman, A. and Medway, P. (eds) (1994) *Genre and the New Rhetoric*. Abingdon: Taylor and Francis.

Gleick, J. (1987) *Chaos: Making a New Science*. New York: Penguin Books.

Graham, S. and Perin, D. (2006) *Writing Next: Effective Strategies to Improve Writing of Adolescents in Middle and High Schools*. Washington, DC: Alliance for Excellent Education.

Graves, D. (1983) *Writing: Children and Teachers at Work*. Porstmouth, NH: Heinemann.

Guskey, T.R. (1986) Staff development and the process of teacher change, *Educational Researcher*, 15(5): 5–12.

Guzzetti, B. and Gamboa, M. (2004) Zines for social justices: adolescent girls writing on their own, *Reading Research Quarterly*, 39(4): 408–36.

Haas, C. (1989) Does the medium make a difference? Two studies of writing with pen and paper and with computers, *Human-Computer Interactive*, 4: 149–69.

Hall, N. and Robinson, A. (2003) *Exploring Writing and Play in the Early Years*. London: David Fulton.

Hall, N., Larson, J. and Marsh, J. (eds) (2003) *Handbook of Early Childhood Literacy*. London: Sage.

Hansen, D.T. (2010) Cosmopolitanism and education: a view from the ground, *Teachers College Record*, 112(1): 1–30.

Hardy, B. (1977) *The Cool Web: The Pattern of Children's Reading*. London: The Bodley Head.

Harris, R. (2007) *The Ghost*. London: Hutchinson.

Harwayne, S. (2001) *Writing through Childhood: Rethinking Process and Product*. Portsmouth, NH: Heinemann.

Hayes, J. and Flower, L. (1980) Identifying the organization of writing processes, in L. Gregg and E. Steinberg (eds) *Cognitive Processes in Writing*. New Jersey: Lawrence Erlbaum Associates, Inc., pp. 3–30.

Heath, S.B. (1983) *Ways with Words*. Cambridge: Cambridge University Press.

Hildreth, G. (1936) Developmental sequences in name writing, *Child Development*, 7: 291–303.

Hillocks, G. (1986) *Research on Written Composition: New Directions for Teaching*. Urbana, IL: National Conference on Research in Englsh/ERIC Clearinghouse on Reading and Communication Skills.

Hillocks, G. (2002) *The Testing Trap: How State Writing Assessments Control Learning* (Language and Literacy series). New York: Teachers College Press.

Honeycutt, R. and Pritchard, R. (2005) Using structured writing workshop to help good readers who are poor writers, in G. Rijlaarrsdan, H. van den Bergh and M. Couzijin (eds) *Studies in Writing: Effective Teaching and Learning of Writing*, 2nd edn. Amsterdam: Kluwer, pp. 141–50.

Horrigan, J. (2005) *Broadband Adoption in the United States: Growing but slowing*. www.pewinternet.org/Reports/2005/Broadband-Adoption-in-the-United-States-Growing-but-Slowing.aspx (accessed 1 November 2010).

Horrigan, J. (2008) *Home Broadband*. www.pewinternet.org/Reports/2008/Home-Broadband-2008.aspx (accessed 1 November 2010).

Hull, G. and Schultz, K. (2001) Literacy and learning out of school: a review of theory and research, *Review of Educational Research*, 71: 575–611.

Hull, G. and Schultz, K. (2002) 'Connecting schools with out-of-school worlds: insights from recent research on literacy in non-school settings', in G. Hull and K. Schultz (2002) *School's Out: Bridging Out-of-school Literacies with Classroom Practice*. New York: Teachers College Press, pp. 32–57.

Hull, G. and Stornaiuolo, A. (2010) Literate arts in a global world: reframing social networking as cosmopolitan practice, *Journal of Adolescent & Adult Literacy*, 54(2): 85–97.

Hull, G., Stornaiuolo, A. and Sahni, U. (2010) Cultural citizenship and cosmopolitan practice: global youth communicate online, *English Education*, 42(4): 331–67.

Hunt, K. (1965) *Grammatical Structures Written at Three Grade Levels. NCTE Research Report No. 3*. Champaign, IL: NCTE.

Hunt, K.W. (1970) *Syntactic Maturity in Schoolchildren and Adults*. Chicago: University of Chicago Press for the Society for Research in Child Development.

Illeris, K. (2007) *How We Learn: Learning and Non-learning in School and Beyond*. Abingdon: Routledge.

Illeris, K. (ed.) (2009) *Contemporary Theories of Learning: Learning Theorists . . . in Their Own Words*. Abingdon: Routledge.

Ings, R. (2010) *Writing is Primary: Action Research on the Teaching of Writing in Primary Schools*. London: Esmée Fairbairn Foundation.

International Telecommunicaiton Union (2010) *Information and Communication Technology (ICT) Statistics*. www.itu.int/ITU-D/ict/ (accessed 1 November 2010).

Jacobs, G. (2008) We learn what we do: developing a repertoire of writing practices in an instant messaging world, *Journal of Adolescent and Adult Literacy*, 52(3): 203–11.

Jakobson, R. and Halle, M. (1956/2002) *Fundamentals of Language*. Berlin: Mouton de Gruyter.

Jeffery, J. (2009) Constructs of writing proficiency in US state and national writing assessments: exploring variability, *Assessing Writing*, 14(1): 3–24.

Jeffery, J. (2010) Voice, genre and intentionality: an integrated methods study of voice criteria in the evaluation of secondary students' writing. PhD dissertation, New York University. Retrieved from Dissertations & Theses: Full Text. (Publication No. AAT 3426956).

Jocson, K. (2006) Bob Dylan and Hip Hop: intersecting literacy practices in youth poetry communities, *Written Communication*, 23: 231–59.

Kell, C. (2009) Literacy practices, texts and meaning making across time and space, in M. Baynham and M. Prinsloo (eds) *The Future of Literacy Studies*. London: Palgrave Macmillan.

Kirkland, D. (2008) Shaping the digital pen: media literacy, youth culture, and MySpace, *Youth Media Reporter*, 2(4): 188–200.

Kirkland, D. (2009) Researching and teaching English in the digital dimension, *Research in the Teaching of English*, 44(1): 8–22.

Kohlberg, L. (1969) Stage and sequence: the cognitive-developmental approach to socialization, in D.A. Goslin (ed.) *Handbook of Socialization Theory and Research*. Chicago, IL: Rand McNally, pp. 347–480.

Kress, G. (1995) *Writing the Future: English and the Making of a Culture of Innovation*. Sheffield: National Association for the Teaching of English.

Kress, G. (1997) *Before Writing: Rethinking the Paths to Literacy*. London: Routledge.

Kress, G. (2003) *Literacy in the New Media Age*. London: Routledge.

Kress, G. (2010) *Multimodality: A Social Semiotic Theory of Contemporary Communication*. Abingdon: Routledge.

Kress, G. and Bezemer, J. (2009) Writing in a multimodal world of representation, in R. Beard et al. (eds) (2009) *The Sage Handbook of Writing Development*. London: Sage, pp. 167–81.

Kress, G. and van Leeuwen, T. (2001) *Multimodal Discourse: The Modes and Media of Contemporary Communication*. London: Arnold.

Kress, G. and van Leeuwen, T. (1996) *Reading Images: The Grammar of Visual Design*. London: Routledge.

Lakoff, G. and Johnson, M. (1980) *Metaphors We Live By*. Chicago: Chicago University Press.

Lam, A.S.L. (2005) *Language Education in China: Policy and Experience from 1949*. Hong Kong: Hong Kong University Press.

Langer, A. and Applebee, A. (1986) Reading and writing instruction: toward a theory of teaching and learning, *Review of Research in Education*, 13: 171–94.

Leander, K.M. and Lovvorn, J.F. (2006) Literacy networks: following the circulation of texts and identities in the schooling and on-line gaming of one youth, *Cognition & Instruction*, 24(3): 291–340.

Lee, J. and Lok, B. (2010) A tale of two Special Administrative Regions (SARs) of China: an overview of English language teaching developments in Hong Kong and Macao, in D. Wyse, R. Andrews and J. Hoffman (eds) *The Routledge International Handbook of English, Language and Literacy Teaching*. Abingdon: Routledge, pp. 448–60.

Leith, P. (2006) Taste of the country, In *Britain's 50 Best Walks, The Guardian* supplement, 20.05.06.

Lenhart, A., Arafeh, S., Smith, A. and Macgill, A. (2008) *Writing, Technology and Teens.* www.pewinternet.org/Reports/2008/Writing-Technology-and-Teens.aspx (accessed 1 November 2010).

Lenhart, A., Hitlin, P. and Madden, M. (2005) *Teens and Technology.* www.pewinternet.org/Reports/2005/Teens-and-Technology.aspx (accessed 1 November 2010).

Lesko, N. (2000) *Masculinities at School.* London: Sage.

Loban, W. (1976) *Language Development: Kindergarten through Grade Twelve.* NCTE committee on research report no. 18. Washington, DC: Office of Education (DHEW) Cooperative Research Program.

Locke, T. (ed.) (2010) *Beyond the Grammar Wars: A Resource for Teachers and Students on Developing Language Knowledge in the English/Literacy Classroom.* New York: Routledge.

MacGill, V. (2009) *Complexity Pages.* http://complexity.orconhosting.net.nz/ (accessed 1 November 2008).

Mahar, D. (2001) Positioning in a middle school culture: gender race, social class, and power, *Journal of Adolescent & Adult Literacy*, 45(3): 200–9.

Mahiri, J. and Sablo, S (1996) Writing for their lives: the non-school literacy of California's urban African American youth, *The Journal of Negro Education*, 65(2): 164–80.

Martino, W. (1998) 'Dickheads,' 'poofs,' 'try hards,' and 'losers': critical literacy for boys in the English classroom, *English in Aotearoa*, 25: 31–57.

Massachusetts Department of Education (2001) *Massachusetts English Language Arts Curriculum Framework.* www.doe.mass.edu/frameworks/ela/0601.pdf (accessed 10 December 2010).

Massey, A.J., Elliott, G.L. and Johnson, N.K. (2005) *Variations in Aspects of Writing in 16+ English Examinations between 1980 and 2004: Vocabulary, Spelling, Punctuation, Sentence Structure, Non-standard English.* Cambridge: Assessment Directorate, Cambridge Local Examinations Syndicate.

Maun, I. and Myhill, D. (2005) Text as design, writers as designers, *English in Education*, 39(2): 5–21.

Maynard, T. (2002) *Boys and Literacy: Exploring the Issues.* London: Routledge Falmer.

McCaslin, M. (1990) Motivated literacy, in *Literacy Theory and Research: Analysis from Multiple Paradigms. The Thirty-ninth Yearbook of the National Reading Conference.* Chicago: National Reading Conference, pp. 35–50.

McKeough, A. and Genereux, R. (2003) Transformation in narrative thought during adolescence: the structure and content of story compositions, *Journal of Educational Psychology*, 95(3): 537–52.

Meek, M. (1983) *Achieving Literacy: Longitudinal Studies of Adolescents Learning to Read*. London: Routledge.

Mellon, J. (1968) *Transformational Sentence-combining: A Method for Enhancing the Development of Syntactic Influence in English Composition*. Urbana: NCTE.

Miller, C.R. (1984) Genre as social action, *Quarterly Journal of Speech*, 70: 151–67.

Moffett, J. (1968/1983) *Teaching the Universe of Discourse*. Boston: Houghton Mifflin Company.

Moje, E., Overby, M., Tysvaer, N. and Morris, K. (2008) The complex world of adolescent literacy: myths, motivations and mysteries, *Harvard Educational Review*, 78(1): 84–106.

Murphy, S. and Yancey, K.B. (2008) Construct and consequence: validity in writing assessment, in C. Bazerman (ed.) *Handbook of Research on Writing: History, Society, School, Individual, Text*. New Jersey: Lawrence Erlbaum, pp. 365–85.

Murray, D. (1968) *A Writer Teaches Writing: A Practical Method of Teaching Composition*. Boston: Houghton Mifflin Company.

Murray, D. (1984) *Write to Learn*. New York, NY: Holt, Rinehart and Winston.

Murray, D. (2003) Teaching writing as a process not product, in V. Villanueva (ed.) *Cross-talk in Comp Theory*. Urbana, IL: National Council of Teachers of English.

Myhill, D. and Fisher, R. (2005) *Informing Practice in English: A Review of Recent Research in Literacy and the Teaching of English*. London: Ofsted.

Myhill, D.A. (2009) Becoming a designer: trajectories of linguistic development, in R. Beard and D. Myhill (eds) *Handbook of Writing Development*. London: Sage, pp. 402–14.

Nagin, C. (2003) *Because Writing Matters: Improving Student Writing in Our Schools*. San Francisco, CA: Jossey Bass.

National Assessment of Educational Progress (2007) *Writing Report Card*. http://nationsreportcard.gov/writing_2007/w0008.asp (accessed 23 September 2008).

Neal, M. (2010) Review essay: assessment in the service of learning, *College Composition and Communication*, 61(4): 746–58.

Newkirk, T. (2002) *Misreading Masculinity: Boys, Literacy and Popular Culture*. Santa Barbara, CA: Greenwood Press.

Ofsted (2005) *English 2000–2005: A Review of Inspection Evidence*. London: Ofsted.

Ofsted (2006) *The Annual Report of Her Majesty's Chief Inspector of Schools*. London: The Stationery Office (TSO).

Ong, W.J. (1982) *Orality and Literacy: The Technologizing of the Word*, New Accents (ed. Terence Hawkes). New York: Methuen.

Patthey-Chavez, G., Matsumura, L. and Valdes, R. (2004) Investigating the process approach to writing instruction in urban middle schools, *Journal of Adolescent & Adult Literacy*, 47(6): 462–76.

Pavel, T.G. (1986) *Fictional Worlds*. Cambridge, MA: Harvard University Press.

Penrod, D. (2010) *Composition in Convergence: The Impact of New Media on Writing Assessment*. London: Lawrence Erlbaum Associates.

Perl, S. (1979) The composing processes of unskilled college writers, *Research in the Teaching of English*, 13(4): 317–36.

Petraglia, J. (1999) Is there life after process? The role of social scientism in a changing discipline, in T. Kent (ed.) *Post-process Theory: Beyond the Writing-process Theory*. Carbondale, IL: Southern Illinois University Press, pp. 49–64.

Potter, E.F., McCormick, C.B. and Busching, B.A. (2001) Academic and life goals: insights from adolescent writers, *The High School Journal*, 85(1): 45–55.

Pritchard, R. and Honeycutt, R. (2006) The process approach to writing instruction: examining its effectiveness, in C. MacArthur, S. Graham and J. Fitzgerald (eds) *Handbook of Writing Research*. New York: The Guilford Press, pp. 275–90.

QCA (1999) *Improving Writing at Key Stages 3 and 4*. London: Qualifications and Curriculum Authority.

Reed, J.H., Schallert, D.L., Beth, A.D. and Woodruff, A.L. (2004) Motivated reader, engaged writer: the role of motivation in the literate acts of adolescents, in T.L. Jetton and J.A. Dole (eds) *Adolescent Literacy Research and Practice*. New York: Guilford Press, pp. 251–82.

Rogoff, B. (1992) *Apprenticeship in Thinking: Cognitive Development in Social Context*. New York: Oxford University Press.

Rohman, G. (1965) Pre-writing the stage of discovery in the writing process, *College Composition and Communication*, 16(2): 106–12.

Rowe, D.W. (2009) Early written communication, in R. Beard, D. Myhill, J. Riley and M. Nystrand (eds) (2009) *The Sage Handbook of Writing Development*. London: Sage, pp. 213–31.

Sainsbury, M. (2009) Developing writing in a high-stakes environment, in R. Beard, D. Myhill, J. Riley and M. Nystrand (eds) (2009) *The Sage Handbook of Writing Development*. London: Sage, pp. 545–60.

Scardamalia, M. and Bereiter, C. (1987) *The Psychology of Written Composition*. Hillsdale, NJ: Lawrence Erlbaum Associates.

Schultz, K. (2002) Looking across space and time: reconceptualizing literacy learning in and out of school, *Research in the Teaching of English*, 36(3): 356–90.

Schultz, K. (2003) *Listening: A Framework for Teaching Across Differences*. New York, NY: Teachers College Press.

Schultz, K. and Fecho, R. (2000) Society's child: social context and writing development, *Educational Psychologist*, 35(1): 51–62.

Scott, D., Encinas, M., Andrews, R., Houssart, J. and Dale-Tunnicliffe, S. (2010) *Curriculum Standards for Basic Education in Mexico*, (Standards Project 2010), unpublished draft, September 2010.

Scribner, S. and Cole, M. (1981) *The Psychology of Literacy*. Cambridge: Harvard University Press.

Sheeran, Y. and Barnes, D. (1991) *School Writing: Discovering the Ground Rules*. Milton Keynes: Open University Press.

Skilton-Sylvester, E. (2002) Should I stay or should I go? Investigating Cambodian women's participation and investiment in adult ESL programs, *Adult Education Quarterly*, 53(1): 9–26.

Smith, A. and Andrews, R. (2009) Toward a comprehensive, contemporary model: writing development. Paper presented in the symposium Hybridity, Multimodality, and New Forms of Composing at the American Educational Research Association, San Diego, California, 13–17 April.

Smith, A. (2009) (Re)Framing development: a review of research on adolescent writing development. Paper presented at the American Educational Research Association, San Diego, California.

Smith, A. (2011) Complicating development: urban adolescent males' transcontextual writing development. Paper presented at the American Educational Research Association, New Orleans, Louisiana.

Smith, F. (1982/1994) *Writing and the Writer*, 2nd edn. Hillsdale NJ: Lawrence Erlbaum.

Snyder, I. (1994) Writing with wordprocessors: the computer's influence on the classroom context, *Journal of Curriculum Studies*, 26(2): 143–62.

Sommers, N. (1980) Revision strategies of student writers and experienced adult writers, *College Composition and Communication*, 31(4): 378–88.

Stevens, L.P. (2008) (Re)framing policy analysis, *Journal of Adolescent and Adult Literacy*, 47(1): 454–61.

Syverson, M. (2006) *The Learning Record*. www.learningrecord.org (accessed 1 November 2010).

Tannen, D. (ed.) (1993) *Framing in Discourse*. New York: Oxford University Press.

The Ghost (2010) film, directed by R. Polanski. Based on the novel by Robert Harris.

Thomas, S., Joseph, C., Laccetti, J. et al. (2007) Transliteracy: crossing divides. *First Monday*, 12(12). firstmonday.org/htbin/cgiwrap/bin/ojs/index.php/fm/article/view/2060/1908 (accessed 13 July 2010).

Torgerson, C. (2003) *Systematic Reviews*. London: Continuum.

Tufte, E. (1997) *Visual Explanations: Images and Quantities, Evidence and Narrative*. Connecticut: Graphics Press.

Turner, J. and Paris, S. (1995) How literacy tasks influence children's motivation for literacy, *The Reading Teacher*, 48(8): 662–73.

US Census Bureau (2010) *Computer Use and Ownership*. www.census.gov/population/www/socdemo/computer.html (accessed 1 November 2010).

Vygotsky, L. (1986) *Thought and Language*. Cambridge, MA: MIT Press.

Walkerdine, V. (1990) *Schoolgirl Fictions*. London: Verso.

Walton, M. (2009) Mobile literacies & South African teens: leisure reading, writing, and MXit chatting for teens in Langa and Guguletu. http://m4lit.files.wordpress.com/2010/03/m4lit_mobile_literacies_mwalton_20101.pdf (accessed 1 November 2010).

Wells, G. (1985) *Language, Learning and Education*. Windsor: NFER-Nelson.

Wells, J. and Lewis, L. (2006) *Internet Access in US Public Schools and Classrooms: 1994–2005* (NCES 2007-020). US Department of Education. Washington, DC: National Center for Education.

Willis, J. (2007) *Foundations of Qualitative Research: Interpretive and Critical Approaches*. London: Sage.

Wilkinson, A., Barnsley, G., Hanna, P. and Swan, M. (1980) *Assessing Language Development*. Oxford: Oxford University Press.

Wilkinson, A., Barnsley, G., Hanna, P. and Swan, M. (1983) Towards a comprehensive model of writing development. In B. Kroll & G. Wells (Eds.), *Explorations in the development of writing: Theory, research, and practice* (pp. 43–68). New York: Wiley.

Wyse, D., Andrews, R. and Hoffman, J. (eds) (2010) *The Routledge International Handbook of English, Language and Literacy Teaching*. London: Routledge.

Index

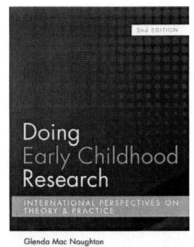

Glenda Mac Naughton
Sharne A. Rolfe
Iram Siraj-Blatchford

DOING EARLY CHILDHOOD RESEARCH

Glenda Mac Naughton

978-0-335-24262-7 (Paperback)
July 2010

"It is rare for any research methodology book to cover so much ground, and contain so many different kinds of resources between two covers."
Journal of Education for Teaching

The book provides a thorough introduction to the most common research methods used in the early childhood context. The book covers a wide range of conventional and newer methods including:

- Observation
- Surveys and interviews with adults and children
- Action research
- Ethnography
- Quasi-experimental approaches

Doing Early Childhood Research explains clearly how to set up research projects which are theoretically grounded, well-designed, rigorously analysed, feasible and ethically based. Each chapter is illustrated with examples.

www.openup.co.uk

OPEN UNIVERSITY PRESS
McGraw · Hill Education

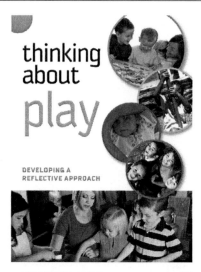

DEVELOPING A
REFLECTIVE APPROACH

Edited by Janet Moyles

THINKING ABOUT PLAY

Janet Moyles (Editor)

978-0-335-24108-8 (Paperback)
2010

eBook also available

This edited collection brings together play and reflective practice and supports practitioners in reflecting more deeply on the play provision they make for young children. This involves analysing and evaluating what makes quality play and learning experiences by considering how current research might impact on practice.

Key features:

- Introduces the concept of 'playful pedagogies' and explains how it relates to practice
- Each chapter starts with an abstract so that readers can dip into issues of particular interest and concern
- Includes questions and follow-up ideas that can be used for CPD experiences and training

This important book supports early years students and practitioners in developing their own thinking, ideologies and pedagogies.

www.openup.co.uk

OPEN UNIVERSITY PRESS
McGraw · Hill Education

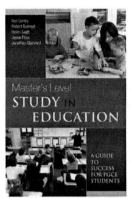

MASTER'S LEVEL STUDY IN EDUCATION
A Guide for Success for PGCE Students

Neil Denby, Robert Butroyd, Helen Swift, Jayne Price and Jonathan Glazzard

9780335234141 (Paperback)
2008

eBook also available

This book offers an insight into the knowledge, tools and skills that need to be developed for a successful outcome in a Master's in an educational context. Using detailed - and real - exemplars, the authors cover the conventions that need to be followed and consider the different elements of Master's level work..

The book will enable you to:

- Understand how to prepare, carry out and write a literature review
- Consider the different methodologies and approaches that are inherent in Master's level work
- Understand the nature of Master's level work within education as a research/evidence based profession
- Appreciate the importance of ethical underpinning when working at this level

www.openup.co.uk

OPEN UNIVERSITY PRESS
McGraw · Hill Education

TEACHING CREATIVE WRITING IN THE PRIMARY SCHOOL: DELIGHT, ENTICE, INSPIRE!

Julie MacLusky & Robyn Cox

978-0-335-24279-5 (Paperback)
September 2011

This book aims to support and develop creative writing activity in the primary curriculum, offering a balanced mix of both theoretical background and practical writing ideas. The book provides various exercises that will help develop creative writing skills, from creating an engaging character to delivering a satisfying ending. The structured and well-tested exercises will help to develop fundamental, transferable tools of story telling that will improve pupil's confidence in all areas of writing.

Key features:

- Providing detailed curriculum links to the National Strategy strands and outcomes
- 20 creative writing templates for activities that can be incorporated into many different areas of classroom teaching

www.openup.co.uk

OPEN UNIVERSITY PRESS
McGraw · Hill Education